Learning Disorders in Children

Diagnosis, Medication, Education

Learning Disorders

in Children

Diagnosis, Medication, Education

Edited by LESTER TARNOPOL, Sc.D.
*Engineering Psychologist, City College of
San Francisco*

WITH 16 CONTRIBUTORS

LITTLE, BROWN AND COMPANY, BOSTON

Contributors

PHILIP R. CALANCHINI, M.D.
Medical Director, Learning Disabilities Center, Institute of Neurological Sciences, and Attending Neurologist, Department of Neurology, Pacific Medical Center, San Francisco

SAM D. CLEMENTS, Ph.D.
Associate Professor, Departments of Psychiatry and Pediatrics, and Executive Director, Child Study Center, University of Arkansas Medical Center, Little Rock

C. KEITH CONNERS, Ph.D.
Associate Professor of Psychology, Department of Psychiatry, Harvard Medical School; Director, Child Development Laboratory, Massachusetts General Hospital, Boston

JOANNA S. DAVIS, M.S.
Instructor, Department of Psychiatry, and Language Specialist, Child Study Center, University of Arkansas Medical Center, Little Rock

ERIC DENHOFF, M.D.
Chief of Pediatrics, Miriam Hospital; Medical Director, Meeting Street School Children's Rehabilitation Center, Providence

JAMES A. DUGGER, M.D.
Department of Pediatrics, Permanente Medical Group, South San Francisco

RUTH EDGINGTON, M.A.
Instructor, Department of Psychiatry, and Education Specialist, Child Study Center, University of Arkansas Medical Center, Little Rock

HELEN GOFMAN, M.D.
Director, Child Study Unit, and Medical Director, Pediatric Reading and Language Development Clinic, Department of Pediatrics, University of California Medical Center, San Francisco

CLEO M. GOOLSBY, M.S.W.
Instructor, Department of Psychiatry, and Chief Psychiatric Social Worker, Child Study Center, University of Arkansas Medical Center, Little Rock

JAMES P. LASTER, M.D.
Chief, Department of Neurology, Permanente Medical Group, Santa Clara; Assistant Clinical Professor of Pediatric-Neurology, Stanford University School of Medicine; Director, Pediatric-Neurology Clinic, Stanford Medical Center, Palo Alto

JOHN E. PETERS, M.D.
Co-Chairman, Department of Psychiatry, and Head, Division of Child and Adolescent Psychiatry, University of Arkansas Medical Center, Little Rock

JAMES C. REED, Ph.D.
Associate Professor of Psychology, Tufts University School of Medicine, Boston

JOHN REYNOLDS, M.D.
General practice, Escondido, California

HENRY S. RICHANBACH, M.D.
Clinical Assistant Professor of Pediatrics, Stanford University School of Medicine, Palo Alto

LESTER TARNOPOL, Sc.D.
Engineering Psychologist, City College of San Francisco, San Francisco

SUSAN STRUVE TROUT, M.A.
Director, Learning Disabilities Center, Institute of Neurological Sciences, Pacific Medical Center; Director, Graduate Programs in Learning Disabilities, and Assistant Professor of Learning Disabilities, University of the Pacific, San Francisco

LEON J. WHITSELL, M.D.
Associate Clinical Professor of Pediatrics and Neurology, and Neurological Consultant, Child Study Unit and Pediatric Reading and Language Development Clinic, University of California Medical Center, San Francisco

Preface

THE SAN FRANCISCO CHAPTER of the California Association for Neurologically Handicapped Children held its third symposium about a year ago. The theme was *Children with Learning Disabilities—Educational and Medical Management*. On the first day, a Panel on Medication under the chairmanship of Lester Tarnopol met to discuss drug therapy for children with learning disabilities. These deliberations were edited for publication together with some of the manuscripts from the symposium which were especially prepared for this volume.

The Panel on Medication considered such problems as developing guides for physicians, parents, teachers, and ancillary personnel. Also discussed were the present state of the art, research guidelines, diagnostic procedures, and medications. Finally, the effects of medication on behavior, attention, impulsivity, and learning were considered.

On the second day, the Diagnostic Team from the University of Arkansas Medical Center, Departments of Psychiatry and Pediatrics, Little Rock, Arkansas, presented *Children with Learning Disabilities—Two Cases*. These cases were subsequently prepared for publication and are included in this volume. The diagnostic team included a clinical psychologist, a speech and hearing therapist, an educator, a psychiatric social worker, and a child psychiatrist.

C. Keith Conners presented a paper entitled "The Psychological Assessment of Minimal Brain Dysfunction (MBD) Children Under Medication" which was rewritten and expanded for this publication as Chapter 7. In order to cover management of children with learning disabilities more fully, Chapters 1, 3, 6, 8, and 9 were written especially for this volume after the symposium was given.

This selection of manuscripts was made in consideration of the needs of physicians and paramedical personnel who wish to become acquainted with the management of children with learning disabilities. Since such management includes educational, psychological, and social as well as medical aspects, the book includes information which physicians require to carry out their roles in conjunction with other professionals. For example, it is most important that physicians be cognizant of the educational and other facilities available to children with learning problems. They must know about both private and public school programs. The most extensive public school arrangement is the Program for Educationally Handicapped Minors in California.

The California school program for educationally handicapped children was the first state-funded program for intelligent children with learning disabilities. California law defines these children as "minors who, by reason of marked learning or behavior disorders or both, require special education programs with the intention of full return to the regular school program. Such learning or behavior disorders shall be associated with a neurological handicap or emotional disturbance and shall not be attributable to mental retardation."

The California State Department of Education estimates that about 5 percent of the school population are educationally handicapped. Other estimates by reputable sources consider that children with learning disabilities may represent as much as 10 or even 20 percent of the population, depending upon how broad a definition is used. At any rate these children represent the single largest category under the umbrella of special education.

The Program for Educationally Handicapped Minors in California includes full-time special day classes, learning disability groups taught by an itinerant teacher who may see a child for an hour each day in a group of four, and home and hospital teaching. This program started in 1963 with about 2,000 children and no state funding. By June of 1970 the program contained about 40,000 children—approximately 50 percent in special day classes, 45 percent in learning disability groups, and 5 percent in home and hospital instruction. The cost of this program to the State of California rose from nothing in 1963–1964 to about $40 million in 1969–1970. Present legislation permits any school district to be reimbursed by state funding for up to 2 percent of its population in this program. Some school districts have no program and others have exceeded the 2 percent limitation. When all the school districts in California reach the 2 percent limitation, there will be about 100,000 pupils in the program.

There are two major aspects to the management of children with learning disabilities. First, a differential diagnosis of the child's disabilities must be made. Second, proper remediation should be based upon a prescription resulting from this diagnosis. Since most children's disabilities tend to be complex, differential diagnoses can be made only by a multidisciplinary team as presented in the cases described in this volume. The team generally consists of a pediatric-neurologist; a psychologist; a speech, hearing, and language therapist; and an educator. Some teams may also include a psychiatrist, social worker, nurse, occupational therapist, and physical therapist.

The physicians who participated in the Panel on Medication agreed unanimously that medication is often a most valuable part of the medical management of children with learning disabilities. They also thought that most pediatricians and general practitioners are not sufficiently aware of the relationship between learning problems and neurological dysfunction, of diagnosis and medical management using medication, and of the relationship of medical diagnosis and management to the educational procedures for these children. Therefore an attempt has been made in this book to cover these matters in some detail in the hope that more physicians will become prepared to work with these children. It is considered by many that *learning disabilities represent the single greatest medical problem of American children today.* Under the circumstances, it is vital that greater numbers of physicians be prepared in this field.

Such terms as *minimum neurological dysfunction* and *learning disabilities* are becoming well known. However, the technical details of the diagnostic procedures are neither well known nor widely used. Nor in many cases are the remedial procedures required to help these millions of children sufficiently understood by physicians, psychologists, and educators. The San Francisco Symposia and the books* which followed them represent an attempt to increase communication among professionals in this most important endeavor.

L. T.

---

* Following the first two symposia, *Learning Disabilities: Introduction to Educational and Medical Management* was edited by L. Tarnopol and published by Charles C Thomas in 1969.

Acknowledgments

THE EDITOR gratefully acknowledges the assistance received from everyone who contributed to this volume. Special credit is due my wife Muriel whose tremendous organizational ability and efforts made possible the symposium from which several of these manuscripts developed. She also read the manuscripts, offering valuable suggestions, and helped read the material for typographical errors. I am also most grateful to Josephine DiStefano and Lynne Tong for typing manuscripts for publication.

The third symposium of the San Francisco Chapter of the California Association for Neurologically Handicapped Children was made possible in large part by a generous educational Grant-in-Aid from CIBA Pharmaceutical Company.

Also gratefully acknowledged are the scholarships to attend the symposium contributed for teachers, school administrators, psychologists, nurses, social workers, and speech and language therapists by the Easter Seal Society for Crippled Children and Adults of California, the Junior League of San Francisco, Inc., and the United Cerebral Palsy Association of San Francisco.

L. T.

Contents

*To Muriel, Matthew, and Daniel
who motivated my inquiry into
learning disorders in children*

Notice

The medications in this book are taken from various sources and do not necessarily have specific approval by the Food and Drug Administration for use in the situations and dosages for which they are recommended. In some instances, the dosages include the adult range. The package insert for each drug should be consulted for use and dosage as approved by the FDA. Because standards for usage change, it is advisable to keep abreast of revised recommendations, particularly those concerning new drugs.

1 Introduction to Neurogenic Learning Disorders

LESTER TARNOPOL

LEARNING DISABILITIES now constitute the most pervasive medical problem of children in the United States. This difficulty seems to affect between 5 and 20 percent of the nonretarded child population, depending upon how learning disabilities are defined. Moreover, the effects of these disabilities may last from several months to a lifetime, even with the best help now available. Thus many physicians have become aware that learning disabilities, if left unaided, usually have more devastating effects on children than most childhood diseases which pediatricians normally treat.

A child who has difficulty learning in school is often called stupid, lazy, or stubborn. Generally if a physician is consulted he will check for mental retardation, physical illness, and hearing and visual acuity. If these tests are all negative, he may suggest that the parents consult a psychiatrist, try a different school, or use more discipline (Meehan 1969).

Usually children with learning disabilities appear normal until they enter school. The parents may have noted that their child started to talk late or was unusually busy and somewhat clumsy.

However, as a rule his troubles really begin when he enters first grade and tries to learn to read and write. Since this intelligent child finds these tasks difficult or impossible, he begins to feel frustrated as he sees others master academic learning which he cannot. Instead of receiving approval for his work, he may feel disapproval and even that he is bad or dumb. To compensate for his lack of academic success, he may engage in boisterous or clowning behavior, or he may withdraw into fantasy. If he is hyperkinetic, he may be scolded and disciplined so that he may become school-phobic. This often leads to aggressive, acting-out behavior, and even truancy and delinquency.

Early identification (preferably preschool) of the child's problems by a battery of medical, psychological, and educational tests can lead to a helpful prescription. Often medication and special teaching methods will help to prevent such untoward educational and emotional results and lead to a happier child who is able to learn and meets with comparative academic and social success. The child, the family, the teachers, and his classmates will all be happier if an effective prescription can be found for this child.

LEARNING DISABILITIES
DEFINED

Research indicates that learning disabilities appear to be associated with *minimal brain dysfunction*. The nature of these dysfunctions tends to be quite subtle when compared with the blind, deaf, cerebral palsied, severely emotionally disturbed, and mentally retarded. Therefore general recognition of this problem has been relatively recent. *Learning disabilities* is the term used to distinguish the problems of those children who are not mentally retarded but who have difficulty learning due to mild central nervous system dysfunctions. Children with such learning disabilities do not tend to exhibit gross psychological or sensory impairment. On the other hand, in cerebral palsy gross motor involvement is common; the blind and the deaf exhibit gross sensory impairment; mental retardation is characterized by general low mental ability; and severe emotional disturbance may be related to a primary functional or psychological disorder.

Recently the term *specific learning disabilities* has been suggested to indicate the nonretarded group of children with learning disabilities while *general learning disabilities* is the term suggested to signify mental retardation.

TERMINOLOGY

Terminology and the identification of these children was the concern of Task Force One of the National Project on Minimal Brain Dysfunction in Children. The deliberations of a committee, composed of nine physicians, two psychologist-educators, and an agency executive, were published by the National Institute of Neurological Diseases and Blindness* (Clements 1966). Thirty-seven different terms had been found which designated this condition, including *dyslexia, perceptual deficit, hyperkinetic behavior syndrome, organic brain damage, minimal cerebral palsy,* and *learning disabilities.* From this array Task Force One selected the term *minimal brain dysfunction* and issued the following statement:

1. Brain dysfunction can manifest itself in varying degrees of severity and can involve any or all of the more specific areas, e.g., motor, sensory, or intellectual. This dysfunctioning can compromise the affected child in learning and behavior.

2. The term *minimal brain dysfunction* will be reserved for the child whose symptomatology appears in one or more of the specific areas of brain function, but in mild, or subclinical form, without reducing overall intellectual functioning to the subnormal ranges. (Note: The evaluation of the intellectual functioning of the "culturally disadvantaged" child, though perhaps related, represents an equally complex, but different problem.)

Some prefer a very broad definition of learning disabilities. They consider that any educational difficulty, regardless of etiology, should be subsumed under an umbrella concept of learning disabilities. Others believe that neurological *dysfunction* is syn-

* Now the National Institute of Neurological Diseases and Stroke.

onymous with neurological *damage,* and that children with neurogenic learning disorders have suffered brain damage.

Unfortunately the problem of terminology has not been settled. There are still several schools of thought concerning the adequacy and usefulness of the various terms used to describe the learning and reading problems of these children. Physicians tend to prefer a term such as *minimal brain dysfunction,* which points to the medical nature of the problem. Educators, on the other hand, tend to prefer a term such as *learning disability, educational handicap,* or *perceptual disorder,* which indicates that the problem is educational in nature. Parents often decry terms which include such words as brain, neurological, cerebral, or even handicap or dysfunction. They tend to prefer the most neutral term possible, such as *learning problem.* Because of the psychological impact of frightening terminology on the lay public, many physicians and educators also prefer the most neutral terms available. Since the use of nonfrightening diagnostic designations seems to encourage parents to have their children tested and placed in remedial educational environments, such terminology is often favored.

Masland (1969) noted that *minimal brain dysfunction* is little different from *learning disability.* Moreover, it is not a diagnosis or a disease. It is a condition or a symptom referring to children with common disabilities requiring a program of management. *Minimal brain dysfunction* points to the requirements of the child and away from the environment as primarily causal.

Masland indicated that there is a group of children who have deviations in nervous system functioning so that they do not react in the way the average child does to his environment and who, therefore, require methods of management and training which are different and often unique for each individual child.

We have carefully avoided characterizing the cause. *It is not desirable for the term minimal brain dysfunction to be equated with brain damage.** In many instances, the child with brain dysfunction has that dysfunction as a result of brain damage. But in many other instances we have no evidence that such damage has occurred. This is not the matter at issue. The matter at issue is the characteristics of the child which are different

* Editor's emphasis [L. T.].

and the characteristics of his learning opportunities and environment which should be different.

AN INTERNATIONAL PROBLEM

Because of the seriousness and the international scope of the problem, the World Federation of Neurology meeting in 1968 in Dallas, Texas, considered terminology related to *reading problems of genetic origin.*

In 1969 MacDonald Critchley, President of the World Federation of Neurology, speaking in San Francisco at the third symposium of the San Francisco Chapter of the California Association for Neurologically Handicapped Children, stated:

The World Federation of Neurology has a special Research Group devoted to the topic of *Specific Developmental Dyslexia,* and our group, which is a small but highly selected one, comprises experts from all parts of the world, including Asia, South America, Europe and the United States.

He then gave the definition of specific developmental dyslexia agreed upon at the Dallas meeting.

Specific developmental dyslexia is a disorder manifested by difficulty in learning to read, despite conventional instruction, adequate intelligence and socio-cultural opportunities. It is dependent upon fundamental cognitive disabilities, which are frequently of constitutional origin.

Critchley continued,

This condition is, I submit, primarily a medical problem. That is to say, the *diagnosis* of the condition is a medical problem. Thereafter it becomes an educational or pedagogic concern. Specific developmental dyslexia constitutes a hard core of cases within the spectrum of poor readers. Just how big is that core? This is something which we are currently trying to determine on a world wide scale. It is currently larger than one first imagines. It was estimated in Sweden, some few decades ago, that possibly 10 percent of all school children have some measure of reading difficulty. But not all children with reading disorders are dyslexics, and especially not developmental or genetic dyslexics. We just do not know the figure. Maybe it differs from country to country.

It has often been proposed that the relatively high incidence of children with reading problems in Great Britain and the United States might be due to the highly illogical spelling of the English language. It was suggested that in those countries where the spelling is logical, as for example in Czechoslovakia, Italy, Spain, Rumania, or Russia, one would not find dyslexia. This was found not to be so, even though the bulk of the literature on this subject has come from three areas, namely Scandinavia, the United States of America, and Great Britain.

Critchley stated:

Developmental dyslexia exists in Spain, Rumania, Russia, France, Italy and Germany. It is also met with in the Orient. This latter is a most interesting observation, because in the Middle East and in the Far East many of the printed languages run from right to left. It is intriguing to observe that when a dyslexic Oriental writes his own language, he perpetrates the same sort of spelling errors, the same reversals and the same rotations as do our dyslexics. Furthermore, the Arabic-speaking dyslexic may, when he writes, confuse such similar sounding syllables as *te* and *ta,* though the graphic symbols for these sounds are quite dissimilar.

In 1967 Dr. Zdenek Matajcek reported in San Francisco on a five-year action research program involving the diagnosis and remediation of children with severe reading problems in the Czechoslovakian schools. Although their spelling is entirely phonetic, Matajcek found that about 2 percent of the nonretarded child population had severe reading problems, with about one-third seemingly of genetic origin. Since their research program was so new, it is doubtful that they have scratched the surface of the problem. For example, they have yet to uncover the large number of children with above-average to genius intelligence levels who suffer from mild to severe neurological handicaps so that they perform in the low-average to average ability ranges in school.

American research indicates that the average IQ of children with learning disabilities is about the same as the average IQ of the total population. The cases reported in this volume demonstrate that severe learning disabilities may be found among children of very superior intelligence. The highest IQ of a child with learning disabilities, reported in one clinic, was 167.

Some children are able to do fairly well until about the fifth grade when they may buckle because of the introduction of abstract logic which may constitute their primary areas of dysfunction. These children tend to be missed in diagnosis because they are beyond the ages at which most diagnostic work is being done. Also many teachers and psychologists do not suspect the existence of neurogenic learning disabilities in children who have been performing well until the fifth grade. They tend to look for environmental causes of such educational failures.

HISTORY

In discussing developmental dyslexia, Critchley observed that neurologists had been aware of this condition since its discovery over 70 years ago when it was referred to as "congenital word-blindness." An English physician, Dr. Little, may have been the first to describe learning problems associated with brain damage. In 1861 he observed some of the sequelae when asphyxiated or apoplectic infants were saved:

The proportion of entire recoveries from the effects of asphyxia neonatorum is smaller than has hitherto been supposed. . . . The muscles of speech are commonly involved, varying in degree. . . . The intellectual functions are sometimes quite unaffected, but in the majority of cases the intellect suffers . . . from the slightest impairment . . . to entire imbecility. . . . The individual may acquire a fair knowledge of music, the memory is good. . . . A fair capacity for arithmetic and languages may be displayed, but there commonly exists a great want of application, a slowness of intellect similar to a slowness of volition. In other cases, where intellectual powers are good, a preternatural impulsive nervous condition of mind exists, combined with an agitated, eager, anxious mode of performing acts of volition. [Cited in Peters et al. 1967.]

In England H. C. Bastain, a British neurologist, is said to have first described *word-deafness* and *word-blindness* in 1869. A patient was described as word-deaf who was unable to understand spoken words even though his hearing was adequate. Word-blindness was described in another patient who had adequate vision but was unable to recognize printed words.

Samuel T. Orton, an American neurologist and psychiatrist, made important contributions to this field from 1925 until his accidental death in 1948. The Orton Society, devoted to the study and treatment of children with specific language disabilities (dyslexia), was founded in his honor.

Heinz Werner and Alfred Strauss, a psychologist and a neuropsychiatrist, investigated the learning characteristics of children with brain damage. Strauss and Lehtinen summarized the previous work in this field and made the first comprehensive presentation of the learning problems of brain-injured children (Strauss and Lehtinen 1947). Studies of the learning problems of brain-injured children revealed basic information about how all children learn and led to the discovery of children with minimal brain dysfunction. Some of the classic works are by Strauss and Kephart (1955), Denhoff and Robinault (1960), and Cruickshank et al. (1961). The field of learning disabilities has received much attention from research workers since then, and during the past decade significant advances have been made in both the diagnosis and remediation of these children.

ROLE OF PHYSICIAN

Masland (1969) discussed the role of the physician in the management of children with minimal brain dysfunction. He stated that physicians must be prepared to make the earliest possible diagnosis since research indicates that the earlier the diagnosis, the better the prognosis. In order to cope with the total management of the children after they are diagnosed, the practicing physician must know what community resources are available to help them. When such resources are lacking and physicians are unfamiliar with the diagnosis, they tend to make two common errors:

The first is to say, "Well, he looks all right to me. Just wait a few years. I think he is going to grow out of it." The second, the other extreme, is to say, "Your child is brain-damaged and there isn't anything that can be done about it, so don't bother me." I think we can get away from these errors if we have in the community the resources available to help such children when recognized and if the physicians become knowledgeable about their existence and location. [Masland 1969.]

Another important task of the physician is to ascertain whether the child has other physical problems which require medical attention, particularly disorders of vision and hearing. Certainly any child who has educational problems would benefit from a searching evaluation of these characteristics. Finally, every child should be examined for other health deficits such as thyroid disorder or some of the subtle defects of metabolism which may also impair intellectual and emotional performance.

It is suggested that the physicians' most appropriate roles are as members of multidisciplinary teams, as described in Chapters 2, 3, 4, and 5. The physicians most likely to see children with learning disabilities are pediatricians, pediatric neurologists, psychiatrists, general practitioners, ophthalmologists, and hearing specialists. Members of these disciplines are becoming aware of the problem from discussions at their society meetings and in their journals.

It is important that the conditions which indicate a high risk for learning disabilities be well known to pediatricians and that they utilize this information to follow such children. For example, since there appear to be genetic learning disorders, family histories which include poor spelling and difficulty in learning to read are indications, if we exclude the culturally and educationally deprived families. Perinatal problems in infants, including any factors which might indicate a period of anoxia or central nervous system insult, should be noted and followed (see Chapter 3, Chart 2). Any unusual developmental histories indicating slow maturation, slow speech and language development, immature social, motor or balance control are noteworthy.

It should also be noted that learning problems appear to be more prevalent in male children than in females, the ratio being from 4:1 to 8:1 in various studies. And finally, the percentage of left-handed children with learning disabilities ranges from 25 to 35 percent in different studies, compared with about 5 percent in the total population.

At the 1969 symposium in San Francisco, Critchley added the following statement concerning genetic dyslexia:

These unfortunate children, born with an innate constitutional difficulty in learning to read—just as organic and just as real as color-blindness—*can* be "cured." The first step in management and treatment is correct diagnosis, which ensures that these children are no longer misinterpreted as being stupid, lazy, naughty, or mixed up. On the contrary, they have a genuine organic problem just as real as the lack of a musical ear. I have found that when this idea is put across and carefully explained to the child, at once the whole scene changes. His frustration goes and his morale rises. This is a most striking and gratifying observation.

The next step is to deal with the teacher who must be persuaded to realize that she has an organic problem on her hands and not just a troublesome, inattentive, or emotionally disturbed child. Individual tuition is called for. I would also plead with teachers and parents not to try and interfere with the dyslexic child's cerebral lateralities, even if they are left-eyed or left-handed. Allow the child to make his own choice as to handedness and eyedness.

I would like to end on two notes of optimism. One is that the future is not too gloomy for these children. Dyslexia can be overcome. I would go further and say that sometimes dyslexics can cure themselves, given the right combination of favorable circumstances, which include: (1) high intelligence; (2) sheer determination on the part of the child; and (3) sympathetic understanding on the part of the parents and the teachers, and also on the part of nonaffected siblings, as well as the contemporary schoolmates. We know from abundant experience that some youngsters who have gone through their school days with reading problems can eventually make good. Quite a number of well-known individuals, household names in science, politics, medicine, art, and literature, have been dyslexics and have mastered their disability. True, they may have remained poor spellers, but this is not necessarily in itself a grave handicap.

The final point that I want to make is to express what I believe to be the ideal. I would like to see certain self-selected teachers who are particularly interested in this topic choosing to specialize in the remedial instruction of dyslexics, in a way that some teachers dedicate themselves to the care of the deaf, or the blind, or the mentally retarded, or the autistic. I can imagine a band of crusading teachers undergoing courses of instruction in the techniques of teaching dyslexics. When trained I can see them given a diploma, and accorded a special status as a *corps d'élite,* with privileges and payment commensurate with their special skill.

EMOTIONAL DISORDERS
AND LEARNING

As a result of the great pioneering work of Freud, both psychoanalytic and psychodynamic theory and therapy were developed. A few clinical cases were reported in the literature in which children with learning problems made considerable progress during the course of psychotherapy. Also the neurogenic aspects of learning disorders were not yet understood. Thus the child guidance movement in America developed with a psychodynamic frame of reference. Attempts were made by means of play therapy in younger children and insight therapy at later ages to determine the underlying traumatic causes of problems which were thought to have produced "emotional blocks" to learning. Therapy was then directed toward the removal of these blocks in an attempt to "free" the children to learn. After many years of such treatment, it was ascertained that relatively little progress was being made.

Therapists then conceived of the idea that since the home environment was considered to be the source of the child's "emotional block" to learning, it would be necessary to change the home environment in order to help the child progress. Family therapy was then instituted, and in some cases the child and parents attended both individual and family group therapy. It was soon discovered that the results were still not satisfactory and so therapists called for a massive increase in the number of child guidance centers and therapists!

Some physicians, psychologists, and educators became suspicious that psychotherapy based on psychodynamic theory might not be the answer for most children with learning problems. Kurlander and Colodny (psychoanalytically trained child psychiatrists), for example, made a study of all their cases of children who had not responded to psychotherapy (Kurlander and Colodny 1969). They discovered that these children appeared to have a number of things in common which could be subsumed

under the general category "minimal cerebral dysfunction."
They suggested that they had discovered a condition which they
termed *pseudoneurosis*. These children had suffered secondary
emotional problems often related to severe frustrations from unsuccessful attempts to learn in school, and their main difficulty
was found to be related to some form of neurological malfunc-
tion. These physicians therefore prescribed a structured environment, medication, and special education for these children
rather than permissive, insight therapy.

The more they studied their total clientele, however, the
more they became convinced that there may not be a neurotic-
pseudoneurotic dichotomy. More extensive diagnostic procedures revealed fewer psychogenic neurotics and a rise in
the number of children exhibiting neurotic behavior as an overlay of some kind of neurophysiological dysfunction. They found
that an increasing percentage of their patients demonstrated
some of the indications of organicity. Consequently, they began
to question many psychodynamic assumptions, such as: hyperkinetic behavior reflects attempts to run away from personal relationships; hypoactivity means flight into fantasy; destructive behavior results from hostility; difficulty in learning to read may
reflect a learning block or hostility toward parents. Simple alternative explanations for these behaviors sometimes appeared
more likely. Hyperactivity was found very often associated with
neurological dysfunction. Hypoactivity could be associated with
either chemical or neuromotor deficiencies. Destructive behavior was often found associated with poor judgment, uncoordinated motor skills, and hyperactivity. Failure to learn was often
found to be related to developmental lags or visual or auditory
perceptual problems. As a result, these physicians concluded
that for most children expensive psychotherapy should be the
last resort.

The role of the psychiatrist should become a more active one,
as Kurlander and Colodny see it. They believe that it is a waste
of much time to enter psychotherapy in order to discover, very
gradually, presumed interpersonal causes for the child's learning
and emotional problems. It appears to be much more effective to
start with a complete medical examination, followed by a neuro-

logical work-up (see Chapter 3, Chart 1), and a complete battery of psychological, language, and educational tests done by a team (see Chapters 2 and 3). The prescription for the child would then be based on the findings of the complete team diagnostic procedure and would tend to be more effective and less expensive than "drifting into open-ended psychotherapy and waiting for a diagnosis to become apparent."

Korner (1965) stated that differences in disposition and temperament among neonates have been clearly demonstrated by research. However, because of the lag between research findings and child rearing practices, these individual differences are still rarely considered by therapists. Problems with children are still often thought of in terms of what the mother has done to her child. Thus, the mother-child relationship is seldom seen as a reciprocal one. Rarely are individual differences among children given sufficient attention. Rather therapists tend to consider only the mother's personality and handling of her child as important to explain the child's deviant behavior.

As an example of the study of innate individual differences among 2- and 3-day-old, normal babies, Korner observed their responses to massive stimulation while sucking a nipple. It was found that under controlled conditions infants responded by sucking vigorously or freezing, or with an overall motor discharge. These different behaviors to the same stimulation on the part of infants could conceivably cause feelings of either acceptance or rejection in the mothers and so trigger quite different responses from them. Moreover, these neonatal reactions suggest possible differences in choice of defense mechanisms to be used in later life.

Korner believes that while the mental health professions deserve credit for recognizing the importance of good mothering, they must also share responsibility for the development of much guilt in modern parents.

Research on newborn babies during the past decade has been proceeding along several different lines to ascertain the type and extent of biologically determined individual differences. Studies have been made of such spontaneous behaviors as startles, rhythmical mouthing, reflex smiling, sobbing inspirations, facial twitches and so forth. These studies should help to improve our understanding of children's behavior and of reciprocal relations between parents and children.

THERAPY

The effectiveness of play therapy, insight therapy, and family therapy has not been determined for children with learning disabilities. If these forms of therapy are to be used successfully, their proponents must perform the necessary research to establish the specific categories of children who may benefit from each.

Behavior modification therapy seems to be receiving more acceptance than insight forms of therapy for helping children with learning disabilities. Behavior modification may be used by both parents and classroom teachers and involves principles of good teaching which every educator should use. An example may be found in the engineered classroom, a concept developed by Haring, Phillips, Hewett, and others. The principles of conditioning derived from Pavlov, Watson, and Skinner are used. Rewards are liberally used to reinforce all learning, and the teaching process is reduced to sufficiently small bits to be learned that success is virtually guaranteed. Negative reinforcement or punishment is avoided. Behavior modification or conditioning therapy has also been used successfully to modify a child's hyperactivity in the classroom to permit him to attend to learning.

The proponents of insight therapy disagree with the behaviorists and say that such conditioning leaves the basic cause of the hyperkinesis unresolved, so that other problems will appear later which may be even worse. The conditioning therapists deny this. They claim, on the other hand, that the insights which clients talk of in therapy tend to coincide with the belief system of each individual therapist and so are not reliable.

Conditioning therapy has been subjected to longitudinal study under controlled conditions in the Santa Monica, California, school system. The approach tested was Hewett's engineered classroom. Some success has been claimed for this technique in teaching both neurologically impaired and emotionally disturbed children. On the other hand, no method so far tested of teaching handicapped children has been completely successful. Refinements of research technique are required to separate the children into categories according to specific deficits in order to determine which teaching methods are most appropriate for each deficit syndrome.

NEUROLOGICAL DYSFUNCTION AND LEARNING DISABILITIES

As long as children with learning problems were sent to child guidance centers, where the dominant philosophy was that such problems were the result of "learning blocks" produced by environmentally induced trauma, the relationship between learning and neurological functions could not be discovered. Therefore our knowledge of this relationship was first derived from the studies of brain-injured children and later from research in the speech, hearing, and language development fields.

Denhoff helped bring to our attention the similarities between cerebral palsied children and normal-appearing children who had learning deficits (Denhoff and Robinault 1960). An important recent contribution to the field comes from the Spastic Centre of New South Wales, Australia, in the form of a book by Brereton and Sattler (1967) and a 16 mm color sound film, "Basic Abilities." Both the book and the film discuss the deficits in neurological learning modalities found in spastic children, as well as specific training plans to overcome each defect. One important value of the film is that the sensory learning deficits are clearly visible in these children so that the reasons for each specific retraining procedure are readily understood. This makes it possible to understand both the nature of the "hidden" deficits and the reasons why each retraining procedure should be applied to normal-appearing children who have these same learning defects. It also becomes quite apparent that such deficits in sensory learning modalities are much more likely to be neurogenic than psychogenic.

Brereton and Sattler propose a basic abilities treatment plan for spastic children which has clear implications for learning disabilities children. They carefully determined the preschool tactile, visual-motor, and auditory perceptual activities which normal children encounter developmentally and which spastic children often are unable to manage without help. The activities selected were those most specifically related to readiness for reading and learning in school. They then developed a basic treatment plan to assist cerebral palsied children through all these developmental stages to prepare them for school. Their treatment plan, which could also benefit many learning disabilities children, includes the following activities:

1. Obtaining information from touching things
2. Appreciation of body position and space
3. Appreciation of distance, position, and order of objects
4. Planning appropriate motor movements
5. Obtaining information from visual observation
6. Selecting objects for attention in static and moving backgrounds

NATIONAL LONGITUDINAL STUDY

The National Institute of Neurological Diseases and Stroke of the U.S. Department of Health, Education, and Welfare has instituted a long-range study of about 90,000 pregnant women and their children. One aspect of this study is to develop more precise information about the etiology and incidence of children with learning disabilities due to minimal brain dysfunction. At least fourteen medical centers across the nation are participating in this research program. They have obtained detailed histories and examinations of the women from early pregnancy through their deliveries. Careful pediatric follow-up of their offspring is continuing at least to school age. Many of the children being followed have already entered grade school.

Both the National Institute of Neurological Diseases and Stroke and the National Society for Crippled Children and Adults cosponsored with the Office of Education, three Task Forces. In 1966 Task Force 1 reported on the terminology and identification of minimal brain dysfunction in children (Clements). Task Force 2 reported on the extent of the need both for medical diagnosis and treatment, and for identification of educational capabilities and methods of educating afflicted children (Charing et al. 1969). Task Force 3 reported on research aspects of the problem (Chalfant and Scheffelin 1969).

PROBLEMS OF PARENTS

Psychotherapists have traditionally used nondirective techniques with most patients. Some pediatricians have adopted this same technique with parents who come to them with questions about their children. For example, a mother said to her pediatrician about her 4-year-old child, "Johnny isn't like other children. He's a very busy child and tends to fall all over himself. This behavior doesn't seem normal to me. What should I do?" To which the pediatrician replied, "What do you think?"

Such a nondirective approach could hardly be expected to help this mother with her child. What this child required was a work-up to attempt to determine the causes of his hyperactivity, clumsiness, and other behaviors, which could lead to a helpful diagnosis and prescription.

In this case because of the persistence of the mother, the pediatrician later advised her to see a child psychiatrist. When the child psychiatrist found the boy to be "a normal Tom Sawyer type" in a one-to-one relationship, the pediatrician next suggested that the mother see a psychiatrist. Fortunately the psychiatrist she saw recognized that the mother did not require psychotherapy.

Since the mother continued to insist that there was something wrong with her child, the pediatrician ordered an electroencephalogram. The EEG showed right occipital intermittent paroxysmal, slow waves, whereupon a neurologist told the mother, "Your boy will never be able to learn. And you will never be able to take a vacation from this hyperkinetic child."

The pediatrician, on the other hand, insisted, "The EEG doesn't mean a thing. Your boy is perfectly normal."

Neither was correct and neither knew how to help this mother and child. What the child needed was a comprehensive diagnostic procedure, as described in some detail in the case discussions in later chapters.

A few years later this child received such a comprehensive diagnostic study and was found to have above 120 IQ in the presence of severe visual-motor disabilities. He was medicated with diphenylhydantoin (Dilantin) and methylphenidate (Ritalin) and placed in a special education class where he progressed with modest success. His best channel for learning was found to be aural, so most of his information was gathered in this manner. His spelling and writing problems persisted and, although he had severe visual-motor deficits, some of his visual learning channels were intact so that much was accomplished through them. Thus if tested orally, he could perform much better than if he was given the same test in printed form. Since many handicapped children have similar problems, some schools and colleges are making provision for such students to have their examinations read to them after which the students write or type the answers; or they may be permitted to take tests orally.

Parents Take Action

Parents have not been able to wait for complete scientific answers to the problems of their children with learning disabilities. Parents have pushed both professionals and schools into furnishing diagnostic and remedial services. The problems of these children have recently come sharply into focus as the result of urbanization and the fact that school dropouts could no longer get jobs. Previously, intelligent children with learning disabilities may have dropped out of school and found their way into the world of work. This is no longer possible since there are very few jobs left which do not require some degree of literacy.

Children with hyperkinetic impulse disorders may present most difficult problems to both their parents and the total family constellation. Often these children are so active and engage in so much impulse-driven, random behavior that they completely wear out any adult who must care for them. Only those who have lived with such children can appreciate the wearing qualities that continuous impulsive, random behavior and perseveration can have on adults. Therefore these parents have banded together and have demanded the services necessary both to help their children and to preserve their own sanity.

In a 1965 San Francisco survey of middle-class parents of children with learning disabilities, it was found that mothers were most often credited with *first* noticing the children's problems. Pediatricians were cited in only 14 percent of the cases. In a 1969 California survey pediatricians assisted in identifying the problem in 46 percent of the cases. However, these particular pediatricians represented a small percentage of those in each community. Most of the parents were referred to specific pediatricians who were considered knowledgeable by school personnel or by other parents who had previously located them.

DIAGNOSTIC TEAMS

Since at least 5 percent of the population of children are believed to have learning disabilities, it will be necessary for a great many more physicians to become prepared to help them. Because of the complexities and multidisciplinary nature of the diagnosis, a great many more teams are needed. Three examples of combined diagnostic and remedial clinics are discussed in this volume: one in Providence, Rhode Island (see Chapter 3); one in Little Rock, Arkansas (Chapter 2); and one in San Francisco (Chapter 6). There are, of course, a great many other such private facilities available throughout the country. San Francisco, for example, has five. Examples of complete diagnostic work-ups are given in the chapters by Denhoff and Tarnopol and by Clements et al. The cases presented in these chapters are given in sufficient detail so that anyone wishing to set up a diagnostic center in a clinic, public school, or private school should be helped by the information available.

The diagnostic examination of the pediatric neurologists has also been set forth in sufficient detail so that a physician who wishes to enter into this type of practice should find valuable information in the text. Since one of the most helpful functions of a physician vis-à-vis children with learning disabilities is prescribing proper medication, several chapters discuss medication in great detail. It is hoped that physicians and other professionals will be encouraged to enter this important expanding field, and that many who are in the field will be able to increase the quality of their work.

EDUCATIONAL PROBLEMS

The number of children with learning disabilities due to minimal brain dysfunction is so great that neither private clinics nor the present special education approach in public schools will be able to give adequate help to all of these intelligent children. If, for example, the number of children involved is only 2 percent, this would represent almost 100,000 public school children in California and over 1 million children throughout the nation. The cost of special classes for 100,000 California children is estimated to be about $120 million per year, which is probably a manageable sum for the State of California. However, if the number of children involved is at least 5 percent as estimated by the National Institutes of Health and the California State Department of Special Education, then the cost of diagnostic procedures and special classes may become unmanageable.

The most reasonable approach to the solution of this problem, therefore, appears to be a multifaceted one. First, special emphasis will have to be placed on developing reading and writing readiness for these children (between 5 and 20 percent of the population) during the preschool and kindergarten years. This will require both preschool and kindergarten screening of *all* children, followed by more extensive diagnostic procedures for those children who appear to have visual-auditory-motor perceptual problems. Based on each child's differential diagnosis, prescriptive teaching should be supplied as, for example, in Brereton and Sattler (1967). Second, it will be necessary for all elementary teachers and some secondary teachers to learn how to teach these children so that most may be retained in the regular classrooms. In order to accomplish this, the teaching methods which have been developed in the field of special education will have to be taught as part of the general education curriculum. This will undoubtedly benefit all children since a great deal of important information about how children learn has been derived from research in special education. Third, a large number of itinerant teacher specialists must be developed to work part time with learning disabilities children who remain in the classroom. And finally, full-time special education classes will be required for a certain number of learning disabilities children whose handicaps prevent them from functioning in a regular classroom. If such classes are started in kindergarten, many of these children should be able to return to regular classrooms with the part-time help of itinerent specialist teachers.

In this manner untold numbers of intelligent children with learning disabilities may be saved to become useful, productive future citizens.

ACKNOWLEDGMENT

Permission to quote Dr. Masland and Drs. Kurlander and Colodny from Tarnopol, L. (Ed.), *Learning Disabilities: Introduction to Educational and Medical Management.* Springfield, Ill.: Thomas, 1969, is gratefully acknowledged.

REFERENCES

Brereton, B. L., and Sattler, J. *Cerebral Palsy: Basic Abilities.* Mosman, Australia: The Spastic Centre of New South Wales, 1967.

Chalfant, J. C., and Scheffelin, M. A. *Central Processing Dysfunctions in Children.* National Institute of Neurological Diseases and Stroke Monograph No. 9. Washington, D.C.: Superintendent of Documents, 1969.

Charing, N. G., et al. *Minimal Brain Dysfunction in Children: Educational, Medical and Health Related Services. Phase Two of a Three-Phase Project.* U.S. Department of Health, Education and Welfare, Public Health Service Publication No. 2015. Washington, D.C.: Superintendent of Documents, 1969.

Clements, S. D. *Minimal Brain Dysfunction in Children.* National Institute of Neurological Diseases and Blindness Monograph No. 3. Washington, D.C.: Superintendent of Documents, 1966.

Critchley, M. *Dyslexia: A World Wide Problem.* Third Symposium of the San Francisco Chapter of the California Association for Neurologically Handicapped Children, 1969.

Cruickshank, W. M., Bentzen, F. A., Ratzeburg, F. H., and Tannhauser, M. T.   *A Teaching Method for Brain-injured and Hyperactive Children: A Demonstration-pilot Study.* Syracuse: Syracuse University, 1961.

Denhoff, E., and Robinault, I. P.   *Cerebral Palsy and Related Disorders: A Developmental Approach to Dysfunction.* New York: McGraw-Hill, 1960.

Korner, A. F.   Mother-child interaction: one- or two-way street? *Social Work* 10:47, 1965.

Kurlander, L. F., and Colodny, D.   Psychiatric Disability and Learning Problems. In L. Tarnopol (Ed.), *Learning Disabilities: Introduction to Educational and Medical Management.* Springfield, Ill.: Thomas, 1969.

Masland, R. L.   Children with Minimal Brain Dysfunction: A National Problem. In L. Tarnopol (Ed.), *Learning Disabilities: Introduction to Educational and Medical Management.* Springfield, Ill.: Thomas, 1969.

Meehan, M.   Learning disabilities (Editorial). *Journal of the American Medical Association* 209:1217, 1969.

Peters, J. E., Clements, S. D., Danford, B. H., Dykman, R. A., and Reese, W. G.   A Special Neurological Examination for Children with Minimal Brain Dysfunctions. Mimeographed. Little Rock: University of Arkansas Medical Center, 1967.

Strauss, A. A., and Kephart, N. C.   *Psychopathology and Education of the Brain-Injured Child.* New York: Grune & Stratton, 1955.

Strauss, A. A., and Lehtinen, L. E.   *Psychopathology and Education of the Brain-Injured Child.* New York: Grune & Stratton, 1947.

2 Two Cases of Learning Disabilities

SAM D. CLEMENTS, JOANNA S. DAVIS,
RUTH EDGINGTON, CLEO M. GOOLSBY,
AND JOHN E. PETERS

THE TWO CASES presented in this chapter represent "mild to moderate" examples from the broad category of learning disabilities which are referred to our clinic.

The Child Study Center is the service and training unit of the Division of Child and Adolescent Psychiatry of the University of Arkansas Medical Center in Little Rock. Perhaps the motto of the University of Arkansas Medical Center best summarizes the variety of programs in which our staff of thirty specialists engages: "To Teach; To Serve; To Search." Our teaching and training responsibilities are directed to medical students, nursing students, residents in psychiatry, residents in pediatrics, social work trainees, educators, interns in clinical psychology, and other mental health specialists.

Although direct service to children, adolescents, and their families takes many forms, including diagnosis, treatment, and consultation to schools and mental health agencies, the bulk of our service is conducted on an outpatient basis. Our Center includes a Therapeutic Day School and a small inpatient unit for children and young adolescents. The age range of the youngsters served is from infancy to 18 years.

The request for service from our Center may originate with the family physician, the school, any community or state agency, or the parents themselves. The original contact may be by telephone, letter, or personal walk-in. Once an experienced staff member accepts a case as appropriate, a set of three forms is sent or given to the contact person. These include a parents' form, a school form, and a family physician's form. These request rather extensive and detailed information about the child and the referring problems. When the three forms are completed and returned, an appointment time is mailed to the parents. We require that both parents, when applicable, be present for the initial evaluation.

The completed forms give us information as to the nature and extent of the problems. This information is used to constitute the team of specialists from our group which seems most appropriate for the particular case. Since ours is a child and adolescent psychiatry department which utilizes a multidisciplinary approach to the diagnosis and treatment of the full spectrum of learning, behavior, and emotional disorders, the individual case determines the number and disciplines of the participating team members.

Approximately one hour before a new case is scheduled for initial appointment, a planning conference is held by the team. During this time the information obtained from the forms completed by the parents, school, and physician is disseminated and discussed, and a diagnostic plan of action is formulated. One half-day is set aside for each new case work-up by a team. In many cases this is sufficient for completion of the evaluation. Others, of course, may require one or several return visits before the team is satisfied that all necessary information and diagnostic procedures have been obtained.

In a written presentation such as this chapter, it seems useful for each team member to present separately his or her involvement with the two cases. Such a format may give the impression that the child and his family are fragmented into distinct segments of investigation as each of us proceeds with our major areas of diagnostic responsibility. This is not in fact true in our Center, where the custom is to share the diagnostic process in its entirety.

Commonly, two of us, any two, go to the waiting room and

introduce ourselves to the family and take them, child or adolescent included, to a room where the total team is assembled. After introductions, we share with the family the manner in which we will proceed with the evaluation that day. The usual pattern is that the child will first accompany the child psychologist along with one or two other team members who will observe or participate, or both, during the psychological evaluation. The parents at the same time go with the psychiatric social worker and one or two others for the initial interview and history taking. All team members move freely in, out, and within any of the parent and child sessions. The parents and the child are informed that this will occur, and in our experience it does not interfere with the evaluation. Rather, this method serves to unify the diagnostic process for the family as well as for the team.

When all necessary diagnostic procedures are completed, the family is asked to return to the waiting room or go for a refreshment break. The entire team then reassembles to share and discuss the accumulated diagnostic data.

The evaluation team then establishes a diagnostic formulation and lists precise recommendations for a program of management. Following this the parents are called in and our information and decisions are relayed to them in a team discussion. The parents are encouraged to ask questions of any of us and are given ample time to do so. Team members are assigned specific areas of responsibility for enactment of the management program and arrangements for its fulfillment and follow-up. With a child of school age, the parent discussion is followed by a separate wrap-up session with the youngster. This gives the child or adolescent the same opportunity to ask questions and to know of any plans for the future.

As indicated, the cases of Darrell and Robert represent "mild to moderate" examples from the broad category of learning disabilities. This concept and this category contain within them a variety of children with many unique profiles of deficits and strengths. In both cases, the chief complaints centered around problems in learning and behavior with impending school failure. Neither case is burdened by complex pathological environmental factors.

The moderate to severe cases of specific learning disabilities (minimal brain dysfunctions) are more conspicuous and, in our opinion, more easily diagnosed. From the standpoint of happiness and productivity of the child and his family, equal importance should be placed on the detection and management of these more subtle symptom complexes which the cases of Darrell and Robert represent.

CASE OF DARRELL

Family-Social History

At the time of evaluation, Darrell was 8 years and 7 months of age. He started school in the fall of 1966 at the age of 6 years and 2 months. His parents saw him as a bright, likeable little boy— not perfect, of course, for he seemed on the immature side. He could not dress himself and his speech was somewhat unclear. His father worried a bit about his lack of coordination; his mother was anxious that the other children might not let him play with them.

In his second year of school, his teacher referred him to the school's Special Services Department for psychological testing "to determine why he was not achieving at the level of average intelligence indicated by a group test." After the evaluation the parents were told Darrell's intellectual functioning was above average, but that he was below average on certain tasks requiring visual perception and visual-motor integration. Testing also revealed he was hyperactive and could not concentrate well. They were advised to have him undergo a complete physical, including hearing and vision examinations; that they should give him more opportunities to accept responsibility; and that if he did not make better progress in the near future, he should be reevaluated in two years.

A year later, in February 1969, his parents had become quite concerned about him. His rate of academic progress was slower than in the previous two years. They had had many conferences at school, always hearing that Darrell was "immature, fidgety, distractible, and unable to concentrate." The teacher said he required constant personal attention and help. They had tried seating him at the back of the room, at the front, and immediately beside the teacher, but nothing seemed to help. The parents were confused and discouraged. They had followed the school's recommendations. His hearing and vision were reported normal; the pediatrician had reported Darrell was a perfectly normal little boy. His parents had worked hard to assist him with homework; they had praised and encouraged him in physical tasks and exposed him to a well-rounded social environment such as Scouting, church, and boys' club sports. His articulation problem persisted in spite of speech therapy.

The following is a direct quote from the father, a nice-looking, personable, 30-year-old college graduate: "I'm concerned mainly about two things; his lack of coordination and his inability to concentrate on anything for over sixty seconds. He wants to compete and to excel in sports—he wants to so badly!—but he can't. He gets his feet mixed up and can't even kick a football. He is uncoordinated; he writes with his right hand, kicks with his left foot."

The mother has a warm, ready smile. She is 29 years old and has a high school education. She expresses in a healthy way her mixed feelings about her son. There was the hint of tears as she said, "It upsets me when he comes home and says the kids don't want to play with him because he's not as good as they are." Later, her irritation came through as she fumed, "He can never find anything to occupy him for longer than a few minutes. He nags me for something else to do, somewhere to go, someone to see. My patience wears out. Sometimes I feel like knocking him down."

She told us about a visit to his classroom this year. It was depressing for her. Darrell was up and down, distracting other children from their work and constantly wiggling. He got very little work done; he couldn't copy things from the board. She felt like shaking him and wondered how the teacher could abide him. And yet she was defensive, of course, because the teacher conveyed to her that Darrell's immature behavior was somehow the parents' fault. This was not true of all his teachers, and in fact this year's principal had been sympathetic and had encouraged them to seek professional help.

As parents, they talked about their home and family life and

Darrell's two younger sisters, one age 2½ years, the other a 2-month-old baby. They were content with the other children and with the way the three of them got along. There was the usual array of play equipment. Darrell and his father spend a good bit of time together and share activities such as football, golf, and fishing. It was my impression that the parents share responsibility and decision-making in all areas. They were not critical of each other's parental or marital roles. Their concern for Darrell was mutual; they seemed in absolute agreement about receiving professional help. In their own words, "We believe there is something wrong, in a physical way, that our pediatrician can't find, and that we can't help Darrell with. We don't know anything else to do."

When I asked for information about Darrell's infancy, the mother exclaimed, "He just wasn't a normal little baby. He spat up his formula and cried for six months with colic. He was underweight. He didn't play or make noise. He never crawled—just scooted a bit. He wanted me to hold him. He slept with us most of his first year; it was the only way we could rest."

The pregnancy was normal except for the mother's alarming 50-pound weight gain. Darrell was a full-term baby, but labor was an exhausting twenty hours and required considerable sedation. Delivery was by instruments. The baby was very blue and his breathing so difficult as to require oxygen for forty-eight hours. He had to be aspirated repeatedly. He was still a bluish color five days later when they left the hospital. It was thought the baby's breathing might have been hindered by the long period of sedation for the mother. Also at birth the anterior ridge of the fontanel was so pronounced it "looked like it was almost pushing through the skin."

Darrell's early motor development was within normal limits; however, speech and language development were delayed in that he never did coo or babble and was almost 3 years of age before he put more than two words together into a sentence. The mother stated, "We thought he never would talk." Also about this age his clumsiness became apparent. He started out using his left hand but gradually switched to the right with no intervention by the parents. He still requires help in tying his shoes and dressing. The mother "checks" him as he goes out the door because he is apt to be buttoned up wrong, have the heel of the sock on top of his foot, or forget his belt.

Darrell's history includes a combined case of German measles and chicken pox at age 2. Other than a seasonal allergy from hay fever, he is healthy. He has never been hospitalized, and his only injury had been a broken nose.

In the area of personality development, Darrell's parents were aware of some mild problems. He was afraid of the dark longer than they expected him to be and he tended to panic in new situations. He was overtalkative once he started and required too much personal attention. Before he started school they recognized he was immature for his age.

Summary. The presenting complaint of learning problems seems to be just that—not a symptom of family pathology or a coverup for more serious problems in the child. The history of birth trauma, the mixed laterality, awkwardness, delayed speech, hyperactivity, and school history all point to the possibility of neurological deficits in a child of good intelligence. The marriage and home situation appear to be within normal limits. The parents are intelligent; their anxiety is justified. Their acceptance of Darrell's problems and their cooperation in following the advice given them in the past indicates a minimum of defensiveness, denial, or scapegoating. I believe them to be a healthy family with good potential for successful treatment, which is enhanced by the availability of excellent resources in the school system and the community.

Psychological Evaluation

From the moment we met Darrell in the waiting room, he could best be described as "effervescent." However, as the day progressed, he became more and more like a long-opened bottle of soda from which time had taken its toll of bubbles. His general enthusiasm and willingness to try, however, never waned. The psychological evaluation was started at nine-thirty in the morning when he was most fresh.

Darrell worked diligently throughout the evaluation and drained off his excess motor energy by fidgeting in his chair, shuffling his feet, and tapping his fingers. As is customary after a few moments of conversation and explanation of procedures, the psychological evaluation was started with the Wechsler Intelligence Scale for Children. This assessment technique, if thought of as something other than an IQ test, can be one of the most powerful of all diagnostic measures for children with learning disabilities. The clinical interchange between child and examiner during the one to two hours necessary for its administration really becomes a microcosm of the language-learning-behavior processes and permits cross-section sampling of communication and social skills as well as cognitive style and power. It is for this reason that other team members frequently observe during this part of the evaluation.

TABLE 2-1.   *Darrell's Scores on the Wechsler Intelligence Scale for Children*

Age: 8 years, 7 months   Grade: 3rd

Test	Scaled Score	IQ
Verbal Scale	65	119
Performance Scale	58	111
Full Scale	123	117

Test	Scaled Score	Test Age Equivalent (years and months)
VERBAL TESTS		
Information	14	10.8
Comprehension	17	13.10
Arithmetic	10	8.10
Similarities	13	11.6
Vocabulary	15	11.0
Digit Span	9	8.2
Sum Verbal Tests	78	
PERFORMANCE TESTS		
Picture Completion	13	10.6
Picture Arrangement	13	10.6
Block Design	11	9.8
Object Assembly	11	9.6
Coding	10	8.4
Sum Performance Tests	58	

As Table 2-1 shows, Darrell achieved a Verbal Scale IQ of 119 and a Performance Scale IQ of 111. By Wechsler's classification, his general intellectual functioning is in the "bright normal" range. Of much greater importance, however, is the manner in which these scores were achieved and the pattern they assume. The Scaled Score column shows that subtest variance ranges from a score of 9 on Digit Span to 17 on Comprehension, with a test age equivalent ranging from 8.2 years to 13.1 years. Little wonder that these children are popularly referred to as "scatter" children. There is a comparative drop in the last three Performance Tests—Block Design, Object Assembly, and Coding—which involve visual decoding, visual-motor organization, and reconstruction in space. Efficiency in these skills is fundamental to all language. An example of an expressive language deficit occurred when in response to the question: How are a plum and a peach alike? Darrell replied, "Got both stems and got both skin." Uncertainty regarding mathematical concepts and computation was also apparent (Arithmetic Subtest), and a deficit in immediate auditory recall and attention was indicated by the Digit Span Subtest. Research indicates that lowered comparative scores on the Wechsler subtest triad of Arithmetic, Digit Span, and Coding are one of the main diagnostic patterns for children with learning disabilities due to minimal brain dysfunctions.

In a one-to-one situation away from the sights, sounds, and pressures of a classroom Darrell was able to sight-read paragraphs at a low third-grade level with good comprehension. In a mildly stressful situation using the strict scoring of the Revised Gray Oral Reading Test, which counts hesitations and repetitions as errors, he scored at the 1.3 grade level. These tests comprise a gross reading assessment and do not yield information regarding the details of the skill of reading.

The reproductions made by Darrell of the Bender Visual Motor Gestalt Test are shown in Figure 2–1. It should be noted that Darrell required seven minutes to copy the designs, whereas the average time for children this age is five minutes.* The reproductions indicate the already stated deficits in visual decoding and visual-motor reconstruction in space.

Following our usual procedure after the two-hour psychologi-

* See Figure 2–2 for an adequate reproduction of these designs.

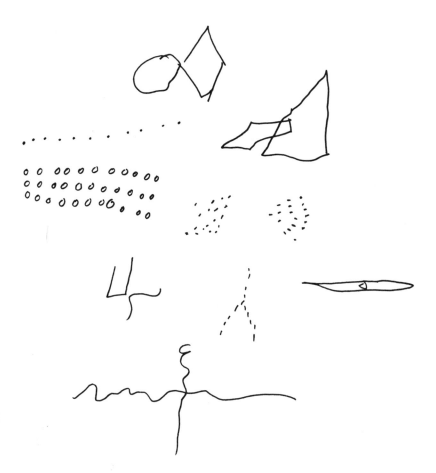

FIGURE 2-1. *Darrell's copy of the Bender Visual Motor Gestalt figures. Shows poor eye-hand coordination for a child of 8 years, 7 months.*

cal evaluation, Darrell was taken to the cafeteria for a refreshment break, as well as for our observations of him in a relaxed social situation. He pranced down the corridor, was quite self-assured, ordered for himself, engaged in animated conversation, and managed to spill only a little of his soft drink as he jogged to the table.

Language Evaluation

In order for a child to engage in the basic language functions of reading, speaking, and writing, it is necessary that he first receive auditory and visual stimuli, then process these stimuli for meaning, and finally store or express this material. The main channels through which we receive information are our eyes and ears; the main channels used in expressing ourselves are our voices and our hands. In a most wondrous and miraculous manner, our brain integrates and processes the information received from auditory and visual sources so that data may be sent out for us to speak or write.

We may postulate one additional language process which is a part of this tapestry of communication. This fourth aspect is referred to as the *automatic language level* and is in evidence when we are involved in such activities as visual and auditory closure, rote learning of items, and blending sounds into a word. Automatic language is still highly organized and integrated but less voluntary than the other language aspects just mentioned.

The following outline delineates the areas which must be included in the language evaluation of a child referred for disabilities in learning.

I. Receptive Language Process: How well a person can recognize or understand what is seen or heard.
   A. Auditory
   B. Visual
II. Integrative Language Process: How well a person can code, sort, select, organize, retrieve, and retain information from different channels of communication.
   A. Auditory-visual-motor-sequential
   B. Auditory-motor
   C. Visual-motor
III. Expressive Language Process: How well a person can express himself in speaking and writing.
   A. Auditory (speaking)
   B. Visual (writing)
IV. Automatic Language Process: How well a person can repro-

duce a sequence seen or heard; how well a person can synthesize sounds in a word; a person's ability in visual or auditory closure, and so on.

   A. Auditory
       1. Closure
       2. Sequencing
   B. Visual
       1. Closure
       2. Sequencing

For purposes of organization the language functions presented in the outline appear separate and distinct. In reality they are very much related, with considerable overlapping and interdependence between and among functions. It is an impossibility to test solely for receptive or integrative or expressive language. One tries to choose tests which are primarily designed to check one of the foregoing aspects of language. Even then at least one other language area is always involved.

In the case of Darrell the measures used to evaluate these language functions were (1) selected subtests from the revised Illinois Test of Psycholinguistic Abilities (ITPA), (2) selected subtests from the Detroit Tests of Learning Aptitude, (3) the Picture Story Language Test by Myklebust, and (4) selected subtests from the Wechsler Intelligence Scale for Children (WISC).

Throughout the language evaluation Darrell was very cooperative. However, his distractibility and short attention span necessitated several "time-outs" during testing—the number of drinks of water and journeys to the men's room was considerable. During the tests for visual and auditory memory, as well as on other items, Darrell found it necessary to "talk himself through" the directions by whispering verbal cues to himself.

The *receptive language* section of the testing was to check how well Darrell understood what he heard and saw. To determine if he understood what he heard, the Auditory Reception subtest of the ITPA was used. In this subtest, a child is given questions to which he answers "yes" or "no." Some of these questions are: Do boys play? Do chairs eat? Do cosmetics celebrate?

Darrell's score of 7 years, 3 months suggests that this type of activity, where *only* auditory information is received, is difficult for him.

To determine Darrell's ability to understand what he saw, another subtest of the ITPA, Visual Reception, was used. A stimulus picture was presented. According to directions, Darrell looked at the picture for three seconds and then he looked at the response page. His job was to find on the response page a picture conceptually similar to the picture he saw first. Darrell missed many items in this subtest, achieving a score of 7 years, 4 months. Again, paying attention to sensations from only one modality, in this case visual, was difficult for him.

Integrative language tests try to evaluate how well a child can organize and put into sequence what he sees and hears, and then how well he can translate this into a proper response preparatory to storage or expression. The Oral Directions subtest from the Detroit Tests of Learning Aptitude was one measure chosen to test integrative language. Darrell was asked to listen to each direction, then do what he was told.

For example, the directions for the first section were: "Put a *one* in the circle and a *cross* in the square; do it now." As a child goes to the other sections, directions become increasingly difficult due to more complex language concepts and the need to retain greater amounts of auditory information.

Other tests given for integrative language were the Information and Picture Arrangement subtests of the WISC. Darrell performed well above his chronological age on the Oral Directions test (10 years) and the two subtests from the WISC (10 years, 8 months and 10 years, 6 months). Of these last two tests, one checked his ability to integrate *auditory* information with a verbal or motor response, and the other test measured his ability to integrate *visual* stimuli with a motor response.

It is instructive to contrast Darrell's performance in the integrative and receptive language areas. As indicated he scored 7 years, 3 months and 7 years, 4 months on the receptive tests, one of which measured his understanding of questions given orally. Yet in the integrative language area, he achieved at least 1½ to 2 years *above* his chronological age on all three subtests. His higher scores on integrative language may have been due to the stimulation he was receiving from the other sensory avenues. In other words, Darrell seemed able to pay more attention and function better when he was getting stimulation from his eyes and his ears as well as his hands. His attention tended to break down when only auditory or only visual stimuli were presented.

In the *expressive language* section of the testing, the Vocabulary subtest from the WISC was used to determine how well Darrell could evoke words spontaneously and to get a sample of his grammar, syntax, sentence length, and vocabulary usage when speaking. Here again he scored far above the norm for his age (11 years). While he was talking, however, it was evident that there was something peculiar about the way he spoke. One's attention was attracted to the child's mouth and what it was doing. One reason may have been because Darrell's words still sounded babyish. He substituted *b* for *v*, so *very* became *berry* and *television* became *telebision*. *Three* was *thwee* and *play* was *pray*. His tongue often thrust forward while he talked and although it did not protrude, one was always aware of its presence. When Darrell tried to make very rapid repetitive movements with his lips, tongue, and jaw, he could only perform these motions slowly—below the norm for children his age. So although he could use words to express himself well, he still showed problems involving the mechanics of speaking.

The Myklebust Picture Story Language Test evaluates a child's ability to express himself through writing a story. Several areas are checked: total words, total sentences, words per sentence, syntax involving word usage, capitalization, punctuation, word order, and degree of imagination used in the story. Darrell was considerably below the 8-year norm (6 years, 9 months) in all areas of written expressive language, as measured by this test.

As a last part of the language assessment, *auditory and visual automatic language* was checked. To evaluate auditory closure (the ability to match parts of spoken words with the whole word) the Auditory Closure subtest from the ITPA was used. Darrell was asked, "Tell me what word this is: *da-y* (daddy); *bo-le* (bottle); *tele-one* (telephone)." Darrell found this a difficult task and made a score of 7 years, 3 months. It is entirely possible that one reason for his poor ability to listen or pay attention to verbal material is due to this problem in understanding partial words.

The second subtest under automatic auditory language in the ITPA is Sequential Memory for Numbers. Darrell scored 8 years, 2 months in this area, indicating that he has some difficulty in holding auditory information in sequential order.

To determine how well Darrell could find partial pictures of objects that were hidden (visual closure ability), the ITPA subtest of Visual Closure was given. His score of 8 years suggests he may have some deficit in this area, a deficit which could affect his ability to see letters as wholes and write them as one unit.

On a test for sequential visual memory, Darrell was asked to repeat in order several different series of letters he saw for only a few seconds (Visual Attention Span subtest from the Detroit Test of Learning Aptitude). He achieved a 9-year mental age on this task, suggesting he is able to remember letter sequences that make up words, a necessary ability for reading.

Summary. Darrell evidences deficits in the areas of auditory and visual reception, auditory and visual closure, and auditory sequencing. He also has some problems in expressing himself through writing. However, when he can receive simultaneous stimulation from his eyes, ears, and hands, he seems to be able to focus his attention much more efficiently, thus allowing his good intelligence to shine through.

Recommendations. Since we believe that many of Darrell's language difficulties hinge on his inability to pay attention, it is hoped that medication will enable him to utilize his good intellectual ability by controlling distractibility.

For short periods at first, and then for increasingly longer times, Darrell should be given auditory material which he listens to and then responds to in some way. For example, he could repeat different series of words that are unrelated—house, boy, train, leaf—and then arrange pictures of these words in the correct order. Later the visual clue of pictures could be removed and he would need to rely totally on auditory memory for the sequence.

Again using familiar pictures for visual clues initially, the names of the pictures could be said to Darrell, but with several sounds or syllables omitted. Could he find the picture when he heard only part of the word? When he improved, the pictures could be eliminated, making it necessary for him to depend solely on the auditory stimuli. Spelling words could also be used for auditory closure practice.

Some activities involving the matching of conceptually similar pictures would be a help for Darrell. Sets of pictures and abstract design patterns could be assembled. For brief periods of three to five minutes, he could try to find which stimulus picture or pattern matched another picture or pattern in a group of several possibilities.

Darrell would be helped by practice with such expressive language activities as defining words and then writing sentences using the words. The task of rearranging different word series to form a meaningful sentence would also be good practice for him.

Educational Evaluation

In the educational evaluation, Darrell was given the Frostig Developmental Test of Visual Perception, Informal Handwriting Evaluation, and the Wide Range Achievement Test.

Darrell is 8 years and 7 months of age; the Frostig Test norms are diagnostic only to age 8. Beyond this age a low subtest score is indicative of a possible disability rather than diagnostic. Darrell's age-equivalent score for the Eye-Hand Coordination subtest was well above his chronological age and his score for the Spatial Relationships subtest was close to his age. The high level of eye-hand coordination, as measured by this subtest, is not in accord with the parents' report, the school's report, or our observations during the testing period.

Darrell held his pencil close to the point and pressed hard on the paper. Even then his control of movement was more like that of a first grader. He made vertical lines more easily and adequately than horizontal lines. When material presented required a horizontal line to be drawn, he rotated the paper so that the line could be made the easier way for him. This maneuver is normal for younger children, usually disappearing around 7 to 8 years of age.

A further inconsistency with low areas of the Frostig is his ability to read at grade level and to spell one grade lower. A one-year lag between reading and spelling is normal for the average child performing at grade level. Children with a disability in reading usually lag two or more years behind in spelling. It is usual, also, for these children to perform better in a one-to-one relationship, such as in our clinical evaluation procedures.

The Informal Handwriting Evaluation included the writing of his name, the date, numerals 20 to 30, and the alphabet in both capitals and lower-case letters, ending with the copying of two short, simple sentences at desk level. Copying from the chalkboard was omitted because Darrell's mother had observed in her visits to the classroom that he was unable to do so. The quality of his handwriting was markedly below that of the average third grader. The speed of his writing was also below average but not too abnormally slow. His coordination was noticeably better than indicated on the Frostig Test. In the writing sample, capital letters were fragmented as the required coordination for complex curves (as in *D, F, G, H, I, J, K,* and *X*) was beyond Darrell's current ability. The letters *K* and *X* were not recognized as being different, either visually or in the movement patterns necessary to write them. The lower case letters *b, d,* and *g,* had poor closure; the letters *m* and *n* were confused in writing.

Observe the range of scores within each subject area of the Wide Range Achievement Test scores. His reading level base is 4.1 and the ceiling is 4.2, while the spelling level has a base of 2.4 and a ceiling of 3.4. The lowest area is arithmetic, with a base of 1.8 and a ceiling of 2.9. The base level is the level of usual functioning, while the ceiling is the top level of functioning.

His teacher says that Darrell can perform at grade level in arithmetic if the conditions are right, that is, when she is sitting by him and he is not distracted by the other children. However, the scores on this arithmetic test indicate that he is at the counting or "tally" level with many gaps in his rote memory for the combinations. He also does not understand the meaning of zero in its function as a place holder. Further, he doesn't know when to "carry" or "borrow"; for example, in one problem he was told to add 14 plus 4 and his answer was 9. In another problem, 14 minus 6, his answer was 12.

During the test inventory, certain characteristics were consistently observed. These were a high degree of distractibility, an abnormally short attention span, and a marked degree of hyperactivity. Darrell has very limited ability to sustain his attention for longer than a few minutes. Even the smallest movements within his visual boundary distract him.

His most intact channel for learning appears to be auditory, which he uses to receive information and to guide the expression of what he knows. He shows this clearly by whispering to himself about what he is to do and to self-monitor his work. His method of working lacks the degree of organization usual by the third grade. From watching Darrell work it requires very little imagination to project his work habits into a classroom with 29 other children. He has many endearing qualities, including a sense of humor; yet his lack of progress and his need for constant reassurance are doubtless puzzling and frustrating, not only to him, but obviously to his teacher and his parents.

Recommendations. Recommendations for retraining are as follows:

First, a learning disability resource room if available; as second choice, a tutor skilled with such children.

Second, general retraining plans should include specific training in visual perception combined with auditory support and kinesthetic reinforcement. Instruction and teaching materials should ensure practice in separating background and foreground, awareness of right and left, and form constancy. Training in recall of sequential tasks must also be provided.

Third, protection from environmental stimuli which conflict with what he is to learn is necessary (e.g., from movements which come within his range of vision). Lesson materials should be free of nonessential features and should be divided into small segments within the limits of his attention span. Instructions may be taped so that he can listen as often as necessary. Whispering the words or instructions to himself is not distracting to Darrell and should be permitted, even encouraged if need be, until he shows signs of voluntarily diminished use as an outgrown crutch for learning.

Fourth, all written work should be clearly organized in a set pattern for completion, for example, beginning with his name, date, subject, and page number. Questions should be answered in top to bottom order, not randomly filled in.

Fifth, all work should be checked as soon after completion as possible. The reasoning for any needed correction must precede the actual reworking (with assistance when needed) and the beginning of any new work. The working pace should be geared to an "Ivory soap" level: 99.44 percent successful.

In subject matter the emphasis of retraining should be on writing, spelling, and arithmetic. Prewriting exercises should begin with developing a better pencil position, fluidity, and rhythm. The latter should progress from using the whole arm while standing, to the forearm and hand while seated. Color-cuing the starting point and the direction of movement would be helpful. Finally the emphasis should be on completing any letters, numerals, and words without fragmentation. Copy work should be done at desk level rather than from the chalkboard until there is definite improvement. He will show the teacher when he is ready to try again from the board by the improvement in desk work.

In spelling, phonetic words from the second- and third-grade lists should precede those which are not phonetic. Sounding word elements while each is being written should be given a thorough trial before resorting to letter-naming. If possible letter-naming should be saved for nonphonetic words. Spelling practice should include writing two short sentences with each spelling word. He should ask for any unknown word to be spelled for him. Each word asked for should be written on a slip of paper for him to copy in his sentence. The demand for increasing sentence complexity should be gradual, in line with his ability to sustain a level of continuous success.

In arithmetic, number concepts need rebuilding by the use of concrete materials that are based on physical units without notches or numerical markings. Avoid practice which reinforces rote learning until number concepts and simple relationships are stable.

Darrell's prognosis seems to be good because of his above-average intellectual capacity and the mildness and discreteness of his disabilities. The control of distractibility and lengthening of attention span will determine the length of time for which resource room services will be needed. Perhaps the time will be as short as a full semester to a year. Without improved control of distractibility and attention span lengthening, the time spent will need to be longer.

Neuropsychiatric Evaluation

A specific contribution which the physician makes to the team work-up, and teaches to residents in psychiatry and pediatrics, is a special kind of neurological examination. It consists of an examination of the neurological integrity of complex motor acts, as opposed to the conventional or routine neurological examination which directs itself more to reflexes, condition of muscle groups, and sensory functions. This special neurological examination evaluates such things as movement coordination, movement organization, motor position persistence, eye tracking, and lack of motor differentiation.

The following are some of the findings which were positive for Darrell. On being asked to stand with arms straight out in front, eyes closed, and to hold this position, his arms spread and drifted too much for an 8-year-old. In our research findings, based on 84 cases of children with minimal brain dysfunction (MBD) and 45 control cases, 33 percent of MBD children showed this sign as opposed to 2 percent of controls.

Facing the examiner with arms outstretched, Darrell was asked to imitate finger movements as demonstrated by the physician. He did this rather poorly, often having to look at his fingers, especially the ring finger. MBD children showed poor copying in 35 percent of cases, and controls in 13 percent.

Darrell hopped poorly on one foot. MBD children, 28 percent; controls, 11 percent.

Though Darrell was able to skip for us, his father told an interesting story of how tangled and confused Darrell becomes when trying to kick a football. He is hesitant over which foot to use. The father has observed that other 8-year-olds seemed to have little difficulty with this activity. He also noted how hard Darrell tries and how much he wants to succeed.

On being asked to touch each finger to thumb in sequence,

first one hand and then the other, Darrell's performance was slow and "sticky," indicating poor control and performance in this type of motor task. MBD children, 50 percent; controls, 6 percent.

On alternating movements of the hand, he was moderately impaired. MBD children, 46 percent; controls, 9 percent.

On directionality testing, he showed that he was still somewhat confused, especially on projecting right-left to objects before him, as opposed to his own body. MBD children, 40 percent; controls, 20 percent.

Darrell has a mild speech defect. MBD children, 22 percent; controls, 2 percent.

When writing dictated materials, Darrell reversed the letter *d* and the numbers *9* and *6*. MBD children, 40 percent; controls, 4 percent.

He showed slow, poor, labored handwriting. MBD children, 98 percent; controls, zero.

When Darrell was with the psychologist at nine-thirty in the morning he was fairly composed, except for his feet which were in constant motion. As the hours passed—including many breaks—he began to show the hyperactivity described by his mother and teacher. Finally he was answering questions with his head on the table one minute, and slipping deep into his chair the next. One might say, "Poor little 8-year-old—of course he is tired." But our evaluation of his activity level rests on a background of examining hundreds of children of all kinds and ages.

   Diagnosis.   Two diagnostic systems for psychiatrists are currently in use. The Group for the Advancement of Psychiatry (GAP) diagnosis would be developmental deviation (moderate) manifest in (1) motor, (2) speech, and (3) cognitive functioning.

Considering the Diagnostic and Statistical Manual of the American Psychiatric Association, Volume II (DSM II of APA): no useful or appropriate diagnostic formulation is possible within this outdated system. The "official" diagnoses contained therein force a hard decision between known organic damage and presumptive or probable organic damage. We prefer a descriptive diagnosis with etiological and contributing factors stated as probabilities.

Even the more sensitive GAP diagnostic system implies that

these developmental deviations are more environmentally caused than organically determined. This makes the process of diagnostic formulation according to prevailing systems a matter of the selection of the lesser of two evils. The DSM II of APA, if used, forces one to abandon the organic contribution and label this child's hyperkinesis as an environmental reaction.

The syndrome of hyperactivity which Darrell displays may be related to complications in the pregnancy: the mother gained 50 pounds; labor was of twenty hours' duration; the child was blue for twenty-four hours and required oxygen and frequent aspiration; and his fontanel was abnormal.

In our opinion neither parental attitudes nor child-rearing practices were significant factors in etiology.

In conclusion, we see Darrell as presenting a case of minimal brain dysfunction, but without a significant language disorder. His disabilities in learning appear to be more a consequence of hyperactivity and short attention span.

Recommendations. Recommendations are as follows: (1) Placement in a public school resource room for learning disabilities, (2) brief family counseling regarding home management techniques, (3) medication: methylphenidate, 10 mg morning and at noon, (4) letter to the school summarizing diagnostic data and treatment plan, (5) follow-up visit to the school and consultation with resource room teacher, (6) Darrell and parents to return to Medication Management Clinic at three-month intervals, after initial dosage is verified by means of home and school feedback reports as adequate to attain therapeutic goals.

CASE OF ROBERT

Family-Social History

At the time of evaluation Robert was 14 years and 11 months of age. He was in the tenth grade in a small-town high school, making D's and F's. Last term he made his first F in algebra, bringing to a head the long-standing concern of the family and school about his learning problems. He was referred to our clinic by the family physician who requested "an evaluation of his learning ability." The physician stated that Robert was in good general health, and that he knew of no personal or family conflict that might contribute to the problem. The school reported Robert to be a poor reader and speller although his intelligence was at least in the low average range. They considered him below average in attention span and in ability to follow directions. The school was not critical of the parents in any way. In the principal's opinion the boy had a "mental block" of some kind; he just "refused" to study. Otherwise he was described as a well-groomed, well-mannered, well-liked boy. The parents' reason for getting professional help was a little more to the point. "Can he learn or can't he?" they wrote. "Robert is a good boy who gives us no trouble except in getting him to study. He seems extremely slow in some ways. He can't snap it up; he lacks the spark and zip that some youngsters have. If only we could motivate him."

We later learned that the main concern had always been his reading problem which had become apparent after the first few weeks of the first grade in school. The school records showed the grades gradually going down from B—'s in the first grade in reading and spelling to C's, C—'s in the sixth grade, and finally to D's and F's in the current year. Robert recalls a second-grade teacher who used to spank him to help him "produce." He said sometimes he knew the words but she didn't give him time to get them out. The mother remembers feeling puzzled because she too felt he knew the words but couldn't express them. She used to take him to the library to encourage outside reading. "He invariably selected advanced books on science or something above his head, and of course he couldn't read a word of it." In fact Robert never read anything voluntarily except comic books until this past fall when he began picking out words and trying to read popular magazines on flying, science, and outdoor life.

No family history of reading disability was uncovered. The parents impressed us as relaxed, comfortable, friendly people. The mother is 51 years old and has a high school and business education. She is editor and business manager of the town's weekly newspaper. The father is a jaunty 65, retired from the poultry business. He wears turtleneck sweaters and a mustache and has a ready wit. He is obviously close to Robert and is affectionate and proud. He told us that in spite of his frustration, Robert never complained about going to school. "Robert's smart in lots of ways. He draws pretty well and he can explain things I don't understand, like atom cracking and space flight, by drawing pictures for me. I think some day he's going to get fired up and really get going."

The mother is not so sure. She seems more discouraged and talks about the frustration and guilt she feels. "I guess we haven't done too well. We nag him for hours every night to go and study. Sometimes we bear down and then we let up. It's a wonder he hasn't broken down under the pressure."

Robert has a 20-year-old married sister who made straight A's throughout school. As far as I could tell, the two of them were friends and there was no special friction. The family has lived in the same house for seventeen years, and they seem quite happy with their small income and rural surroundings. They are rather relieved Robert has not "matured" enough yet to chase around with the other boys and girls. He doesn't date and hasn't asked for the family car as yet. There is no conflict in discipline except in trying to get Robert to study.

As for Robert's early history, the pregnancy and birth were within normal limits. The parents didn't recall any complications in development. He had chicken pox, measles, and mumps between ages 3 and 5. He was never seriously ill and sustained no major injuries. They felt he was well coordinated, and he was never confused about which hand to use. Speech and language development were all reported as within normal range. In fact he was a pleasant child who presented no special problem of any kind until he started to school at age 5½ years.

Summary. The team's conclusions based on the family interview were as follows. The family and individual strengths were impressive. They were a stable, close-knit group with a good sense of humor. The father's pride in the boy was a bright spot; the mother's concern and frustration were within normal limits and well balanced by her good sense and the capacity to channel her energies into other outlets. Whatever pressure they had applied to Robert was apparently not so intense nor of a nature to cause serious emotional conflicts. Even though at times Robert may have felt like a "dumb kid," the parental acceptance had helped him develop a relatively healthy self-image.

Recommendations. A few supportive sessions to clarify the diagnosis and plan for management were suggested. In view of Robert's reluctance to study and the mother's frustration about this, any parental help with homework should be done by the father. One problem might be the difficulty of finding the right tutor for Robert in their small community.

Psychological Evaluation

Robert is a rather shy, sincere youngster who is undergoing the variety of changes which will take him from childhood to manhood. At present he is suspended somewhere in between. Since the information from the parents' form indicated that he had always been a quiet, nonverbal child, our emphasis was on activity rather than conversation during the early stages of the evaluation.

Robert sat quietly and listened intently for instructions. He was an excellent worker who got right to the task at hand. He had nothing but good to say about his teachers and school in general. With regard to his poor school achievement and failure, he blamed no one, but rather had concluded that he simply did not have the ability, and except for concern over a vocational choice, he seemed resigned to this fate.

As indicated in Table 2-2, his scores on the Wechsler Intelligence Scale for Children show that he has ability. Robert achieved a Verbal Scale IQ of 114 and a Performance Scale IQ of 122, with a Full Scale IQ of 120. The last two scores, according to Wechsler's classification, are in the "superior" range of intellectual functioning or the top 7 percent of the population. This pattern of low verbal and high performance scores, though not dramatic in Robert's case, is typical of youngsters with severe reading disability who—along with a specific cluster of symptoms, including nonhyperactivity and even-tempered disposition —are frequently referred to as having *primary reading disability* or *developmental dyslexia.*

TABLE 2-2.   *Robert's Scores on the Wechsler Intelligence Scale for Children*

Age: 14 years, 11 months   Grade: 10th

Test	Scaled Score	IQ
Verbal Scale	61	114
Performance Scale	66	122
Full Scale	127	120

Test	Scaled Score	Test Age Equivalent [a] (years and months)
VERBAL TESTS		
Information	14	15.10
Comprehension	14	15.10
Arithmetic	13	15.10
Similarities	11	15.10
Vocabulary	9	13.8
Digit Span	12	15.10
Sum Verbal Tests	73	
PERFORMANCE TESTS		
Picture Completion	14	15.10
Picture Arrangement	15	15.10
Block Design	15	15.10
Object Assembly	12	15.10
Coding	10	14.2
Sum Performance Tests	66	

a Ceiling age is 15 years, 10 months.

It should be noted that Robert's verbal responses are slow and deliberate, and time is required for him to retrieve the words with which he wishes to express himself. The evaluation of such a child requires extreme patience, and the examiner cannot assume that an answer is not known just because delivery is not immediate. A classroom teacher who is not aware of the difficulty such a youngster has in expressive language is apt to bypass him in class discussion and recitation and will presume that the child does not know the answer or is lacking in sufficient knowledge to contribute. This kind of teacher approach simply reinforces the child's feelings of frustration and inadequacy.

Robert's reading was painfully slow and laborious. Sight-reading of paragraphs was at the fifth-grade level with adequate comprehension. On the Revised Gray Oral Reading Test, which is strictly timed, his reading was at the fourth-grade level.

As you might suspect from Robert's superior achievement on the visual-motor tasks of the Wechsler Intelligence Scale, his reproductions of the Bender Gestalt geometric designs are excellent (see Fig. 2-2). These were executed in five minutes and ten seconds.

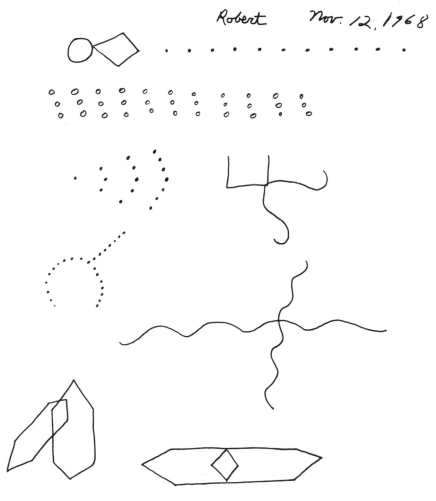

FIGURE 2-2. *Robert's copy of the Bender Visual Motor Gestalt figures. Shows adequate eye-hand coordination for a child of 14 years, 11 months.*

Robert obviously enjoyed the testing experience and, indeed, asked if there were not other things we wanted him to do. As we finished this part of the evaluation, he hung his head slightly and said, "I hope you can help me do better in school." With a youngster such as Robert, we spend considerable time assuring him of his ability level and that indeed we do intend to help him through this situation.

Educational Evaluation

Robert was administered the Wide Range Achievement Test and the Informal Test of Written Language Expression. Robert is 15 years old and in the tenth grade, the sophomore year in high school.

His reading level has a base score of 5.3, a ceiling of 6.4—four to five grades lower than the average high school sophomore. His spelling base level is 3.2 with a ceiling of 5.3, five to seven grades below average; however, his arithmetic level, the highest of the three subtests, ranged from a base of 6.7 to a high of 8.1, which is two to four grades below average. These findings would be serious enough for a child of average ability. For a child in the superior range of intelligence, they are tragic.

Observations of test behavior were revealing as a miniature picture of how he responds to reading, spelling tasks, and arithmetic. In reading he did not sound out unknown words audibly or with lip movements. He would simply wait until he had applied the phonetic skills he could command internally and then attempt the pronunciation. In spelling he used the same style of approach, waiting if he were unsure of how to spell the dictated word. In a few seconds he would write down his attempt.

The pattern of internalizing the process was repeated on the arithmetic subtest. He was told, even encouraged, to use the space below the problems for figuring out the answers. Examples ranged from simple addition to decimal fraction equivalents, such as $34/100 = .34 = 34\%$. He became confused when multiplying fractions and multiplied denominators with numerators. The division of fractions and the averaging of groups of numbers to find percentages of the whole numbers were not understood. He did not make any marks on the paper other than his answers, again internalizing the total process. Extra time in reviewing these processes would be of considerable help.

Since he has had to learn most of what he knows by listening, supported by some visual aids such as pictures or drawings, it was surprising he did not use crutches such as whispering to himself in these subjects or some kind of external aid for improving accuracy in arithmetic.

The Informal Written Language Evaluation was made from a story written about a picture which was shown to Robert. He asked me only one question: "How should I write the story?" I explained there were several ways to do this: describe what he saw in the picture, or perhaps imagine what had happened before this scene and what might happen afterward. He was told he could use one of these approaches or write it in any other manner he wished. He looked at the picture for a few minutes and began.

The story which resulted was written in the first person and the style was direct and informal. The sequence of the events was clear and logical. There were three time divisions, past, present, and future. The ten sentences used averaged fourteen words in length.

Robert's writing was large, uneven in size, and more round than is usual for boys his age, but the results were easily legible. A third of the sentences began with "so." The spelling errors were *where* for *were* and *help* for *helped*. An example of reversed word-order appeared when he wrote "He had to right go home." The level of language patterns used were at the fifth- to sixth-grade level, or perhaps at the average seventh-grade level for informal teen-age communication.

During the testing procedures Robert worked quietly with minimal movements. His attention span was adequate and his attention was not distracted by minor movements or sounds. Brief rest periods were given to reduce fatigue and help him function at his optimal level.

Robert is a quiet fellow who answers politely, but with a minimum of elaboration. He does not appear self-conscious, just naturally a person who does not talk much. He has a sense of humor, smiling or chuckling when joked with. To keep a conversation going questions are needed, even though the topics discussed were ones in which he is very interested, such as civil defense, flying, space travel, science, and architecture. He did tell me in some detail about the first aid kit he was collecting for civil defense. He has spent about eleven dollars on the kit so far and is justifiably proud of its elaborateness. He thinks now he would like to be an architect.

Recommendations. Some compassionate helper should be found to read aloud to him his subject matter assignments. He can learn by listening and should not have his comprehension impaired by trying to read tenth-grade texts with fifth-grade reading skills. The reading should be done at a reduced speed for maximum retention of information. Even though his parents have helped him in the past and can try the reading aloud, they should be watchful for signs of possible resentment, delaying tactics, and poor retention of information. If these symptoms appear someone else should be found, a friend perhaps. Taping an especially difficult lesson for him to replay several times is a very useful technique.

If at all possible, his examinations at school should be given orally. He should be graded for mastery of content and not penalized for being unable to read the examination questions or for his inability to spell, neither of which is his fault.

In other written work grades should be based on his knowledge and logical order of thinking. He has to spell phonetically and makes mistakes, but his phonetic spelling is not difficult to interpret and correct spelling should not be a grading penalty.

Patience and understanding plus tutoring will enable him to continue progressing. Occasional reassurances that he is not "stupid" will be helpful, too. He has been wonderfully patient and willing to continue the struggle to learn, without "kicking over the traces." Many children his age would have long since given up and expressed their frustrations through disruptive behavior. Long periods of failure and self-doubt can be very taxing and troublesome to all concerned.

A tutor should be found to work with him to improve his basic levels of functioning in reading and spelling. The general approach to both subjects should be multisensory and on the basis of parts to whole (e.g., word elements taught separately should be blended into wholes). Motor patterns should be used to form a link between visual and auditory learning. The sessions should be a minimum of an hour in length, preferably four times a week. Less time than this will not be as effective or make progress as smooth and efficient in relation to time and money expended.

The prognosis for retraining and adult functioning is good, based on his intellectual capacity, pleasant personality, and willingness to continue putting forth maximum effort to increase academic learning. Further, the prognosis can be enhanced by keeping expectations in line with what he can reasonably fulfill.

Language Evaluation

Since there are no standardized language tests for children over 10 years of age, selected items from other test batteries were used to evaluate Robert's performance in the areas of receptive, integrative, expressive, and automatic language functioning.

Receptive language was tested using the Peabody Picture Vocabulary Test to check auditory understanding. A stimulus word is given and the subject chooses a picture from a set of four that best matches the stimulus word. Robert scored above 18 years, indicating he has no trouble decoding simple auditory signals. To determine the boy's ability to understand visual stimuli, we used the reading assessment given by the education specialist (see section on Educational Evaluation).

Integrative language was tested by means of the Detroit subtest of Oral Directions. The testing revealed that Robert has some difficulties in this area of integrating sensations from all modalities. His score is 13 years, 9 months—15 months below the norm for his age. When both auditory-motor and visual-motor aspects of integrative language were investigated, Robert performed 10 months above the norm for his age. He scored 15 years, 10 months both on the Comprehension and Information subtests (auditory) of the WISC and on the Picture Arrangement subtest (visual) of the WISC.

Testing in the area of *expressive language* indicated that the boy has many problems in word-finding and often in the formulation of ideas during both speaking and writing. Auditory expressive language (speaking) was checked through the Vocabulary subtest of the WISC. Robert's score was only 13 years, 8 months, the lowest of the WISC Verbal Scale measures. Although the boy's definitions were accurate on the majority of the items, the quality of expression was suggestive of a much younger child, and the phrases and sentences were usually short and without elaboration. Visual expressive language (writing) was tested by the education specialist.

Language testing was concluded by the administration of two subtests to check *automatic language:* Digit Span from the WISC and Visual Attention Span for Letters from the Detroit. Robert's auditory memory and sequencing abilities, factors necessary for repeating digits, were 15 years, 10 months—above the 15-year norms. However, his ability to retain a visual sequence of printed letters was at only the 10-year, 6-month level, or almost five years below the norm for 15-year-olds. Interestingly enough, on this test Robert still evidenced an instance of letter reversals, calling *b, d.* This score seemed particularly significant as it might point to one of the reasons for Robert's poor reading. A child who cannot retain a visual sequence of letters while trying to match it to an auditory pattern will find the mastery of reading the written word an almost impossible task.

What do the foregoing scores tell us about Robert's language? First, he learns best when material is presented aloud. His score on the Peabody indicates he receives and decodes simple auditory stimuli readily and well. Also his performance on sequential auditory functions points to good ability to attend to auditory stimuli and then to recall these stimuli immediately. Further corroboration of his better-than-average ability to learn aurally is his performance on the Information and Comprehension subtests of the WISC.

Language testing also indicated some discrete and subtle language deficits. Following complex oral directions involving visual as well as auditory decoding, selection and storage of information are somewhat difficult for Robert. Expressive language, especially writing, shows many problems. Visual attention span for letters was five years below the norm for his age.

Recommendations. Retraining suggestions given to Robert's parents and tutor include the following:

All assignments should be read aloud or put on tape for him to listen to. In this way he will not be penalized because he cannot read the material for himself.

Some time should be spent during each lesson on vocabulary. Robert should define new words in his assignments orally. He should then write sentences using the new words.

To improve syntax, practice in finding the misplaced words in sentences (words that change the sentence's meaning) might prove helpful. For example, "He went right now home," or "You get a dollar for ten rides" are sentences that mean something entirely different when wording is changed. In this activity Robert should orally state the sentence correctly, then write the sentence.

Practice to increase his visual attention span should also be an important part of Robert's lessons. Devices such as a "Flash-X" or other controlled reading devices could be very useful in helping the boy to increase his visual attention span.

At frequent intervals activities involving complex oral directions should be given. These would provide additional practice for Robert so he might better learn to manage longer and more complicated units of oral material and sequential elements, as well as the language concepts involved. These activities stressing oral directions could contain new vocabulary, sequences of letters, and phonic elements.

Neuropsychiatric Evaluation

Robert performed perfectly on the special neurological examination except for a solitary and minor error: he called a *9* a *6* when it was traced out on the palm of his hand. This is a surprising residual of a defect in memory for directions in space—up-down, right-left, before-after—which was probably a pronounced problem when he was age 8 or 9. It will be recalled that a serious deficit in his memory for sequences of symbols was found when they were presented visually only. This brings to mind the reason why the California pioneer in dyslexia, Grace Fernald, developed a specific multisensory approach for dyslexics—namely, tracing letters and words with the finger while pronouncing them. If there is a deficit in either visual or auditory memory and their integration, this method allows the bits of information to be slowed down to an easy absorption rate and then to become associated by the motor act of tracing with the finger.

Robert's uncertain grasp of letter combinations which are not words but which are common in English was typified in material elicited by the language specialist: For the syllable *oke* as it appears in the word *broke,* Robert read *oik;* for *ome* as it appears in *home,* he read *oim;* for *age* (standing alone or as it appears in *bondage*), he read *edzi.* Some syllables which contain a silent *e* were pronounced correctly; however, for *ize* as in *size* he said *i-zee.* For *uit* as in *suit* he said *it;* for *eet* as in *feet,* he said *it;* for *eek* as in *seek* he transposed the *k* and said *keek,* i.e., a sequence contamination; for *og* he said *udz;* for *ent* he said *et;* for *ith* he said *itch.*

The fact that Robert performed so well in the special neurological examination is not surprising, in view of the fact that deficits in motor integration are *not* a common feature in the type of severe reading disability with which he is afflicted. As a point of interest, but not related to the case of Robert, our research with the mixed type of MBD children shows that most of the "soft" neurological signs begin to drop out rather rapidly between the ages of 10 and 12 years.

Note that Robert's interest and attention span have always been very good, despite the frustrations he has experienced through the years because of difficulty in breaking the reading code which his friends were able to do with ease. Would that the poor boy had had the opportunity to use a consistent code such as the Initial Teaching Alphabet.

Diagnosis.   Referring to the two diagnostic systems we get for the Group for the Advancement of Psychiatry (GAP): Developmental Deviation—Cognitive.

The Diagnostic and Statistical Manual of the American Psychiatric Association, Volume II (DSM II of APA), No. 306.1 gives—Specific Learning Disturbance. This DSM II diagnosis is included solely for its interest value, if any, since this code number and designation appear within the section called "Special Symptoms" which *cannot* include any related to organicity.

In our Center the condition which is so handicapping to Robert is called *primary reading disability* or *developmental dys-*

lexia. In our opinion the etiology is genetic. We do not believe that the attitudes or behavior of the parents are in any way responsible.

Recommendations. Recommendations are these: (1) Parents to secure a private tutor for Robert from the local community, (2) education and language specialists from our Center to arrange an in-person consultation session with the tutor to outline in detail the teaching approach for Robert, (3) education specialist from our Center to arrange for the taping of appropriate texts used in Robert's high school, e.g., history, literature, social studies, so that he will have the opportunity to absorb the content of the courses and participate in class discussion by a method which would detour his severe reading handicap, (4) our Center to send a letter to the school summarizing diagnostic data and outlining specific approaches for the teachers to use in the academic management of Robert, (5) follow-up appointment in two months so that Robert and parents can report on progress with the plan and so that team members can pursue any aspect of the case which requires handling.

Letter to the School

Following is the letter that was sent to the principal and teachers at the public high school Robert attends. It is similar to the letter we write on each school-age child diagnosed in our Center as having learning disabilities.

Mr. ————————, Principal
———— High School
————, Arkansas

Re: Robert ————
Born: 12–16–53

Dear Mr. ————:

Robert was seen in our Center on November 12, 1968 for evaluation of long-standing poor academic achievement. It had been noted by his teachers from first grade on that reading disability seemed to be the source of his school difficulties. He has always been described as a nice, cooperative youngster who has presented no conduct or discipline problems.

As part of our evaluation, Robert was given the Wechsler Intelligence Scale, and he achieved the following scores:

Verbal I.Q.   114
Performance I.Q.   122
Full Scale I.Q.   120

As you know, this places Robert in the "Superior" range of general intellectual functioning. His sight reading ability, which is slow and laborious (and painful to watch) is roughly at the fifth-grade level with adequate comprehension. His spelling skill is also at about the fifth-grade level. Robert was a diligent worker, but is somewhat shy and nonspontaneous.

Our evaluation indicates that Robert is a rather typical case of "primary reading disability" (which is also referred to as "developmental dyslexia"). This condition is considered to be of genetic origin resulting in deficits in the discriminatory and integrative functions of language acquisition over which the youngster has no control. It is not because of noninterest; poor motivation; failure to study sufficiently; or "emotional block." It is simply that he is a *different* learner because his learning apparatus for reading and spelling is impaired.

It is amazing how such children, who have experienced failure and frustration throughout their school career, can maintain such a good attitude about it all. In Robert's case, we feel very fortunate because the parents have located someone to tutor him on a regular basis.

An appointment has been set for the tutor, Mrs. ———, to meet with our educational specialist for the purpose of designing a training program for Robert. Specific techniques for teaching such youngsters have been developed during the past few years. Progress, we feel, will be somewhat slow since he is so far behind.

Meanwhile, we have some recommendations which we hope can be carried out for him at school. We realize the difficulty and extra burden this will place on some of his teachers. However, we feel that it is important that Robert be given this extra measure of help and assurance.

1. His parents were requested to read aloud to him the bulk of his outside reading assignments. This is for the purpose of acquiring the content of his studies such as civics, etc., since he is able to learn the material through his ears. He should not have the added burden of struggling through material written for tenth grade when his skills at the present time are at fifth-grade level.
2. If at all possible, his examinations should be given orally,

and he should be graded for his fund of information and knowledge rather than penalized for not being able to make out the written exam questions.

3. Since his spelling is poor, "correct" spelling for him should not be stressed. Again, he should be graded for the content of written work and not marked off for spelling, which undoubtedly has reduced many of his grades to an "F." As you know, he tends to spell phonetically, and though frequently not correct, it is usually easy to interpret.

4. With patience, understanding, and tutoring, the skills which are holding him back from achievement at his high level of intellect should begin to progress nicely.

5. An occasional "B" on an oral exam would do much to lift his spirits, and in some small way begin to pay him back for the years of frustration and self-doubt that he has endured.

If we can be of any further service, please let me hear from you.

CONCLUSIONS

In the first presentation, the case of Darrell, our etiological formulation is that of minimal selective brain damage. In the second case, that of Robert, we suspect genetic causation. Both qualify for the term *learning disability,* and for the term *minimal brain dysfunction.*

We believe the conclusions which follow are pertinent to the diagnosis and management of children who are included in these overlapping and complementary categories.

The following is a list of the underlying processes wherein deviations in specific cognitive, motor, and integrative functions may appear:

1. Attentional defects
2. Specific time-function memory defects
3. Activity level abnormalities
4. Emotional modulation defects
5. Symbolic and abstractive defects
6. Space, directionality, time, and sequencing defects

7. Motor organizational defects
8. Musicality defects

All these may be included in the concept of higher-order brain integrations as funneled through and processed in the final common path, attention.

Next is a list of the specific and mixed entities which may be expected to appear in the group of children said to have specific learning disabilities or minimal brain dysfunctions. Here, based on clinical estimation, the highly delimited, specific entities comprise a small percentage of the whole group, whereas the mixed types make up the majority:

15% {
1. Relatively pure hyperactivity and impulsivity
2. Relatively pure hypoactivity (often with a specific learning disability)
3. Relatively pure motor integration deficit
    a. With only "soft," integrative neurological signs
    b. With some "hard" signs indicating minimal cerebral palsy
4. Relatively pure dyslexia (reading deficit)
5. Relatively pure dysgraphia (writing deficit)
6. Relatively pure dysorthographia (spelling deficit)
7. Relatively pure dyscalculia (arithmetic deficit)
8. Relatively pure dysphasia (language deficit)
}

85% {
9. The many mixed types of learning disabilities or minimal brain dysfunctions
}

Historically this diverse group of children, having in common the two facts that they are not mentally retarded and that each child manifests one or more specific deficits in cognitive, motor, and integrative functions, was approached by each professional discipline in the manner of the seven blind sages who set out to learn, each for himself, the nature of the elephant. Each found a fragment of the truth.

An English physician found a "word-blind" child. The psychiatrist was preoccupied with the hyperactive and impulsive child. The physiotherapist and physical educationist focused on the clumsy child. The neurologist found dyslexia and motor-integrative signs. The psychologist found fluctuations in cognition and alterations in that "hot-point" of consciousness, attention, in short- and long-term memory, and in cross-modality integrations. The language development specialist found that various specific symbolic functions were faulty. The educator found an exaggeratedly jagged and unique profile of deficits and talents in each academically handicapped child. Individuals in each discipline found ways, many of them overlapping, to help these children. Most methods are based on techniques of capturing the child's attention, feeding the parcels of information simultaneously through two or more sensory channels, giving him very small increments on which to work, and quick reward for each effort.

The present official diagnostic system in child psychiatry does not give much leeway in setting out the phenomenology of these children. And it tries to force us to decide in favor of either an organic brain syndrome with an ascertained etiology, or a reaction-type diagnosis with a heavy weighting of environmental causation. Variation among specific functions on a genetic basis is largely ignored in considering these deficits. The system tries to force us to formulate an exclusive etiology when child psychiatry is not in a position to do so. We are doing well to be able to map out the phenomenology in a fairly precise manner. Beyond this, the system should allow us to express ourselves in terms of *probable etiologies,* not one exclusive etiology. There is good reason to think that many of our specific learning disabilities—minimal brain dysfunctions—cases represent a final product of predisposing genetic factors, selective mild brain damage at prenatal, perinatal, or early childhood stages, and of inflexible or ill-matched environmental expectations and pressures. *We visualize the final product, the particular MBD child, as the result of a dynamic, ongoing interaction between the child's specific profile of deficits and the environment's specific profile of demands.*

Though one's practice can be conveniently limited to pure cases of developmental dyslexia with good IQ's, or a research endeavor can be limited to hyperactive children, the schools are faced with the multitudes of nonpure cases—the jumbled mixtures of two, three, or more deficits and deviations, often complicated by environmental vicissitudes.

It has been our good fortune, as a team that has worked together for a long time, to see many cases of both the pure and the mixed types. For example, we have seen cases with pure hyperactivity with no specific learning disability. Rather, the child in his headlong rush stumbles across words, people, and chairs in indiscriminate haste. He has inadequate brakes, his inhibitory circuits do not function well. When decelerated with a proper medication such as methylphenidate or amphetamines, he reveals that he does not have a reading, arithmetic, or memory deficit. We have seen pure developmental dysphasias and aphasias wherein the intelligence was judged normal and activity level was not especially deviant. We have seen cases of pure deficits in motor coordination with no hyperactivity or learning disability.

But by far the majority of these perplexing children are mixtures of the listed deficits. There has been heuristic value in considering them as a group and giving them a broad label: (1) for calling attention to the existence of this large, neglected category of children, (2) for the remediation approaches they often share, (3) for providing the schools with a framework to organize classes, individualize instruction, and train teachers, (4) as a corral of research steers waiting to be lassoed singly, and (5) to rescue this large and heterogeneous group from the grasp of those who would, by reflex, place the major blame on parent-child interactions. (The "psychotic" child has not as yet been rescued, though many are rushing to his aid.)

Here is another important consideration: A large number of children who qualify for the terms *learning disability* and *minimal brain dysfunction* have only a moderate problem with attention, reading, and activity level. For them we do not necessarily think in terms of brain damage or a markedly abnormal genetic causation. We see them as having naturally occurring, mild deviations in the pace of maturation of different systems within the brain—actually a modest extension of the venerable concept of (discrete) individual differences—which education and educational psychology worshiped for many years, yet failed to believe in when it stood before them in the flesh. That great idol, that great abstraction, "the average child," progressing step by step and year by year in phalanxes of thirty, demolished the intricately patterned and fragile profiles of the individual child. His downward spikes were real and painful, his upward spikes were used against him, the accusation being that "He is not working up to capacity." He disappeared into the mathematical average. Deeply frustrated and humiliated, he usually gave up and started on one or another of the thousand downward paths to inadequate living.

The majority of these mild to moderate cases of children with specific learning disabilities can best be remediated on release time from the regular class. In Arkansas these special teaching units are called *resource rooms*. The specially trained teacher has 2 to 4 of these children for one to two hours at a time on a daily basis. She tutors them and helps the regular teacher select material and methods which take the deficits and strengths of such a student into account: books at appropriate interest levels, but with a lower-level vocabulary; oral examinations; compassionate helpers from upper grades, from home, from volunteer groups, to read to him, to pour into him the content, the information he so often can indeed acquire through his ears. In fact, as for the blind, tapes and records should be made available to the schools for use with this child. He usually can't take group instruction, so it is time-saving and nerve-saving for the teacher to plan to render a repeat set of directions in "slow talk"—i.e., slowly spaced words at such a speed that he can catch each word and process it. Lastly, his grades in his deficit areas should be for effort, not for his capacity.

On the horizon are television methods of visual instruction, tailored into small increments, well spaced, but highly kinetic, highly animated. Vocational programs must reach down to these children at a younger age and dislodge them from the rigid track of the abstract scholar, for which they are so ill suited. The alternative to these approaches is individual and social waste.

3 Medical Responsibilities in Learning Disorders

ERIC DENHOFF AND LESTER TARNOPOL

LEARNING PROBLEMS IN CHILDREN of normal intelligence are becoming more evident because of improved identification. In many cases difficulty with scholastics is a psychological symptom of an underlying biological, neurological, sociological, or economic disturbance (see Table 3-1). Often such basic difficulties are reflected in school disorders in verbal or written communication or behavior problems, or both. Failure to learn to read adequately has reached epidemic proportions: it affects between 10 and 20 percent of the young school population. Moreover, effective remedies cannot be prescribed until the causes are clear.

In the past physicians did not generally consider school performance to be a medical responsibility. Often they had not been alerted to the fact that a young child required visual and auditory perceptual skills and coordination to learn efficiently because this had not been part of medical education. Thus, when called upon to make a judgment of neurological status in an academically stressed child, they usually disregarded subtle inefficiencies which are now known to affect learning.

The pediatrician, who develops a special neurological assessment and a thorough knowledge of its relation to school problems, may provide meaningful medical clues and specific help for medical problems which may be contributing to the child's

TABLE 3-1.   *Causes Contributing to School Failure*

EXOGENOUS FACTORS

Physical illness resulting in prolonged absence from school

Acute: ear, throat, rheumatic fever, gastroenteritis

Chronic: meningoencephalitis, cystic fibrosis, rheumatic fever, metabolic disorders, anemia, parasites

Emotional

Anxiety: unstable home conditions, marital, financial, frequent moves, death, direct parental influences, underprivileged minority with hostile attitudes, middle-class striving, school phobia

Poor motivation: overdependency on mother, active or passive rebellion against authority, depression, acting-out, psychosomatic complaints

Peer influences: conflicts from attitudes of poorly adjusted friends

Symptom: projects blame on others

Major psychiatric disorders: psychoses, severe neuroses

ENDOGENOUS FACTORS

Genetic: chromosomal

Perinatal: fetal encephalopathy, poor intrauterine climate, anoxia, birth trauma, postnatal trauma, residuals of infection, metabolic error

Syndrome of cerebral dysfunction resulting from above:
Cerebral palsy, mental retardation, convulsive disorders, neurosensory disorders, hyperkinetic impulse disorder, visual-auditory-perceptual motor disabilities, language disorders, some psychiatric disorders

MIXED FACTORS

Neurological dysfunction

Associated with emotional overlay

Associated with poor environment

SOURCE: Adapted from J. E. Bradley (1968) with permission.

school failure. He may also help minimize the confusion of educators and parents concerning the reasons for poor achievement.

MEDICAL ASPECTS

Individual Evaluation

An appropriate history may provide differential clues to the causes contributing to school failure. A medical examination should be used to rule out illness, and a neurological evaluation to assess functions which relate to academic efficiency. Laboratory studies, including an electroencephalogram, may provide support for clinical impressions; psychological screening tests may suggest areas for more intensive study. An example of a history and examination form is shown in Chart 3-1.

CHART 3-1.   *Neurological Examination*

Name:
Parents' names:
Street:
City, state:
Age:
School: Grade:
Date of visit:
Referred by:
    Address:
(Circle appropriate findings)
CHIEF COMPLAINT. This _____ year old
  (a) white   (a) male   was referred because of _____ _____
  (b) Negro (b) female
  (c) _____ ___

FAMILY HISTORY
There are _____ siblings. (a) They are problem-free.
                                 (b) Problems are:

The neurological background is (a) noncontributory.
                                  (b) suspect. Describe:

The emotional climate is (a) normal.
                         (b) abnormal. Describe:

PREGNANCY HISTORY
There were (a) _____ previous miscarriages. _____ sibling deaths.
          (b) _____ miscarriages after birth of patient.
Pregnancy was (a) uneventful.
          (b) characterized by vaginal bleeding, virus infection, toxemia, trauma, during the 1st, 2d, 3d trimester.

OBSTETRICAL HISTORY
Patient was born on _____ at _____ Hospital.
Birth weight: _____ lb. _____ oz.
The labor was (number of hours) _____. The delivery was (a) normal.
                                       (b) precipitate.
                                       (c) prolonged.
                                       (d) cesarean.
Oxygen (a) was required.
         (b) was not required.
There were (a) no complications.
               (b) complications. Describe:

POSTNATAL PERIOD

In the early days of life the baby was (a) normal.
  (b) overly quiet.
  (c) irritable.
  (d) colicky.

In the early months of life the baby was (a) normal.
  (b) overly quiet.
  (c) irritable.
  (d) colicky.

There were problems in (a) sucking.
  (b) swallowing.
  (c) feeding.
  (d) food sensitivity.

ACCIDENTS AND INFECTIONS

There were no serious accidents or illnesses.
The child had the following:

DEVELOPMENTAL LEVEL

Development was (a) normal with walking unsupported at _____ months.
  (b) delayed with walking at _____ months.
  The child said single words at _____ months and 2- or 3-word sentences at _____ months.

SYSTEMIC COMPLAINTS

The systemic complaints were (a) noncontributory.
  (b) abnormal.
Except for: frequent colds, ear infections, pica encopresis, enuresis (diurnal, nocturnal).

Seizure history was (a) benign.
  (b) characterized by
  convulsions.
  generalized eye blinking.
  unexplained outbursts.
  nightmares.
  sleepwalking.

Behavior history was (a) benign.
  (b) characterized by
  hyperactivity.
  short attention span.
  mood swings.
  acting-out.
  passivity.
  withdrawn.
  head rocking.
  head banging.
  nail biting.
  facial grimaces.
  self-mutilation.

PHYSICAL EXAMINATION
Wt. _____ Ht. _____ in. Head _____ in. Chest _____ in.
Blood Pressure _____/_____ Hgb _____%
Vision checked (a) with glasses.
          (b) without glasses.
Far vision is (a) 20/20 bilaterally.
          (b) _____/_____ on the right; _____/_____ on
               the left.
Near vision is (a) normal.
          (b) abnormal.
Hearing is
          (a) normal by   audiotest.
                          clacker.
                          bell.
                          tuning fork.
                          whisper.
          (b) diminished on the right at _____ freq. _____ by dB.
                          left at _____ freq. _____ by dB.
The child was friendly, passive, confused, alert, irritable, uncooperative.
The child follows directions well, poorly.
The general physical findings were (a) noncontributory.
                          (b) revealed the following:

Congenital stigmata are (a) absent
                          (b) as follows:
                          epicanthal folds.
                          pilonidal dimple.
                          crossed toes.
                          webbed fingers.
                          high arch palate.
                          telangiectasis.
                          curved fifth digits.
                          straight palmer crease.

The Neurological Examination includes testing of balance and coordination, gross and fine motor skills, cranial nerves, deep and superficial reflexes, muscle strength, and sensory-parietal intactness, sidedness, perceptual skills, and position sense.
Only the pertinent abnormal findings are reported here.

POSITIVE FINDINGS
The skull is (a) enlarged.
          (b) not enlarged.
Fontenels are (a) open.
          (b) closed.
Transillumination is (a) negative.
                     (b) abnormal.
Ocular movements are
          (a) normal.
          (b) abnormal. Pupil reflexes _____ accommodation _____.

Extraocular movements are (a) normal.
      (b) sluggish.
      (c) discoordinated.
Visual fields are (a) grossly normal by confrontation.
      (b) abnormal.

Binocular fusion is (a) adequate.
      (b) inadequate.
Examination shows (c) strabismus.
      (d) nystagmus.
Discs and media are (a) visualized and normal.
      (b) could not be visualized.
      (c) abnormal disc and media. Findings are: _____
Color vision red/green is normal/abnormal.
There is foreground difficulty; background.
Tongue movements are (a) normal.
      (b) sluggish.
      (c) abnormal with thickening; inability to move tongue upward, down, laterally.
There were no fasciculations.
Deep reflexes were
(a) active and normal.   (c) symmetrically/asymmetrically.
(b) increased, diminished. (d) symmetrically/asymmetrically.
Reflexes of the upper extremities are (a) normal.
      (b) atypical.
      (c) describe.
Reflexes of the lower extremities are (a) normal.
      (b) atypical.
      (c) describe.
The abdominal reflexes are (a) active and equal.
      (b) greater on the left than on the right.
      (c) greater on the right than on the left.
      (d) diminished.
Tonus is generally (a) normotonic.
      (b) hypertonic.
      (c) hypotonic.
Achilles tendons are (a) normal   on the (d) right.
      (b) hypomobile   (e) left.
      (c) hypermobile   (f) bilaterally.
Muscle strength is (a) normal.
      (b) weak.
Major involvement is in (a) hands
      (b) upper girdle
      (c) trunk
      (d) lower girdle
The spine is (a) normal.
      (b) kyphotic.   There is a mass of hair in the (a) sacral area.
      (c) lordotic.   (b) lumbar area.
There is/is no evidence of myotonia.

There are (a) no pathological reflexes.
        (b) equivocal pathological reflexes.
        (c) pathological reflexes.
There are Babinski reflexes (a) right (b) left (c) bilaterally.
        Clonus less than 5 beats; 5 beats or more.
Postural reflexes are (a) physiological.
        (b) immature.
        (c) abnormal.
The reflexes include (a) Moro.   (e) placing.
        (b) T-N-R.   (f) parachute.
        (c) Landau (prone, supine).   (g) vestibular.
        (d) extensor.   (h) optokinetic.
Overflow movements of the hands and fingers are (a) absent/present.
        (b) mild.
        (c) moderate.
        (d) severe.

The Romberg is normal, fair, abnormal.
Balance is normal, fair, poor.
Coordination is (a) normal by finger-nose and/or finger-finger test.
        (b) fair.
        (c) poor.
There are good/poor bilateral synchronous skills.
There is no dysdiadochokinesis on the right, left, bilaterally.
Additional cranial nerves are normal.
  Abnormal cranial nerves are:
    I   Response to odors (a) appropriate (b) absent right/left.
    V   There is (weakness) (deviation) of muscles of face, jaw, right/left.
   VI   There is abnormal sensation of forehead, cheeks, chin.
  VII   There is lid weakness, weakness of upper/lower part of face.
   IX   Palate is asymmetrical, gag reflex is weak/absent.
   XI   Sternocleidal muscle strength is poor. There is poor shoulder op-
        position.
Sensation: There is normal/diminished/excessive response to a pinwheel/
brush.

DIAGNOSIS

There is normal/abnormal response to position sense.
Right to left discrimination is (a) normal.
        (b) abnormal.
        (c) immature.
Sensory-parietal tests are (a) normal.
        (b) abnormal on the right/left.
The abnormal tests include (a) face/hand.
        (b) double tactile stimulation.
        (c) finger agnosia.
Graphesthesia to traced figures, key, coins is (normal, physiologically im-
mature, abnormal) on the right/left.

PERCEPTION
The Archimedes Spiral was (a) normal.
    (b) physiologically immature.
    (c) suspicious.
    (d) abnormal for occipital lobe (perceptual) dysfunction.

DOMINANCE AND LATERALITY
(a) The child is left-eyed; left-handed; dominance is left.
(b) The child is right-eyed; right-handed; dominance is right.
(c) The child is left-eyed; right-handed; dominance is mixed.
(d) The child is right-eyed; left-handed; dominance is mixed.

SCREENING PSYCHOLOGICAL TESTS
At age _____ yrs. _____ mos., Wechsler Verbal IQ _____.
Performance IQ _____.
Full Scale IQ _____ Range of Wechsler subscale scores _____.
Visual-perceptual function on the Bender was: (a) mature.
    (b) immature.
Goodenough drawings were (a) normal.
    (b) abnormal.
Handwriting was (a) normal.
    (b) abnormal.
Reading level was _____ in grade _____.

IMPRESSIONS
1. Cerebral dysfunction
    (a) visual-perceptual
    (b) visual-perceptual-motor
    (c) language; receptive, integrative, expressive
    (d) specific learning disability
2. Convulsive disorder
    (a) generalized
    (b) petit mal
    (c) minor motor
    (d) psychomotor
    (e) mixed
3. Delayed development
    (a) genetic
    (b) congenital
4. Mental retardation
5. Behavior disorders
    (a) hyperkinetic
    (b) withdrawing
    (c) overanxious
    (d) unsocialized
    (e) runaway
    (f) group delinquent

RECOMMENDATIONS
(a) EEG
(b) Psychological tests
(c) Visual/perceptual evaluation
(d) Language evaluation
(e) Differential learning analysis
(f) Psychiatric evaluation
(g) Counseling—parent/child
(h) Hospital studies
(i) Laboratory studies
(j) Audiological examination

DISCUSSION

The information obtained from the medical evaluation should be incorporated into the school record, which should include detailed psychological, visual and auditory perceptual, and language information. This provides the basis for team discussion and recommendations for a remedial program.

The child who is failing to learn at his mental ability level may have one or more of these deficiencies revealed by the following examinations:

1. *Physical.* Visual acuity may be substandard. Auditory acuity may suffer from high or low frequency hearing loss.

2. *Neurological.* Inefficiencies may occur in gross and fine motor skills, sensory functions, reflexes, body organization, and sensory-parietal (intake) skills such as face-hand and 2-point discrimination. Agraphesthesia (inability to discriminate printed symbols on the palm of the hand) and astereognosis (inability to distinguish forms and shapes) may be found.

3. *Psychological.* Large differences may be found in Wechsler Verbal and Performance Intelligence Test scores and wide scatter in Wechsler subtest scores. Inefficiencies in visual perception, visual-perceptual-motor function, auditory discrimination, auditory sequencing, language skills, and distortions in projective tests may occur. Related psychoeducational tests for reading and writing skills may be atypical.

4. *Laboratory tests.* Abnormalities in the electroencephalogram, or abnormal metabolic functions such as low thyroid function or glucose function, may be found.

From this profile may emerge recommendations such as:

1. Correct vision with glasses.
2. Seat child in front of the room with his better ear to the teacher.
3. Provide a regime of special physical exercises to help overcome body clumsiness.
4. Provide specific educational remediation as required, related to the needs indicated by the psychological tests.
5. Provide psychological guidance or counseling for child and parent as needed.
6. Help modify hyperactivity, short attention span, or mood variability by medication.
7. Correct specific deficiencies revealed by the laboratory tests.

The physician must be able to translate the findings and recommendations to the parents, work closely with the school, and provide medical services that can help speed the learning process.

Group Screening Tests

The increasing number of suspected cases of learning disorders makes it impossible to provide detailed assessment for each. Therefore screening techniques have been developed to help bridge the gap between potential school difficulty and likely candidates for school failure. Ozer (1968) has contributed a screening test for neurological problems, suitable for use by the physician. Educationally oriented tests for screening children with learning disabilities or minimal cerebral dysfunction are also available (de Hirsch 1966, Frostig 1964, Slingerland 1962, Tarnopol 1969).

A number of preschool readiness tests for assessing reading or scanning readiness are being developed and some are in use. Hainsworth and Siqueland (1969) discuss their values and limitations in a publication that describes the teachers' form of the Meeting Street School Screening-Test. Standards for items that test neurological efficiency are most difficult to obtain below the age of 5 because of inconsistencies in performance in such young children. An attempt is being made to develop such items.

Building bridges. Development of the Meeting Street School Screening-Test for early identification of children with learning disabilities was begun in 1960. The Meeting Street School Children's Rehabilitation Center Team, which was dedicated to the diagnosis and management of cerebral palsied young children, started to build a bridge to transmit information learned from cerebral palsied children to normal-appearing children with learning problems (Denhoff and Robinault 1960). *Important similarities in clinical and psychological findings were found in both cerebral palsy and learning difficulty cases.*

Based upon a 36-item screening test culled from among items used by the team to test cerebral palsied children for learning deficits, it was possible to predict with 89 percent accuracy that 19 percent of 355 normal first-grade children would fail either the first or second grade (Denhoff et al. 1968). Eighty-four percent of the school failure group had intelligence test scores in the average or higher range. On this test four to six items failed indicated suspicion of neurological inefficiency; seven or more items missed indicated probable grade failure. In a follow-up study of 105 children with either one or no items missed, only 1 child failed school; of 241 with three or fewer missed, only 5 failed to pass; while of 108 with four or more missed, 57 (53%) failed. In the group of 33 children with seven or more items failed, 26 (79%) were not promoted and 32 (97%) did not attain a grade achievement score of 2.0.*

Not all the children were immediate school failures. However, those who were prone to fail had a constellation of deficiencies that were significant in providing early diagnostic clues. These included:

1. Inefficient balance, poor fine and gross motor skills
2. Poor auditory discrimination and retention skills
3. Poor symbol recognition ability
4. Poor position in space and visual perception

* This score is the grade equivalent. Thus 2.0 represents grade 2.0 work.

5. Poor form reproduction
6. Behavior problems such as hyperactivity, short attention span, anxiety, or poor motivation

The 36-item screening test has been standardized for 5- to 7½-year-old children.

Screening Instrument for Office Practice

The items (and instructions to patients) listed below serve as a simple screening instrument for office practice since 95 percent of the 6- to 7½-year-old population successfully passed this test.

1. *Balance.* Stand straight, eyes closed, for fifteen seconds.
2. *Gross motor coordination.* Hold arms out in front equally for five seconds. Arms straight above head without deviation for five seconds. Arms out front, turn hands over and back smoothly, four times.
3. *Fine motor coordination.* Touch tip of little finger to nose accurately (eyes closed) two times.
4. *Motor speech.* Open and close mouth smoothly five times.
5. *Extraocular motility.* Follow a pencil smoothly without turning head; laterally, up-down, and diagonally.
6. *Stereognosis.* Discriminate a key, coin, and button in either hand with eyes closed.

Additional screening items of significance. The physician may want to employ all or some of the following tests:

1. *Gross motor skills.* Skip across the room, walk around the room, run around the room. The physician watches for awkward, shifting patterns.
2. *Fine patterned movement.* With eyes open, touch each finger to thumb, both hands simultaneously at one-second intervals; repeat with eyes closed. Say "Puh-tuh-kuh" at rate of one per second for each sound; repeat in sequence three times without error.
3. *Perceptual motor.* Draw a diamond in both a vertical and horizontal plane without deviation.

4. *Sensory integration* (graphesthesia). Show the child the following sequence: circle, cross, square, triangle. He then closes his eyes and the examiner draws the patterns on the right forearm, then the left. The child identifies them.
5. *Language skills.* (1) Articulation: Ask the child to repeat the sentence, "The girl thinks the cowboy on TV is real." Circle errors in the *s* and *r* sounds. (2) Auditory discrimination: Select the proper word in "Jack has a (fat) (sat) (hat)." Repeat this sentence after listening once: "Tom has lots of fun playing ball with his sister." (3) Symbol recognition for auditory visual association: Read the words or name the letters: *He, Come, Big, See.*
6. *Complex integrative skills.* With eyes closed, raise the left arm, right leg, touch right ear with left hand. Examiner determines awareness of right-left discrimination.

Persistence of immature performance of these skills beyond age 7 is an excellent indication of potential scholastic difficulty. A word of caution concerning the developmental nature of the test is appropriate. In many children ability to perform certain items improves by age 7, and erroneous predictions are possible unless there is an awareness of the maturational nature of these skills. The items are gross motor skills, hop, skip, run; fine auditory discrimination and auditory-visual association; muscle trunk strength, sit from supine; position in space, circle the figure that is different in a group all alike except one. Table 3-2 provides further information about maturational changes in the 6- to 7½-year range.

When a child has a suspicious rating on the group screening tests, he should receive a detailed individual neurological and psychological evaluation. The Meeting Street School team is developing neurological test items which can be rated objectively. They are being standardized against a normative population.

Additional Neurological Tests

The following list describes some items in areas related to neurological function which can strengthen the standard neurological examination.

TABLE 3-2. *Maturational Characteristics of Selected Items Contributing to Learning Efficiency*

ITEMS MOST STABLE OVER AGE RANGE 6–7½ YEARS

Gross motor skills
 Changing gait patterns, skipping
Fine motor skills
 Bilateral synchronous skills, touching forefinger to thumb, both hands simultaneously
Visual-perceptual skills
 Foreground-background discrimination, tracing a star superimposed upon another star
Visual-perceptual-motor skills
 Drawing a square, a diamond
Language skills
 Symbol recognition, reading words and naming letters, writing name

ITEMS THAT CHANGE OVER AGE RANGE

6–6½ Years
Gross motor skills
 Balance, hopping along line on one foot, then the other
 Trunk strength, sitting up from supine
Fine patterned movements
 Eye-hand coordination and finger dexterity, picking up 10 sticks and placing them in a box within 10 seconds; winding a 12-inch length of thread on a spool in 12 seconds

6½–7 Years
Visual-perceptual-motor skills
 Ability to draw a line down middle of a curved road without touching the sides
Language skills
 Abstract reasoning, filling in appropriate words to complete sentence
 Auditory retention, repeating a sentence correctly

NOT ESTABLISHED IN AGE RANGE

Laterality
 Mixed dominance
 Right-left discrimination

Gross motor skills

1. Balance on one foot: Stand in place on the right foot with the left foot at knee level. Stand in position for ten seconds. Repeat on the left foot.

2. Finger-nose: With eyes closed and arms outstretched laterally, use tip of little finger of right hand to touch tip of the nose. Repeat for left hand.
3. Hopping in place: With the position assumed for balance on one foot, hop in place five times at a rate of one hop per second for each foot.

Fine patterned movement

1. Articulation: Repeat the following sounds three times in succession without error.
   a. Puh-tuh-kuh
   b. Tuh-puh-kuh
   c. Kuh-puh-tuh
2. Bilateral synchronous finger skills:
   a. With arms outstretched in front and hands extended, simultaneously touch index fingertip (finger No. 2) to ball of thumb, then fingertip 3, 4, and 5, smoothly and precisely.
   b. Repeat in the following order: 5, 2, 3, 4.
   c. Repeat again: 4, 2, 5, 3.

Sensory integration (graphesthesia)

1. Show the child a picture of a circle, cross, and triangle. Using a blunt-tipped wand, draw each figure on the plantar surface of the palm on the child's right hand. The child names each figure drawn. Repeat on the left.
2. If successfully done, repeat using the digits 1, 3, 9, 6, 7.

Complex integration

1. Visual motor skills: Have the child copy a square, a triangle, a diamond.
2. Auditory-motor: Tap out sequence (hand hidden from view); have the child repeat with his own tapping
   (1) $--$ (2) $---$ (3) $-----$ (4) $----$ (5) $------$.

There are some abnormal signs which, collectively, appear to relate to poor visual-perceptual-motor functions and consequently to poor written work. There are other signs which suggest a language dysfunction and difficulty in verbal performance. These are yet to be standardized against a normative population and must be used cautiously in differential diagnosis (Denhoff 1969).

GENESIS OF A DEMONSTRATION
PROGRAM

Findings in cerebral palsied children helped provide the clues for the group screening tests and portions of the objective neurological evaluation. This population also contributed to the concepts involved in developing a demonstration program for children with neurologically based learning difficulties but with normal intelligence and potentially normal achievement.

Over the years the Meeting Street School diagnostic team noted a gradual infiltration of children not overtly handicapped but referred for diagnosis and management. The presenting complaints were learning difficulties or behavior problems, or both. When a sufficient number of cases had been accumulated for analysis, striking similarities as well as marked differences were found in the cerebral palsied and "hidden"-disability populations (see Table 3-3).

There was an over-one-third incidence of presumed genetic or constitutional factors in the learning problem population. The incidence of socio-environmental disruption such as emotional instability (psychiatric or neurotic disorders) in parents or siblings was 23 percent. Parents of cerebral palsied children evidenced some emotional problems which appeared to be related to the problems encountered in coping with a handicapped infant. Divorce and adoption problems, a feature found in the learning disorder group, were not encountered as a major occurrence in the small but representative group of cerebral palsy cases. The effects of "hidden" neurological dysfunction in children may have been much more drastic on the emotional lives of parents than clearly visible cerebral palsy.

Complications of pregnancy were twice as high in cerebral palsy, but complications of delivery were relatively high in both groups. Anoxia and respiratory distress were strikingly higher in cerebral palsy cases. The incidence of prematurity was thirtyfold higher in cerebral palsy. The percentage of accidents and serious injuries in the learning problem group was more than twice as great as in the cerebral palsy population. A high risk perinatal profile may be used as an early index of suspicion (Chart 3-2).

It appeared that a fair number of the learning problem cases

TABLE 3-3. *Comparison of Associated Factors Between Children with Cerebral Palsy and Children with Learning Problems*

Family History	Cerebral Palsy (N = 100)		Learning Problems (N = 48)	
	No.	% [a]	No.	% [a]
Presumed genetic				
Specific reading problem	0	0	7	14
Chronic neurological disorder	10	10	10	21
Socioenvironmental				
Emotional instability	15	15	6	12.5
Divorce	5	5	2	4
Adoption	0	0	3	6
Perinatal history				
Pregnancy complications	48	48	11	23
Delivery complications	37	37	14	29
Neonatal complications	50	50	9	18
Prematurity	30	30	2	4
Infancy history				
(Accidents or infections prior to age 3)	11	11	19	39

[a] Multiple causes give total percentage in excess of 100%.

belonged within the syndromes of cerebral dysfunction because of the much higher incidence of perinatal complications in the learning problem group than in a control group of 504 newborns. In the controls, family history factors evidenced less than 10 percent neonatal complications, with pregnancy and delivery complications between 10 and 15 percent and the incidence of prematurity 5 percent (compare with Table 3-3). In the learning problem group, neonatal, pregnancy, and delivery complications ranged from 18 to 29 percent.

Data concerning a representative sample of newborns, who were part of the Brown University–Rhode Island Collaborative Study,* are being tabulated comparing perinatal data and a seven-year neurological-psychological follow-up against Meeting

* Brown University–Rhode Island, National Institutes of Health Collaborative Study for Cerebral Palsy, Mental Retardation and Sensory Disorders, Bethesda, Md.

Chart 3-2 High Risk Perinatal Profile

MOTHER

Gravida. Less than 16 years, more than 40 years old

Primigravida. More than 35 years old

Mother. Unmarried, short, thin, malnourished, sterility problem, uneducated, low income, nonwhite

Prior history. Abortions, stillbirths, neonatal deaths, placenta-abruptio or circumvallette, renal-hypertension, proteinuria, nephritis, bacteriuria, diabetes, phlebitis, cervical incompetence, contracted pelvis, polyhydramnios

Labor. Precipitate, prolonged, cesarean

INFANT

Gestational age. Less than 34 weeks

Birth. Liveborn/stillborn, birth weight less than 5 pounds (2000 gm), poor condition, unusual appearance, poor color, low Apgar score, cyanosis, resuscitation required, respiratory distress in infants under 5 pounds, small heart volume

Neonatal. Incubator/oxygen needed; difficult sucking/feeding; cry or activity atypical; injury/anomaly; asymmetry face and extremities; jaundice, tonus, seizures; weight gain poor; vomiting, fever

Early infancy. Feeding difficulty, choking, sleep reversals

Street School Screening-Test scores. The results of the study should help to clarify an important question. Do children with learning problems have a substantial portion of the syndromes of cerebral dysfunction, or are such children a mixed group with unclear etiologies?

We were convinced of the similarity between the cerebral dysfunction and learning disabilities populations, and consequently we developed a consulting team which provided educational diagnostic services for such children. Soon state legislation was passed which required appropriate educational services to be provided for children with various categories of learning disabilities (Rhode Island State Board of Education 1963). One category was designated as *neurologically impaired.* Such a child was identified as one without serious locomotor problems who tests within the normal range of intelligence and demonstrates unusual perceptual and conceptual problems.

A DEMONSTRATION PROGRAM

In the endeavor to improve educational facilities for these children, it is necessary for education, medicine, language therapy, and psychology to join in mutual programs of comprehensive diagnosis and management. The Governor Center School is one example of how professionals have merged to provide a diagnostic and treatment facility for middle-class children classified as neurologically impaired.

The Governor Medical Center and its satellite, the Governor Center School, were developed because parents complained to a child psychiatrist and a pediatrician of the lack of facilities for their academically distressed children. Their frustrations when attempting to get diagnoses and guidance pushed them to join forces and develop a Center where diagnosis and management could be provided under one roof. The physicians they consulted encouraged their professional colleagues to join the venture. The result was a multidisciplinary and interdisciplinary private practice facility composed of professionals from pediatric neurology, psychiatry, psychology, social work, optometry, physical therapy, speech and hearing and language therapy, with a bridge to these disciplines through special education.

The following condensation of the Center's brochure expresses what it is doing for children who are failing in school and in social adjustment.

Governor Medical Center

The Governor Medical Center provides a comprehensive diagnostic, evaluation, and treatment service for children and adolescents who have emotional disturbances, disorders of growth and development, problems of deviant physical and behavioral functions, and learning disorders.

The Center was developed to provide a unified approach to difficult diagnostic problems. By bringing the capabilities of various qualified professional persons to bear on a given problem, a comprehensive treatment plan is developed which meets the needs of individuals and families alike.

Diagnostic services. The diagnostic services available at the Center are neurological evaluation, psychiatric evaluation, clinical psychological testing, electroencephalography, and clinical laboratory studies. Facilities are also provided for special educational assessment; analysis of speech, language communication, and hearing disorders; surveys of patterns of growth and development; evaluation of gross and fine motor coordination skills, and the analysis of sensory and perceptual disorders. Social service casework facilities are also provided. The clinical staff is particularly interested in the areas of sensory and motor handicaps, delayed speech and developmental aphasia, and problems of children who are school failures.

Treatment facilities. Treatment facilities include medical and related therapeutic procedures for neurological disorders. Psychotherapy and counseling are provided for both individuals and families who have emotional and behavioral disturbances. Special educational facilities are available in the form of individual tutoring or small classes at the Governor Center School.

Governor Center School

The Governor Center School is an integral part of the treatment program. It is dedicated to the concept that with sympathetic understanding and individual instruction planned for each child, these children can reach their highest potential. The school welcomes all children on the basis of their handicaps and needs.

Included in the program are remedial, occupational, and physical therapy for disorders affecting fine and gross motor coordination, speech correction, auditory training, lip reading, and language therapy for disorders of communication. Special training techniques for perceptual-auditory-motor deficits are also offered, thereby rounding out a comprehensive therapeutic program.

Primary classes. Each primary class is limited to 6 children and meets for three hours, Monday through Friday mornings. Some children are fortunate enough to have their difficulty spotted before the first grade. Many future problems can be avoided by a year of special work at this time. These children require much help in developing preschool readiness skills such as expressive language or muscular coordination, which the ordinary child is expected to have when he enters kindergarten or the first grade. At the appropriate stage in each child's development, reading, writing, and number readiness work is begun.

Elementary classes. The elementary classes meet five afternoons a week. In addition to the prereadiness skills which these children may lack because of their disability, specialized remedial reading and arithmetic are given along with other academic subjects suited to their needs.

Part-time groups. Part-time classes, each limited to 4 children concurrently attending other schools, combine opportunity for individual work with the advantages of working in a carefully selected group. The children meet for an hour or an hour and a half twice a week after school, and in addition each child has half an hour a week alone with the teacher. Children are assigned to the groups after careful consideration of their ages and personalities as well as their particular learning difficulties. The teaching is carefully adapted to each child's needs and emphasizes a multisensory approach and integration of auditory, visual, and kinesthetic perception.

Individual tutoring. For high school students and some younger children, individual tutoring may be the answer. Such instruction can be arranged after school or on Saturday. Parent conferences with the teacher are held twice a year. A complete report on each child's progress is made at that time.

Admission procedure. Application for admission to the school is through the child's physician or the school department. Children are admitted to the school only after a detailed analysis of their problems has been made at the Governor Medical Center to determine whether they would benefit by this program. The results of the tests are used to help place each child correctly and in planning individual instruction.

The diagnostic procedures generally required for admission are outlined in Table 3-4. To demonstrate the depth of the diagnostic process, a detailed case record covering several years is presented. The case of Roy is an example of an extremely bright

TABLE 3-4. *Neurological Deficits in 48 Nonretarded Children with Learning Disorders*

Deficits	No.	Group Totals No.	Group Totals %
BALANCE AND COORDINATION			
Gross motor skills		43	89
Inability to stand on 1 foot 10 seconds	26		
Precise finger-nose	9		
Adiadokinesis	7		
Romberg	1		
Fine motor skills		17	35
Finger skills inept	9		
Bilateral synchronous finger skills poor	6		
Mirror movements of hands	2		
REFLEXES, TONUS, MUSCLE STRENGTH		34	70
Deep			
Increased	12		
Diminished	3		
Superficial abdominals, asymmetrical	2		
Babinski, equivocal	9		
Muscle tonus			
Hypertonic	3		
Hypotonic	1		
Muscle strength, upper girdle	4		
CRANIAL NERVES			
Visual inefficiency (III, IV, VI)		45	95
Extraocular	20		
Acuity	11		
Binocularity	6		
Strabismus	3		
Optic pallor	2		
Nystagmus	2		
Photophobia	1		
Auditory inefficiency (VIII)		10	20
Hearing, midrange abnormalities	3		
High frequency loss	2		
High/low frequency loss	2		
Low frequency loss	1		
Other	2		

Deficits	No.	Group Totals No.	%
Tongue (X, XI)		22	46
Sluggish movements	7		
Thickened	7		
Apraxic	6		
Fasciculation	2		
Facial (V), asymmetrical		2	4
SENSORY INTAKE FUNCTIONS		16	33
Face-hand, 2-point discrimination	11		
Astereognosis and agraphesthesia	5		
DIRECTIONALITY AND POSITION SENSE		25	54
Right-left indiscrimination	16		
Finger agnosia	6		
Finger position sense	3		
DOMINANCE AND LATERALITY			
Mixed	20 (42%)		
Left	18 (37%)		
Right	10 (21%)		
CONGENITAL ANOMALIES		4	8
Skull			
Hydrocephalus	1		
Craniostenosis	1		
Heart, congenital malformations	1		
Winged scapulae	1		

child with neurological deficits who has great difficulty learning to read. This case demonstrates that a child may score IQ 138, placing him in the top 1 percent of the population, and still have severe learning deficits. It is interesting to note that his poorest intelligence and language development test scores often were average for the population. In order to achieve these average scores he probably had to work exceedingly hard to overcome severe visual and auditory perceptual and integrative central nervous system deficits. Thus for this child, average test scores may have represented the effects of severe handicaps. This case history also indicates how much we still have to learn about how to diagnose and teach these children.

We chose to present this case rather than a nicely successful one, because it is sometimes possible to demonstrate more this way. The case of Roy realistically illustrates the extent of the struggle of both parents and professionals to help such children. This case was worked up by the Governor Center diagnostic team.

CASE OF ROY

Diagnostic Summary

Roy: Age 7½, elementary school, grade 2.

Chief complaint.   This 7½-year-old, white male was referred because of reading difficulty. He struggles with reading and the teacher cannot understand the reason. He is not a discipline problem, but he is hyperactive, fidgety, and has poor attention span. He was overactive even as a toddler. He has never been happy. He had some speech difficulty in kindergarten and was seen by an orthodontist and a speech therapist. However, this was dismissed as not being a problem.

One year ago he received visual-perceptual training for an entire summer because of "eye fatigue." Glasses were also prescribed but there has been no appreciable improvement in reading.

Family history.   There are three siblings. They are without problems. The gross neurological background appears noncontributory and the emotional climate is normal.

Perinatal history.   There were no previous miscarriages. The pregnancy was devoid of stress factors. Birth was uneventful except for a precipitate three-fourths of an hour labor. He weighed 8 pounds 10 ounces. There were no complications. The early days and months of life were uneventful.

Accidents and infections.   Roy sustained a fractured clavicle at 6 years of age.

Developmental level. The developmental milestones were normal.

Systemic complaints. Nocturnal enuresis started at 3 years and persisted until recently.

Physical examination. Weight, 50 pounds; height, 47½ inches; head, 20 inches; chest, 23¼ inches; hemoglobin, 82 percent. The patient was a hyperactive male who followed directions competently. He was alert and responsive. There was no gross evidence of body clumsiness and gait was normal.

General physical findings. All findings were within normal limits. There were no congenital stigmata.

Pertinent neurological findings. Gross and fine motor skills showed fair balance and fair bilateral synchronous finger skills.

Sensory examination showed vision far and near 20/20; hearing, mild low tone loss (500 cps) bilaterally. Ocular and extraocular movements were normal as were tongue movements. Testing of sensory intake skills indicated mildly atypical face-hand and 2-point discrimination tests. Astereognosis to key, coins, and buttons.

Reflexes were normal except for equivocal Babinski bilaterally.

Other test results were as follows: Right dominant; good auditory sequencing and automatic sequential skills; good cross-modality skills. Good tactile awareness. Archimedes Spiral for visual perceptual function normal.

Electroencephalogram. The EEG showed basic 10/sec frequency with scattered 4/sec with irregular runs bioccipital. No focal abnormalities or seizure discharges.

Impression: For the age, not significant, but 4/sec runs will be significant if they persist.

X-ray. X-rays showed skull and bone age-normal. Thyroid studies were normal.

Ophthalmological examination. Unaided visual acuity was 20/20 in each eye. Cycloplegic refraction was normal. The report stated, "There was a slight lag suggesting hyperthyroidism. The reading problem is not related to the eyes."

Screening psychological tests. The Bender Visual Motor Gestalt Test (copying geometrical figures) was mildly atypical for a 7½-year-old. His verbal level was equivalent to about 10 years and his score on the Similarities subscale of the Wechsler was equal to about that of a 14-year-old child. On the other hand, his Wechsler Arithmetic and Information subscale scores were equivalent to about age 8, indicating a rather broad spread of scores.

Different administrations of the Digit Span test of immediate recall by three examiners gave a range from 3 to 7 digits recalled. Such discrepancies tend to indicate a problem which may be neurogenic, psychogenic, or both.

Impression. Findings suggested the following:

1. Specific reading difficulty and question of underlying language disability
2. Hyperkinetic impulse disorder
3. Visual-perceptual motor and auditory-perceptual problems
4. Anxiety associated with learning disorder and perhaps with parental attitudes

Discussion with parents. The findings were discussed with the parents and it was agreed to pursue the following plan:

1. Medication to control hyperkinesis. The prescribed drugs were methylphenidate (Ritalin), 20 mg morning and noon, and imipramine (Tofrānil), 25 mg at night for enuresis.
2. School placement in an experimental third grade class in a demonstration school where supportive tutorial help would be received.
3. Child and parent counseling.

Clinical course. With the child on medication, the teacher but not the parents noted improved attention span.

The following are reports from the diagnostic team members at the time of the initial examination.

Psychological Report

Roy is a cute, rather shy, 7½-year-old boy. Although he is highly verbal, he hesitates to talk about himself. He is somewhat hyperactive; nevertheless he concentrates well on tests. In general he relates appropriately and with some spontaneity, but occasionally he becomes restless and impatient. At times there is a "girlish" quality about Roy as reflected in some of his mannerisms, and during fleeting moments his behavior appears infantile.

Tests administered. The following tests were administered:

Wechsler Intelligence Scale for Children (WISC)
Rorschach
Sentence Completion
Draw-A-Person
Bender Visual Motor Gestalt

Test interpretations. On the WISC Roy obtained a Verbal Scale IQ of 129, a Performance Scale IQ of 140, and a Full Scale IQ of 138, placing him in the very superior range of intellectual functioning. The subscale pattern was as follows:*

Information	12	Picture Completion	13
Comprehension	17	Picture Arrangement	14
Arithmetic	11	Block Design	19
Similarities	19	Object Assembly	17
Digit Span	14		

Roy is obviously a brilliant child as demonstrated, for instance, by his extraordinarily high scores on Similarities and

* Standard scores: 10 is average, 19 is 3 standard deviations above the mean. It is too bad that the Coding subtest was not included, as the Arithmetic, Digit Span, Coding triad appears to be diagnostic of learning disabilities due to minimal brain dysfunction.

Block Design. His relatively lower score on verbal as compared to performance tasks might indicate one or both of two possibilities: that Roy had difficulty learning in school due to a learning disability, or that he has problems concerning interpersonal communication and initiative. He is barely above average on Arithmetic and Information, suggesting that he has not worked anywhere near his potential. He had a problem in organization on performance items, such as a tendency to become confused on the Block Design test and an initial reversal of sequence on Picture Arrangement. However, when the error was pointed out to him, he made appropriate corrections.

The Bender Gestalt reproductions are slightly inferior for his ability, and the quality of his figure drawing is considerably below expectations. In fact this test reflects a great deal of constriction and compulsiveness.

The projective tests, although somewhat immature, are typical of a youngster with a highly superior intellect. His Rorschach responses are of high level in terms of vocabulary, conceptualization, and creativity. There is no evidence of flagrant psychopathology; however, he does have a great deal of trouble with affect. The reasons for his inability to integrate feelings are not clear. There is some evidence of preoccupation with nurturance, but more in the area of sexual preoccupation. He is confused about his own identity, sexual and otherwise. He appears uncertain what a boy is all about. In part this may be a result of an unsuccessful resolution of oedipal problems, as well as trouble with inner aggression. His angry feelings are extremely frightening to him and therefore may be solidly repressed. His inner hostility appears to reflect itself as self-assertion.*

Although the psychodynamic meaning of Roy's school problem is unclear, one could speculate that it may be related to his tendency to be infantile and his fear of assertion. It is possible that he associates academic accomplishment with aggression and that it frightens him. On the other hand, Roy's learning problems may be the result of specific learning disabilities. Since it is unclear what his school problem really is, it is recommended

* Since these impressions appear to have been based on projective tests that have not been validated for such interpretations, one might question their practical usefulness [L. T.].

that Roy and his parents be observed psychodiagnostically in a few sessions to clarify the psychological problem and to provide therapeutic support if it seems required. A complete diagnostic test battery for learning disorders is recommeded, especially related to visual and auditory perceptual functioning. With such information we should be in a position to make specific educational recommendations.

Visual Perceptual Report

Visual acuity. The results of the visual acuity tests were as follows: Unaided Snellen at far. OD and OS 20/20 minus, OU 20/20. Unaided near point visual acuity 20/20.

Ophthalmoscopy. Ophthalmoscopic examination showed the fundi and external ocular movements negative, the optic discs and maculae well defined.

Pupillary reflexes. There was normal response to light and normal accommodation.

Dominance. Tests for dominance indicated use of right hand, eye, and foot. Occasionally he used his left foot. Dominance not fully established.

Ocular motility. Ocular pursuit movements were somewhat jerky, but saccadic fixations and voluntary ocular movements were executed with good neuromotor control.

Binocular functions. Accommodation/convergence, fusion, macular discrimination, and stereoscopic discrimination were all within the normal limits.

Bilateral hand-eye coordination. He did not manifest any difficulty in direction or simultaneous movement. Overall performance was up to level.

Form perception. Reproduced geometric tachistoscopic forms were somewhat immature but fairly well organized.

There was only one error in direction of a line within the basic figure.

Digit span. His digit span was just at the low normal level of three digit numbers.

Summary. Roy has had vision training for an accommodative problem and has lenses to be worn for near point visual tasks. At this time no problem is evident in this area. Form perception was a little immature with only one error in direction of a single line within a basic figure. On digit span he is at the low normal level. He did not present a binocular problem nor a problem in hand-eye coordination. On the controlled reader he manifested a problem in continuity and recognition of basic vocabulary. There was also substitution and insertion of words. Roy is quite typical of a case not showing serious visual perceptual difficulties but with a basic problem of inattention and poor concentration plus reading difficulties. Specific reading training at the Governor Center School or visual reading skills training with the controlled reader, or both, seem to be the academic help most needed.

Language Assessment

Tests administered. The following tests were administered:

Peabody Picture Vocabulary Test, Form B
Goodenough-Harris Draw-A-Man Test
Illinois Test of Psycholinguistic Abilities, experimental edition (ITPA)
Ammons Full-Range Picture Vocabulary Test, Form A

Communication. On the ITPA Roy scored above the norms on four of the subtests, and above norms for the test as a whole. By interpolation of the score, he achieved a language age of 10 or higher. If his mental age is similar, his IQ should be 130 or higher. However, he did not do that well on any of the screening tests administered today.

On the Peabody Picture Vocabulary Test he earned IQ 104,

and on the Ammons IQ 112, indicating normal or slightly better receptive capacity. On both of the decoding subtests of the ITPA he was above the norms; thus he scored higher on them than on the vocabulary tests.

On the Goodenough-Harris Draw-A-Man Test, Roy earned IQ 88, which was his only below-average score. The figure was drawn in profile, which is somewhat unusual for his age. On the expressive sections of the ITPA he performed from 1 to 2 years above his own age level. In general his expressive language seems good. He kept up a stream of conversation which sometimes interfered with the testing.

His lowest ITPA score, Auditory Vocal Automatic, was almost exactly at his chronological age level. This is a test of knowledge of the formation of plurals, participles, and comparative forms of adjectives. While the score is low for him it is normal for his age. His sequential scores were good, especially the Auditory-Vocal (digit span). The Visual Perceptual Report noted a low normal digit span of three numbers. However, today he repeated six numbers easily, and even succeeded with seven numbers. (On the ITPA, digits are given at the rate of two per second, which may make a significant difference in some cases.) He counted well, said the days of the week well, but omitted *s, t, y,* and *z* when reciting the alphabet. When giving the months of the year he had to be primed with January, and he omitted May and September. Thus the test scores present a contradictory picture.

Impressions. Roy does not seem to have a language problem. He appears hyperactive and aggressive. During the Visual-Motor Sequential test, he accused me repeatedly of cheating to make it harder for him. His attention fluctuations were most obvious on this test since attention is one of the elements being tested. He often tried to turn the cards over before his five-second observational time period was over. When he failed a sequence and repeated it, he would insist that he had originally done it properly.

Summary and recommendations. Roy's testing yields inconsistent scores. This may be due to his hyperactivity and inattention, or there may be emotional factors involved. He certainly gave evidence of hostility. However, there appears to be no evidence of a language problem.

Language training is not indicated. If he is going to repeat the second grade, it would be well to let him have the summer off for play. If psychometric testing points in this direction, psychotherapy for the child or casework for the parents would be advisable. I doubt the Governor School will be necessary. However, if he continues to fall behind in reading, this may be advisable.

Special Education Report

General observations. Roy, a good-looking, friendly boy, accompanied the examiner to the testing room without any hesitation. He smiled frequently, sometimes inappropriately. This might be a manifestation of tension and anxiety. He was somewhat hyperactive and quite easily distracted. He could not remember his address even after some help from the examiner. Spontaneous speech was adequate, although at certain times it became excessive and was delivered in a "driven" manner, suggesting that Roy was unable to control it.

Automatic speech was adequate for the numbers and days, but he had difficulty with the alphabet and the months, omitting several in each case. His writing was poorly organized on the paper and though he could write the numbers acceptably, he had considerable difficulty writing letters. He was very unsure of himself during this activity and hyperactivity increased significantly. He began squinting and making facial grimaces. He commented several times that he gets "mixed up" on some letters and there was obvious confusion. For example, he reversed the *J*, wrote *U* for *Q* and *R* for *B*. In most instances he was aware of his mistakes but did not know how to correct them. Roy said the name of each letter as he wrote it, although generally the visual symbol he produced was not appropriate to the auditory symbol. He held his paper at an unusual angle and seemed to be looking at the paper from an unlikely angle as well. Although he had difficulty keeping the paper immobile, he never made any attempt to use his left hand for this accommodation. Attention span was somewhat limited, but it could be extended with structure.

There were indications of right-left confusion, although not consistently. He seemed to be able to project these concepts on the examiner more adequately than on himself. In addition, performance in this activity improved when the examiner pointed to a part of the body, and requested him to identify it as left or right, as opposed to giving him a direction which included one of these directional concepts, suggesting the possibility of auditory confusion affecting performance. Tests for dominance revealed complete right preferences.

Tests administered. The tests administered were the following:

Ammons Full Range Picture Vocabulary Test, Form B
Metropolitan Readiness Test (selected items)
Metropolitan Achievement Test (selected items)
Gray Oral Reading Test
Memory for Designs Test (selected items)
Eisenson Examining for Aphasia (selected items)

Test results. On the Ammons Roy earned a mental age of 10.5 with an equivalent IQ of 135, indicating his intellectual ability to be within the superior range. These findings agree closely with previous WISC scores but are considerably higher than the previously administered alternate form of the Ammons. The achievement profile of this test showed inconsistencies and was suggestive of an emotional or other problem.

The results of the Copying subtest of the Readiness Battery are poorly formed and suggest spatial disorientation as well as tension and anxiety. He called the diamond a triangle but copied it adequately. His final reproductions were sometimes "tipped" to one side or another and there appeared to be evidence of a visual-motor difficulty. The Matching subtest revealed several errors and he held the booklet in an almost vertical position. His working speed on this test was high and the errors may have been due to a lack of attention.

Roy became obviously disturbed when the reading materials were introduced, especially Gray's oral reading. He was not able to read even the first paragraph acceptably and made omissions, insertions, and substitutions. He does not appear to have any organized method of word attack. In some instances a Gestalt approach appeared evident, while in other cases he seemed to be attempting to utilize the phonetic method. However, there is confusion and deficit in both sensory modalities and therefore little success was achieved. The Word Discrimination subtest of the Metropolitan Achievement Test indicated difficulty in auditory skills, while the Word Knowledge subtest suggested a breakdown in the visual approach. An evaluation of the boy's ability to associate the sound of a letter with the corresponding visual symbol revealed much confusion and substantiated previous findings suggesting a breakdown in both the visual and auditory processes.

Arithmetic achievement is on a higher level than his reading, both in computation and problem-solving, although the latter is obviously affected by poor reading skills. When the problems were presented from an aural stimulus, he was able to solve each one quickly and accurately without the use of visual symbols.

Summary and recommendations. This evaluation revealed a 7-year-old boy of superior intellectual ability, currently enrolled in a third grade. In spite of his superior ability Roy's achievement in the language arts is below grade placement, and this fact caused school authorities to recommend repetition of the second grade. However, because of high ability he was promoted to the third grade.

The results of this assessment suggest organicity, as well as emotionality. There are indications of the hyperkinetic syndrome with resulting learning and behavior problems. Based on his performance during this evaluation, a multiplicity of problems in the learning process appear to be present. There are indications of visual-perceptual, visual-motor, and auditory-perceptual difficulties. In addition there are breakdowns in transferring from one modality to the other, resulting in general confusion and limited achievement. There is no evidence of a consistent approach to the language arts and it was not possible to determine which teaching method is most appropriate. However, the need for a special education approach is indicated, and diagnostic teaching after placement is made should follow.

Casework Interview with Parents

A half-hour interview was held with Roy's parents to evaluate the area of concern and to see how we could be of help. They were a very pleasant couple, conveying an impression of warm and concerned parents. They spoke of their son's being presently in the second grade and facing the possibility of repeating the grade due to his inability to read. A decision will have to be made shortly, namely, should the school promote the boy and expose him to even greater struggles in reading in the third grade or should he be permitted to repeat the grade? In either case, the parents wanted to know how to handle any resulting anxiety. Generally they felt that the child needed some help with reading and they wished to discover the causes of his difficulty.

Roy does well in school in arithmetic but reading and spelling seem to be beyond his comprehension. He was tutored briefly last summer but with no positive results. He has had some eye training and is wearing glasses.

Both parents felt that while Roy was a fairly easy child to handle, he was hyperactive. He had a speech defect in kindergarten but has outgrown it. He is the second oldest of four children, all doing well. Roy seems to have friends and forms relationships easily. He gets along with his siblings and is very close to his brother.

The parents spoke of attempting to help the boy with reading but he would just sit and cry, so they felt that they needed outside help as they are too closely involved with the child. The boy presently likes school but had difficulty in separating from his mother in the first grade.

Generally both parents felt that they definitely needed some help in regard to school. They spoke of feeling that the boy, although not a behavior problem, was anxious over his inability to read and that he was immature in many ways. They were ready to proceed with whatever was indicated to get help and guidance. Although there may be an emotional factor, it was felt that the organic component may be primary and that the situation would be best handled by helping the child with the learning problem first.

Two-Year Interval: Case Work Reports—Parents

The parents were seen over a period of two years. At the last meeting they stated that since they had been seeing the caseworker they felt that some progress had been made by their son in school. However, at home he is a problem; he seems to be stubborn and asserts a lot of independence. He wants to have his own way. His mother cited as an example the time that he had refused to go to catechism.

The father stated that he and the mother tend to get upset with Roy. Also, the youngster clashes with his brother and this seems to be intensified by sibling rivalry since they are close in age. However, he gets along well with the children in the neighborhood. He is presently in a regular fourth-grade class and his report card seems to be good. His only deficiency is in spelling.

The parents said that the teacher told them he is a normal child in the class. However, the parents said that they check often with the teacher to insure Roy doesn't lose control at school. They both feel that he has made educational progress and likes school. For three years he had been in a special class. This is his first year in a regular class and this seems to please him. The parents recognize that the behavior problems have been confined to the home environment. We discussed getting a caseworker for Roy and they agreed that he should have therapy. The parents were later interviewed separately and jointly over a period of three months by another caseworker. A summary report follows.

They continue to be extremely resistant to an exploration of their own part in Roy's problems.* Mrs. A is a passive, somewhat anxious woman who at first tended to deny that she might handle Roy differently. She has, however, been able to reach the point of admitting that she has difficulty controlling the boy. Mr. A, on the other hand, seems disinterested and defensive and would like to confine Roy's difficulties to reading. He questions whether or not the boy is socially isolated at school.

---

* Since the previous caseworker noted that these parents were actively seeking help, perhaps another interpretation is possible. The resistance may partly be related to guilt and anxiety generated by what the parents may have interpreted as blame for Roy's problems [L. T.].

Both parents have feelings about setting limits and controls. Maternal and paternal grandparents were overly restrictive. Mr. A did not develop a close relationship with his father or brothers but felt identified with his mother. He projects many of his own feelings onto Roy. He rationalizes Roy's behavior as being "individualistic" and projects the boy's difficult adjustment in school onto the teacher.* Because of business demands, the father has limited time to spend with the boy. In many ways both parents may be unconsciously fostering Roy's acting-out behavior. Treatment has been concentrated on helping the parents see their role in the relationship and setting limits with Roy. Mrs. A may be more receptive than her husband. About a year later, a joint interview was held with Mr. and Mrs. A to review plans for termination. The parents felt that therapy has helped in Roy's relationships at home but hasn't really made a difference in school. They are concerned that he will be able to attend this school for only another year and then they must make other plans.

What really came out of this interview was Mr. A's admission that he has difficulty relating to Roy. His own father saw his role as supporting the family financially but not really spending much time with the children. Mr. A's father was authoritarian and worked compulsively night and day running two businesses. Mr. A continues to follow this role model but I feel he's not too comfortable with it. Perhaps some of Roy's learning difficulty is related to identification with his father.† Mr. A did not go on to college because of similar learning difficulties, and his ambivalence about this gets expressed in relation to Roy.

Therapy Progress Report – Roy

Roy started in therapy and was seen weekly from age 9 to 11 when sessions were reduced to every other week. The reasons for this reduction were based on two factors: (1) Contacts with the

* Since the Special Education Report previously cited stated that Roy's academic achievement could be improved by using teaching methods appropriate to his strengths and deficits, the father's feelings may not have been entirely unrealistic "rationalizations" and "projections" [L. T.].

† Or it may be genetic [L. T.].

family revealed that Roy had improved noticeably and that the parents were ready to terminate therapy, and (2) Roy made significant gains in therapy and seemed ready for a reduction of treatment hours.

Roy's hyperactivity, his continued need to test and push limits decreased noticeably in our therapy hours over the past four months. He appeared better able to concentrate in play activities and began to use many of our hours to verbalize his feelings. For example, he was able to describe some of his difficulties in school, his problems with authority, and his feelings of being pushed beyond his expectations. He seemed to come to the realization that he had to learn and to do well in school because this was important for himself and that, although it might please his parents, he would be the one to benefit the most. This change in attitude was accompanied by improved grades, new interest in school subjects, and his often bringing tests to therapy so we could discuss what he was learning. He talked about his hopes to become a sports writer and we spent much time checking out what one needs to know to do this job well. After his last report card he talked with pride about his friends' wonderment about his improved grades.

According to Roy his home situation has improved somewhat but not as much as he would like. There are fewer arguments over his refusal to do chores or homework, but his parents still become upset when he expresses anger or disappointment. He sees his mother as being warm and loving but too busy to be happy. Father, he feels, is never around and he spends most time with him when he accompanies him for therapy sessions. Roy is somewhat fearful of his father yet enjoys teasing him about things such as his choice of clothing and cars, and the fact that he always naps when at home.

In some of our play sessions Roy revealed that he sees himself as a small, ineffective boy who could never grow big and strong, and that he can manipulate people only by outwitting them, teasing, or pushing limits. He feels that what he needs most is a "good friend" and for this reason he particularly enjoys therapy. Initially he found it difficult to accept the reduction of hours, but he came to accept this as a realistic step toward eventual termination, which he now accepts as an ultimate reality. I would like to continue seeing Roy for at least six months on an every-other-week basis, with the goals of strengthening his self-image, helping him to understand how he relates to his parents, and consolidating his new-found academic interests.

Academic Progress Summary

While the therapy designed to help the emotional overlay appeared to be progressing well, the parents became very upset when the Stanford Achievement scores for the 3-year academic period were shown to them. A summary of this report is listed:

Grade Level Scores

Roy's grade in school:	Third	Fourth	Fifth
Word meaning	2.6	4.6	4.7
Paragraph meaning	4.3	3.7	3.6
Spelling	2.6	3.2	4.7
Language	3.8	3.1	4.0
Arithmetic computation	4.1	5.0	5.2
Arithmetic concepts	4.0	4.6	5.6
Social studies	3.6	4.5	4.5
Science	4.3	3.4	3.7

A report from his remediation teacher provided insight into the education problem.

Teacher's Report

Roy entered the special school in November as a full-time day school pupil. He was in a special experimental third-grade class until June.

In September he entered a regular fourth grade. Since the school had no special education programs at Roy's level during that school year, he remained in the regular classroom without any special help.

The next September he entered the fifth grade and has received help from me in a special education resource room program. From 8:30 to 10 o'clock each morning Roy and 6 other boys at the fifth-grade level have participated in a tutorial or group experience which emphasized reading, language, spelling, and writing. While I have seen progress this year, I have also considered the possibility that another educational environment might be more beneficial.

The following is a survey of the methodologies used. Roy revealed disabilities in visual and auditory perception, visual-motor, expressive language, and sequencing. Since Roy had no consistent learning modality, diagnostic programs were initiated. More success was attained when a multisensory approach, which emphasized the auditory factor, was utilized. Therefore a combination and modification of the Gillingham and Fernald methods became the basis of his reading and spelling programs. Some difficulty was observed when he had to supply the appropriate word or in sequencing the days of the week, months, or year. The paucity of language, sentence structure, and sequencing were well below his ability level. Development in these areas was structured on the basis of his experiences, using commercial language kits such as Peabody and Ginn, tapes supplied in these kits and tapes made by Roy himself, language games, and puppets. While growth in this area has been noticeable it is still not commensurate with his ability.

To sum up, we have a child with superior ability who has multiple learning problems and resulting emotional problems. We have seen great improvement in his ability to interact with his peers, remain relatively emotionally stable, and show slow progress in the academic areas despite his learning problems. We have also been aware of his need for intellectual stimulation. In this program his cognitive abilities have been stimulated in the regular classroom while his learning disabilities and academic problems have been helped in the resource room program. In a situation which does not provide intellectual stimulation Roy becomes lethargic and disinterested. Therefore we would like to find an educational environment that would fulfill these requirements.

Case Conference

A case conference was held and it was felt that, in spite of the massive efforts already described, apparently the key to the problems had not yet been found and that perhaps placement away from home in a fully qualified special-education preparatory school might be considered. As a trial Roy was sent away for the summer to an educational camp which was run by such a preparatory school.

Their report and recommendations are of interest.

Summer Camp School

Roy has improved a great deal in all areas this summer. His successes have built toward a basic command of spelling, composition, and handwriting, and a most satisfying improvement in his reading. In reading he has progressed through Merrill Linguistics Readers 1-4. Walking around during the sessions with these readers helped a great deal. He has read 1-4 of the Coleman and Berres series of books about submarine adventures. With a simple syntax and a phonetic approach, these books did a great deal to build up his confidence and ability. By my pointing to each word with a pencil, along with his following with his finger, he achieved success. There was no verbal reproval for mistakes; the pencil just rested on the mispronounced word. I also read to him and had him follow along to catch my errors.

In spelling we used card games with Gillingham cards; *Read, Write and Spell;* tracing on masonite board with fingers; Phonovisual Consonant card; nonsense syllables, and RRI sheets. Initially a straightforward approach to vowel sounds was a failure. I worked out a system of placing short vowel words on cards, vowels and consonants in different colors, and then having him make sentences, with any extra words willingly supplied.

In composition Roy still needs work. By dictating his compositions to me and then writing them from my dictation, with help in syllables and sounding out words, a good composition can be achieved.

In handwriting Roy needs improvement. We used Johnson Handwriting cards in class each day. His improvement tends to fall off under stress. He is aware of his writing problem and his ability to improve it.

Movement is a necessary part of the entire program. Jumping jacks, throwing, catching, jumping, and walking were used.

Discussion and recommendations.   Roy's case history suggests many early indications that "something was wrong," but testing failed to elicit any specific problem. However, testing indicated that he is extremely bright. His Wechsler in 1965 indicated that he was in the superior to very superior range in almost all functioning. Despite this high intellectual potential, however, he is a consistent underachiever in school and simply has not learned the language skills of reading, writing, and spelling. Spelling and writing are both far below his intellectual potential, and they are much more appropriate for a third-grade child than for a boy in the sixth grade. He is having particular difficulty in organizing his thoughts for written output. When he does attempt to write, sentences are often confused or run together.

In the tutorial process he was found to have extreme difficulty with any type of decoding skills, and his ability to handle serial order material was extremely low. He was also found to have difficulties in auditory discrimination and particularly in blending tasks. This auditory difficulty did not seem to be related to acuity, but rather represented a problem in handling auditory input.

Unfortunately earlier testing had not revealed this except in a very gross way. In our initial testing, the sequencing problem was still apparent just as it was in 1965. For example, his problem in getting letter sequences correctly formed was so intense that he was able to spell correctly only 3 out of the 7 days of the week.

Because no new WISC scores were available within the past two years, it was decided that a new administration should be undertaken at the close of the summer session. The results of this test are as follows: Verbal IQ 97; Performance IQ 136; and Full Scale IQ 117. Subscale breakdowns are given and compared with his 1965 scores.

Wechsler Subscale Scores

Verbal Scale	1965	1969
Information	12	7
Comprehension	17	9
Arithmetic	11	11
Similarities	19	10
Digit Span	14	14

Performance Scale

Picture Completion	13	17
Picture Arrangement	14	10
Block Design	19	18
Object Assembly	17	18
Coding	—	13

The remarkable drop in verbal ability during the past four years is of major significance. We have frequently observed a massive drop in Verbal IQ in children who do not learn to read, so it is not surprising to have Roy show such a precipitous decline. In a sense this precipitous fall in Verbal IQ is a tragic example of what happens to the child with an *untreated perceptual-motor disorder*.* It is highly improbable that he has "lost" any IQ. He simply has not been able to develop the potential that was there earlier, before reading became the dominant factor. It is particularly tragic to see a potentially brilliant child sink into mediocrity because he is unable to acquire the skill of decoding the written word. We are quite sure that the potential is still available, but it is highly unlikely, if he does not acquire the language arts, that he will develop into the gifted individual that he might be.

At the present time Roy is in a fair way to becoming one of the "creeping educational disaster cases" whom we frequently see in middle or late adolescence as high school dropouts. Unable to read or write within normal limits, they limp through until legal leaving age allows them to escape from the scene of continuing defeats.

In Roy's case there was evidence this summer that he can be taught the language arts skills. Unfortunately the seven weeks of the summer program ended before he had been able to make any massive gains, but we were able to see many evidences that he is eminently teachable, and consideration should be given to placing him in a private school which is specifically tailored to his needs.

It has been our general experience that when a very bright boy fails almost completely, there often builds up a great deal of resentment and frustration not only in the child but in the staff

* My emphasis [L. T.].

of his school as well. A fair amount of frustration and emotional overlay has built up in Roy's case, and we feel that this is another reason why getting a fresh start in a residential situation would probably be indicated for him.

Conclusions

This case demonstrates well the complexities that are associated with a learning disorder in a very bright boy. Roy may be suffering from a neurogenic learning disability. This can be inferred from the very severe reading problem associated with visual-motor and auditory-perceptual deficits in the presence of a very high IQ. Also characteristic is the large differential between his Wechsler Performance and Verbal IQ scores. He also demonstrates a variety of other problems which are often seen in such cases. These include the slow 4-per-second waves on his electroencephalogram, confusion on the Block Design and reversal on the Picture Arrangement test, a slightly inferior Bender Visual Motor Gestalt Test, difficulty on the Draw-A-Man test, dominance not fully established, high and low scores on the same test taken at different times, wide variations on the subscales of both the Wechsler Intelligence Scale and the Illinois Test of Psycholinguistic Abilities, problems with sequencing, and difficulty with certain letters and sounds. Finally, the lack of positive effect on his reading and spelling development of both psychotherapy and previous educational experience tends to confirm this diagnosis.

Most of the problems evidenced by Roy during testing appeared minor. Taken individually they would probably be of little consequence. However, when added together they seem to constitute a fairly formidable barrier to ready learning in this child. The teachers who used the Fernald and Gillingham approaches seemed to be on the right track and they made progress with Roy. He appeared to respond to a multisensory teaching approach.

If he becomes successful in his schoolwork one can expect the secondary emotional problems to dissipate gradually. The parents seem typical of many adequate parents in their behavior patterns and one should note the lack of emotional problems in the other three children.

The future for this boy is still questionable in spite of the hopes held out by a faculty of earnest, well-meaning professionals running a full-time school. Hopefully their offer to accept this boy will help solve the problem, but we are not in a position to guess the future.

In retrospect we were not originally sufficiently influenced by the organic aspects of the case, primarily because of the psychologist's psychodynamic orientation and the benign report of our visual-perceptual expert. Would the outcome have been better if we had used a visual- and auditory-perceptual bombardment approach? Would we have had a better outcome if we had concentrated upon placing this child at age 7 at Governor Center School rather than at a superior regular school where he received some supportive help?

From experience we can only conclude that the very bright child with a learning disability may respond dramatically with a minimum of help, or he may present a very frustrating and complicated picture which must be handled in a variety of ways based on an adequate differential diagnosis.

PROFILE OF 48 CHILDREN

A profile of 48 full-time students at Governor Center School with problems comparable to those described in Roy's case history provides some insight into the common but complicated issues of academic underachievement and the hyperkinetic behavior syndrome.

Demography. There were 43 boys and 5 girls in the group. They were first referred between 6 and 14 years of age. One-half of this group were first referred between 9 years and 11 years, 6 months. Although their intelligence scores ranged from superior to untestable, half the group were in the low normal range (90–99 IQ) but with wide scatter on the Wechsler Verbal and Performance subtests. Most of the children stemmed from the white- and blue-collar middle class.

Major complaints. School problems, hyperkinetic behavior, difficulty in expressing thoughts adequately, and a scattering of other complaints are listed in Table 3-5.

TABLE 3-5.   *48 Children with Learning Disorders*

Presenting Complaint	%
School difficulty	33
Hyperkinetic behavior	25
Expressive difficulty	17
Miscellaneous:	
Reading and writing difficulty	7
Slow or clumsy	6
Comprehension	4
Others	8
Total	100

History. Fourteen percent of the families had members who had difficulty learning to read or write. Twenty-one percent of the families reported neurological stigmata such as convulsions and mental retardation; in 14 percent, unstable parents or siblings created poor home conditions. An unusually high number of abnormal stress factors (74%) were described by parents as occurring during pregnancy, delivery, and immediately after birth. Serious infections and head injuries during the first three years were present in 19 cases (39%). (See Table 3-3.)

Development. Delayed onset of two- or three-word sentences was reported in about half the cases, and delay in onset of single words in about one-quarter. Motor development (walking) was normal in most. The similarity in percent of cases of delayed start of sentences between the learning disorder and cerebral palsy cases is interesting (see Table 3-6).

Physical examination. Clumsiness, i.e., a mild impairment of balance and coordination, could be observed in

TABLE 3-6. *Developmental Milestone Comparison Between Cerebral Palsy and Learning Disability Children*

Development	Delayed Onset	
	Cerebral Palsy (N = 100) %	Learning Disorder (N = 48) %
Walk unsupported	77	6
Speech		
Single words	74	23
2–3-word sentences	46	47

most cases. Minor changes in reflexes, tonus, and muscle strength were also found, as well as poor fine-motor skills. Impaired directionality and position sense were found in one-half of the group and sensory intake skill impairment occurred in one-third of the cases. Ocular or extraocular pathology occurred in 45 cases (93%). Acuity deficiencies were found in 22 percent and impaired tongue mobility occurred in 22 percent. Dominance and laterality mixtures were found in 41 percent and left-sidedness in 37 percent (see Table 3-4).

Electroencephalograms. EEG's were consistent with convulsive disorders in 10 percent and with cerebral dysfunction in 35 percent of the cases (see Table 3-7).

TABLE 3-7. *Findings in 48 Children with Learning Disorders*

Procedure	No.	%
Electroencephalograms	31	100
Abnormal consistent with cerebral dysfunction	11	35
Suspicious of cerebral dysfunction	11	35
Convulsive disorder	3	10
Normal	6	19
Archimedes Spiral aftereffect	48	100
Abnormal	13	27
Normal	35	73

Diagnosis. When all test results were analyzed, communication skills (language or visual-perceptual-motor or both) difficulties accounted for over one-half of the cases. Behavior disorders were found in 30 percent, and cerebral palsy or mental retardation was found in 8 percent of the children.

Specific learning disability was found in 6 percent. This diagnosis was made when there was a family history of learning difficulty, evidence of a deficit in reading (dyslexia), writing (dysgraphia), or arithmetic (dyscalculia), and a neurological examination that was relatively normal.

Results. Of the 48 children, 31 percent entered a regular class, generally at anticipated grade, after one or two years at Governor Center School. Three children were placed in special education classes in public schools for the intellectually normal, and 3 were placed in classes for the mentally retarded. One-half of the group remained at the School for further treatment.

ROLE OF MEDICATION

If the ability to pay attention is a prime requisite of learning, then every attempt must be made to develop this ability in a child who lacks it. Medication, behavior modification, and psychotherapeutic counseling are the main approaches to help children. In certain children the proper choice of medication will control hyperactivity and increase attention span and thus save many months of hard work on a one-to-one basis between child and therapist.

There are three groups of children who appear to benefit from medication.

1. Those with convulsions, or with electroencephalograms which suggest convulsive or subconvulsive tendencies. Such children often also have the hyperkinetic behavior syndrome.
2. Those with the hyperkinetic behavior syndrome.

3. Those with behavior disorders which reflect anxiety, aggression, or neurotic behavior.

Hyperkinetic Impulse Disorder

The child who appears to respond best to medication is the one with *hyperkinetic syndrome.* Such a child may exhibit the following behavior characteristics, found most often in boys.

1. *Hyperactivity.* Involuntary and almost constant overactivity beyond the norm for the age.
2. *Short attention span.* Attention span of one to five minutes on a single activity with frequent shifting to other activities.
3. *Variability.* Unpredictable behavior with wide fluctuations in the same activity from day to day, hour to hour, or minute to minute.
4. *Impulsiveness.* Inability to delay gratification. "He wants what he wants when he wants it," and he does things on the spur of the moment.
5. *Irritability.* Low frustration tolerance is characteristic.
6. *Explosiveness.* Tantrums which reach unpredictable heights and include irritability and low frustration tolerance.
7. *Poor school work.* Behavior interferes and school work suffers.

The behaviors described are often associated with child perinatal-infancy stress complications and resulting maternal stress. A history of prematurity, precipitate delivery, prolonged labor, or breech labor is commonly found. A history of serious illness, especially meningoencephalitis and head trauma during the first three years, is not unusual. Older children who suffer from head injuries associated with automobile accidents may demonstrate such behavior within three to six months after the accident. One hypothesis is that such behavior may stem from diencephalic dysfunction due to cellular change resulting from anoxia or trauma to the sensitive ganglia within the diencephalon which produce norepinephrine. The electroencephalogram is generally but not necessarily abnormal in these cases.

Since both hyperactive and hypoactive behavior may result from primary emotional causes, without an adequate history differentiation may be difficult. Often in such cases there may be a mixture of both organic and emotional factors which contribute to the behavior pattern. Secondary emotional factors develop early in the hyperkinetic, impulse-disordered child. When this remains unrecognized and untreated, withdrawing behavior or, more likely, acting-out for peer-group approval develops which covers the basic hyperkinetic disability (Denhoff and Robinault 1960).

Medication is an early and effective step in differential diagnosis as well as treatment. Proper drug selection and use will modify some components of the syndrome and make educational and social behavior management easier. In mild cases effective drugs taken by the child can often help a teacher achieve rapid educational progress with him. In more complicated cases, the drug will make an impact only on the symptom, and intensive guidance work will be required to correct the behavior and the associated disabilities which contribute to scholastic failure.

The drugs which are useful in this syndrome as well as in hyperkinesis from other causes are the following:

Psychotropic Drugs
  1. Psychomotor stimulants (amphetamine-like)
     dextroamphetamine sulfate (Dexedrine)
     amphetamine (Benzedrine Sulfate)
     methylphenidate (Ritalin)
  2. Antidepressants (imipramine-like)
     imipramine (Tofrānil)
     nortriptyline (Aventyl)
  3. Major tranquilizers (chlorpromazine-like)
     chlorpromazine (Thorazine)
     thioridazine (Mellaril)
     fluphenazine (Permitil)
Anticonvulsants
  1. Major motor seizures

primidone (Mysoline)
diphenyhydantoin (Dilantin)
2. Minor motor seizures
ethosuximide (Zarontin)
phensuximide (Milontin)

There are many other drugs which are believed to be useful in hyperkinesis. However, only those with demonstrable efficacy, based upon reports in the literature, will be discussed. For a summary of the research on drugs, see Table 7-1.

Methylphenidate and amphetamine-like drugs. The stimulants increase arousal mechanisms in a normal nervous system. In children with diencephalic dysfunction, methylphenidate and the amphetamines appear to promote cerebral control over attention. Several articles have been published to demonstrate by double-blind study the efficacy of methylphenidate (Ritalin) and dextroamphetamine (Dexedrine) over placebo (Conners et al. 1963, 1967; Millichap et al. 1968). The dose requirements are not large and vary from 2.5 to 20 mg two or three times a day.

Chlorpromazine and chlorpromazine-like drugs. Such medications as the chlorpromazine-like drugs are sedatives and create reduced attention span and reduced motor activity. However, in some children they may help. Mostly they are used to help reduce anxiety. Often chlorpromazine (Thorazine) is used initially to reduce anxiety and make it possible to use amphetamine or methylphenidate with effectiveness for increasing attention span.

Thioridazine (Mellaril) has been a popular antihyperkinetic sedative drug. It appears to have some of the benefits of amphetamine without the side effects. Whereas amphetamine (methylphenidate less so) almost invariably reduces appetite and makes it difficult for a child to fall asleep at bedtime, thioridazine promotes appetite and sleep. Many children become so obese while on thioridazine that an adrenal-cortical side effect is suspected. They lose weight when the drug is omitted.

Imipramine (Tofrānil) is also valuable, not because of its antidepressant qualities but because it appears to have a potentiating effect with amphetamine to increase attention span.

Anticonvulsants. There is a close relationship between convulsive states and the hyperkinetic impulse disorder. Children who have seizures often exhibit hyperkinetic behavior. On the other hand, when children with hyperkinesis have abnormal EEG's which suggest convulsive or subconvulsive patterns, appropriate anticonvulsant medications may be used together with methylphenidate or amphetamine for better behavior control. There appears to be good evidence that there are close relationships between abnormal behavior in children (psychotic, emotional, hyperkinetic) and abnormal electroencephalograms (Stevens 1969).

Two drug studies using a 10-mg capsule of Dexedrine spansule were carried out by Denhoff on the same 27 learning-disorder children. In the first study parents gave the drug out. They reported a benefit in 54 percent of the cases. In the second study the teachers administered the capsule at the start of class. The teachers reported a 78 percent benefit, mostly in reduction of hyperactivity and increased attention span (see Table 3-8).

TABLE 3-8. *Effect of Dexedrine Sulfate on Neurologically Impaired Children*

| | Administered and Reported | | | |
| | by Teachers | | by Mothers | |
Benefit Reported	No.	%	No.	%
Excellent	4	15	1	4
Moderate	8	30	5	19
Fair	9	33	8	31
None	6	22	12	46
Total	27	100	26	100

CONCLUSIONS

In the management of children with learning problems, the medical responsibilities relate to: (1) correcting deficiencies stemming from acute and chronic physical illness, (2) discovering neurological disorders or dysfunctions which depress skills relevant to learning, (3) appropriate referral for psychiatric problems, (4) prescribing and controlling overall supervision, and (5) translating to parents the findings and the processes involved in the remediation program.

The physician must develop an ability to evaluate developmental skills in children as they relate to school and social activities. He should be able to evaluate the significance of reports from allied professionals and help fit them into the overall pattern. He must be able to comprehend the search for answers by a variety of nonmedical allies and encourage such attitudes. When contributions appear irrelevant, interchange based upon the professionals' comprehensive and objective views may provide the basis for a meaningful team learning process. At the same time, *it is most important that all professional personnel remain open to suggestions and new information which may contradict their previous training and understanding.* It is important for the physician to recognize that a subjective analysis based upon either parental or professional views, glimpses of a child in an office session, and laboratory tests which evaluate a function over a short period of time are not adequate bases for proper diagnosis. He must encourage the development of and participate in multidisciplinary centers where longitudinal diagnoses and remediation proceed simultaneously.

Currently there seems to be no better way than the comprehensive multidisciplinary approach to dam the flood of school children who are emerging into adulthood with poor writing and reading skills, with a poor self-image, and with a self-defeating attitude, as the result of early traumatic school and social experiences.

REFERENCES

Bradley, J. E. Symposium: School problems and the physician. *Current Medical Digest* 35:147, 1968.

Conners, C. K., and Eisenberg, L. The effects of methylphenidate on symptomatology and learning in disturbed children. *American Journal of Psychiatry* 120:458, 1963.

Conners, C. K., Eisenberg, L., and Barcai, A.   Effect of dextroamphetamine on children. *Archives of General Psychiatry* (Chicago)
17:478, 1967.

de Hirsch, K., Jansky, J., and Langford, W.   *Predicting Reading
Failure.* New York: Harper & Row, 1966.

Denhoff, E., and Robinault, I. P.   *Cerebral Palsy and Related Disorders.* New York: McGraw-Hill, 1960.

Denhoff, E., Siqueland, M. L., Komich, M. P., and Hainsworth, P. K.
Developmental and predictive characteristics of items from the
Meeting Street School screening test. *Journal of Developmental
Medicine and Child Neurology* 10:220, 1968.

Denhoff, E.   Detecting potential learning problems at pre-school
medical examinations. *Texas Medicine* 65:56, 1969.

Frostig, M., Lefever, D. W., and Whittlesey, J. R. B.   *The Mary-
anne Frostig Developmental Tests of Visual Perception.* Palo
Alto, Cal.: Consulting Psychologists Press, 1964.

Hainsworth, P. K., and Siqueland, M. L.   *Early Identification of
Children with Learning Disabilities: The Meeting Street School
Screening Test.* Providence: Crippled Children and Adults of
Rhode Island, 1969.

Millichap, J. G., et al.   Hyperkinetic behavior and learning disorder. *American Journal of Diseases of Children* 116:235, 1968.

Ozer, M. N.   Standardized Motor Examination of Pre-School Children. Presented at American Academy for Cerebral Palsy, Miami
Beach, Fla., Dec. 11, 1968.

Rhode Island State Board of Education.   General Regulations
Governing Special Education of Handicapped Children. Providence, 1963.

Stevens, J. R.   Clinical and EEG correlates of 100 children hospitalized for psychiatric disorders. *Electroencephalography and
Clinical Neurophysiology* 28:90, 1970.

Slingerland, Beth H.   *Pre-Reading Screening Procedures to Identify First Grade Academic Needs.* Cambridge, Mass.: Educators
Publishing Service, Inc., 1969.

Tarnopol, L.   *Learning Disabilities: Introduction to Educational
and Medical Management.* Springfield, Ill.: Thomas, 1969.

4

Proceedings of the Panel on Medication

Medicating Children with Learning Disabilities

Part I

SAM D. CLEMENTS, C. KEITH CONNERS,
JAMES A. DUGGER, HELEN GOFMAN,
JAMES P. LASTER, JOHN E. PETERS,
JOHN REYNOLDS, HENRY S. RICHANBACH,
LESTER TARNOPOL, AND
LEON J. WHITSELL

CHAIRMAN TARNOPOL: The purpose of this Panel on Medication is to bring together physicians and psychologists who have had many years of experience working with children who have learning disabilities. Our primary purpose is to pool our experiences so that they can be shared with others who are interested in the medical management of these children, but who may not have had as much experience with them.

The United States Department of Health, Education, and Welfare has issued a statement to the effect that about 5 percent of school children have learning disabilities which appear to be associated with neurological dysfunction. "The word *dyslexia* is sometimes used to describe children with such symptoms, but there is as yet no general agreement about the definition of this term. Also *minimal brain dysfunction* is loosely used to explain a variety of learning problems, sometimes including dyslexia. In any case the many variations in type and severity call for diagnostic study by a team of collaborating professionals. The earlier the diagnosis, the greater is the likelihood that instructional efforts will be successful." *

On the other hand, pediatric neurologists variously estimate the incidence of neurological dysfunction in the presence of learning disabilities to include from 5 to 20 percent of the population. Clearly the disorder under discussion has not been adequately specified diagnostically, and adequate prevalence studies are lacking. At any rate, learning disabilities as diagnostic entities requiring medical management have been recognized certainly since Dr. Samuel T. Orton's work in the 1920's and have become generally accepted as a pediatric problem during the last decade.

This panel is primarily concerned with the medication management of these children. During the past ten years there has been sufficient controlled research on drugs to make it possible for physicians to suggest that their colleagues may find that they can help a great many of these children with properly prescribed medications.

We wish to discuss the various medications that have proved useful in the management of children with different types of learning problems. It is also important to indicate the precautions required when using medication. To the extent that we are aware of possible untoward effects that may occur with various drugs, we wish to discuss those effects.

We are also interested in examining the various approaches which you have developed for gathering diagnostic case histories. You may wish to discuss how you work with the families of these children and with their teachers, psychologists, and schools in a total management program.

Dr. Richanbach has a brief introductory statement for us.

Dr. Richanbach: An appropriate opening statement for this panel discussion on medication might be to note that drugs

---

* *The Child with a Reading Disorder*. U.S. Department of Health, Education, and Welfare, Oct. 1968.

are often effective in altering and improving behavior and school performance.

The paradoxical effect of stimulant drugs in hyperkinetic children was noted by Bradley (1937) over thirty years ago, but interest seemed rather dormant until recently. There are a limited number of drugs which may be extremely useful in altering behavior and performance, particularly the symptoms of hyperkinesis, attention span difficulties, and useless activity. School performance and ability to learn and socialize may also be enhanced. Symptoms such as anxiety, withdrawal, and depression are also treatable.

It is extremely important that the use of medication be more widely understood in the medical community. Many of us have been trying to accomplish this for years. It seems, however, that many people are misusing the drugs. Many physicians, parents, teachers, and others are responding to limited knowledge and overly enthusiastic lay literature and publicity in a way that is rather distressing. We are all familiar with the parent who comes in with a child in one hand and a magazine article in the other asking for the little pill that will solve all their problems. And there is also the physician who, without much more information, prescribes the pills.

However, the fact that the drugs can be remarkably effective at times permits one the possibility of changing a child's entire life style and character. Drug usage must be extremely careful and should be based upon a great deal of knowledge about the patient and the circumstances in which he must function, as well as information about the drugs. In addition, one would like to be able to utilize any change or improvement in behavior or performance in a constructive way. Inability or failure to observe and follow up children on medication adequately may lead to an effect's being unnoticed, lost, or misused.

The necessary extent of the examination of a child is that which is appropriate to the needs of the child and his circumstances. It is perhaps most useful to have a multidisciplinary team, including teachers, social workers, psychologists, psychiatrists, and so on. Although an experienced practitioner who already knows the patient and his family may act intelligently after a single office visit with a new complaint, a severe learning or communication problem may take weeks or months of observation and management to elucidate.

The various categories such as *minimal brain dysfunction, neurological handicap,* and so on, have no specific diagnostic or remedial value. I participated in one of the pilot studies on neurologically handicapped children in San Mateo County nine years ago, which led to the present California legislation for *educationally handicapped* children of substantially normal or higher intelligence with neurological or emotional problems. Personally, at the moment I find it more satisfactory to call them *developmental disorders* when talking to families, since the etiology is still uncertain.

Since one of our reasons for being here is our enthusiasm for the use of drugs, I would like to express some of my concerns. Abuse occurs at all levels, and the problem was most succinctly stated by Dr. Shirkey (1967) in an article on drug abuse with the facetious observation that life is a drug deficiency disease. The message from the mass media is that one must take something for everything; there is chemical management for everything from body odor to the various kinds of headaches and tensions.

The medical profession must share the guilt in creating the need for treating everything. Though much specific drug therapy is available, it should be used judiciously with a diagnosis and goals in mind. Management of any disorder is dependent on the adequacy of the diagnosis, and should be appropriate to the needs of the child, his circumstances, and the services available to him.

An adequate diagnosis that permits me to define for the family those things which the child is contributing to his problem creates the opportunity to make a major impact on the situation. This may sometimes be expressed by the remark, "You mean, he isn't doing it all on purpose?" Parents are victimized by a society which blames the parents, and particularly the mother, for everything that goes wrong. A good example is *Summerhill* by Neill which has as its thesis that there is no such thing as a bad child, only bad parents.

Many parents have to live with children who are difficult to be around and unrewarding as offspring. Acknowledging and defining the child's contributions as well as those of the parents and the schools *without establishing guilt,* but rather offering reasonable courses of action which may include medication, can be a most gratifying and productive function for the pediatrician.

Dr. Gofman's (1969) concept of *school failure as a serious occupational hazard,* a hazard that can have as serious consequences as many diseases or injuries which are given much attention by physicians, is a most useful one. A good work-up, including psychological testing and discussion time with the family, may cost less than the care of a broken bone.

Cooperation with the schools is a vital dimension in both diagnosis and management. A sophisticated and sympathetic teacher is my most valuable aid in determining the effect and dosage of medication. Parents may be unaware of subtle changes that affect behavior and performance in school. If objective evidence can be obtained that the child is quite capable of more acceptable performance, this can be utilized with him and with those who deal with him.

Professional counseling can be immensely effective if the referral is appropriately made and if the counselor recognizes the organic determinants of behavior and the significance of the school situation. School is where the child must make it in our society, and *a well-adjusted school failure is a contradiction in terms.* The community I work in is relatively rich in sophisticated child psychiatrists and psychologists, though never as many as could be used. There are also many knowledgeable school administrators, teachers, and so on, who can be of help. State law permits up to 2 percent of the California public school population to receive special education with state funding in the Program for Educationally Handicapped Minors, and many school districts are providing at least this much.

As to specific drugs, my personal preference is for the amphetamines, though methylphenidate (Ritalin) is probably the smoother drug. Amphetamines are less expensive; their longer duration of effect with sustained-release preparations permits a single dose to be given in the morning. This permits the medication to become routine and attracts less attention. The experience of having a teacher ask about medicine in front of the class, or a little sister at home (bright little sisters can be a terrible burden), may be devastating. Taking medicine is a child's own private business and he should be so instructed.

If there is to be a lasting beneficial change in a child's behavior or performance, it is imperative that something in the environment reward and reinforce this success. Thus the medication can be regarded as temporary help to be used until the child matures and learns to use his own abilities, motivation, and inner controls.

Duration of therapy, when it is effective and accepted, may run a year or two, but I have had some patients on continued therapy for over eight years. I do not believe that maturation or growing out of the need has anything to do with puberty itself. Social and academic expectations are different for adolescents.

I have limited experience with other drugs. The phenothiazines may be very useful, particularly trifluoperazine (Stelazine). Trifluoperazine in combination with methylphenidate or amphetamine may be useful. The greater toxicity of the phenothiazines is of some concern.

In summary, the drugs do work and their usage must be based on a working diagnosis and some goals of management. It is essential that the effect be evaluated at regular intervals and that the physician be responsible. Once the dosage is established I insist that I see the child after three to six months. I like a regular dosage every day including weekends and vacations so that the child knows what to expect of himself on a regular basis, and to avoid the family's using the pills for symptom relief.

CHAIRMAN TARNOPOL: Let's take a look at some of the drugs that are used and start listing them, so that we have a list of medications for discussion.*

DR. PETERS: I'll be glad to give our rather extensive list. I would like to explain first, though, that we have a fairly large outpatient clinic and a number of residents working with us. The children often have to be seen by residents who are new to them, since the residents change about every four months. I

* See Chapter 9 for a list of medications which includes generic and trade names, dosages, and cautions [L. T.].

and my Staff supervise these new residents as they are getting acquainted with each child and his prior treatment.

We have at present 45 children on dextroamphetamine (Dexedrine); thioridazine (Mellaril), 27; methylphenidate (Ritalin), 17; trifluoperazine (Stelazine), 6; perphenazine (Trilafon), 2; amitriptyline (Elavil), chlordiazepoxide (Librium), diphenylhydantoin (Dilantin), and diphenhydramine (Benadryl), 1 each.

This covers many more than just hyperactive children. There is quite a range of kinds of diagnoses. Some combinations used are Dexedrine and Mellaril, 13; Ritalin and Mellaril, 5; Stelazine and Ritalin, 3; chlorpromazine (Thorazine), and Dilantin, 2; fluphenazine (Prolixin) and Ritalin, 1; Stelazine and Dexedrine, 3; and various other combinations of stimulants and imipramine (Tofrānil), 10.

DR. CONNERS: There is a recent report from Emory University that combinations of methylphenidate and diphenylhydantoin led to toxic elevation of blood levels of diphenylhydantoin in 1 patient.

DR. REYNOLDS: I have a patient who has been on this combination for almost two years now, seemingly with a great deal of success and no obvious toxicity.

DR. CONNERS: One issue is what you consider to be toxicity and how you monitor it. Most patients are not likely to be monitored closely. It is my understanding, for example, that levels of diphenylhydantoin above 20 μg are likely to produce some of the early toxic side effects. In some of these children who have such a diversity of symptoms, it may be difficult to detect actual toxic effects.

DR. DUGGER: Would you clarify whether it is side effects or toxic effects?

DR. CONNERS: Toxic effects. I think myospasm, ataxia, and disequilibrium are the early effects.

CHAIRMAN TARNOPOL: Does anyone else have medications to present?

DR. REYNOLDS: I am interested in the area of tricyclic anti-depressants. I see in my own limited practice a number of children who are not hyperkinetic, but they are very unhappy—depressed, if you will. I have had 6 or 8 children on nortriptyline (Aventyl) and imipramine (Tofrānil), some with good results. These are not drugs I routinely recommend for children.

DR. RICHANBACH: Tofrānil is a remarkably effective drug in treating enuresis.

DR. REYNOLDS: This was often why I first prescribed it, and then subsequently found I was dealing with a very depressed child who was beginning to withdraw. In retrospect I am not sure what I was treating.

DR. RICHANBACH: I give it just at bedtime, and the side effect seems to be that next day some kids feel funny and upset, and the dosage has to be cut.

DR. CONNERS: There are three reports within the last two years on the use of tricyclic drugs with hyperkinetic children. Two of them are on imipramine and 1 on amitriptyline, I believe. One of the reports concerns a fairly substantial number of children and makes fantastic claims of 80 to 90 percent cure.

DR. DUGGER: Of hyperkinesis or enuresis?

DR. CONNERS: Hyperkinesis. It is obvious that a study with such a high percentage of cures needs to be controlled.

DR. DUGGER: I would take a very strong position on using something like imipramine for enuresis. It is exceedingly toxic and produces the same result as the amphetamines, which is lightcned sleep.

DR. WHITSELL: There is some doubt about whether it does produce exactly the same effect. There is a slight difference in the part of the reticular activating system which is affected by these two types of drugs. Apparently the major activity of amphetamine and methamphetamine is on the mesencephalic (midbrain) portion of the reticular formation (see Fig. 6-10). On the other hand, the tricyclic compounds have been shown to have more activity at the pontine (lower) level of the reticular system. This site of action is inferred from sleep studies which show changes in the level of sleep from these drugs—there is particularly a change in the rapid eye movement (REM) phase.

Apparently one of the significant effects of the tricyclic drugs is to allow the child to waken more readily when his bladder is full. Long experience with the use of tricyclic drugs in adults, as well as in children, indicates that these are very tricky, *very unpredictable drugs from the standpoint of exactly what may be accomplished.* But there has been very wide use of imipramine throughout the world now for a number of years. It has been available on prescription in this country since 1959. It is interesting that the F.D.A. has not released imipramine (Tofrānil) for use in children under 12 years—according to the package insert it is not recommended for younger children. Nortriptyline (Aventyl), a product introduced several years later than imipramine, has been accepted for use in younger children.

There has been a controversy as to whether these drugs are really any more effective than a placebo. I think this has finally been settled by a number of double-blind studies which seem to indicate drug effectiveness.

I believe it is agreed that one of the actions of these drugs on the bladder may be anticholinergic, particularly in enuresis. But the point I would like to bring out from my own experience with using tricyclic drugs for children with enuresis is that I think almost invariably when it has been effective for enuresis it has also had a favorable effect on behavior.

DR. REYNOLDS: This is also my experience.

DR. WHITSELL: I haven't really tagged it as the drug of choice for behavior problems, but I have gotten enthusiastic about it if the child has enuresis. If enuresis is one of the complaints I put it on top of the list.

DR. DUGGER: Since we are discussing school children and school problems and enuresis, I think that comparing dextro-amphetamine (Dexedrine), which is virtually free of toxic effect, and the tricyclic drugs, which are considerably more toxic, for the specific purpose of mood elevation, I would be very reluctant to use the tricyclic drug on a hyperkinetic child without having exhausted the other drugs first.

DR. CONNERS: There is another application for tricyclic drugs—severe school phobia. Klein in New York has been treating school-phobics, kids who simply will not go back to school, and he thinks that the component of depression, which is very strong in these children and accounts for the fear of going to school, is effectively treated with these drugs. He is conducting a double-blind trial now.

DR. CLEMENTS: If I may, I would like to turn the conversation in a different direction. I would like to hear discussed three major areas. One, the indications for the use of medication in children reporting disabilities—*minimal brain dysfunction, neurological handicap,* or *developmental deviation.* Two, the objectives which hopefully will be achieved by the use of medication, and three, how can these objectives best be measured?

I am sure each of you, as you evaluate a child, has built-in detectors for selecting children whom you would like to see as part of the management program and using medication. I would like to hear some other kinds of indications besides hyperactivity that would lead you to prescribe for a child with learning disabilities.

CHAIRMAN TARNOPOL: What kinds of children do we see who have learning disabilities, and what indications are there for medication for the different types of children?

DR. REYNOLDS: As I mentioned earlier, there are a number of children whom I see who are not hyperkinetic, who have shortened attention span, distractibility, difficulty in school, and maybe but not necessarily behavior problems. They are unhappy children and these are the ones to whom I was referring. On these I try the tricyclics and get good results.

I am concerned about these comments on toxicity. I wonder if the amphetamines are really as nontoxic in the long run as some think they are. I have been impressed with the number of children I have seen with hemorrhagic cystitis due to amphetamines. In my experience this is not uncommon. Certainly one sees it a great deal with adults.

DR. RICHANBACH: With the doses we are talking about?

DR. REYNOLDS: Yes, I'm talking about doses of 5 to 15 mg per day.

DR. DUGGER: You are talking about methamphetamine?

DR. REYNOLDS: Methamphetamine or dextroamphetamine. One sees adults on many combinations that are available for appetite suppression. I find myself writing prescriptions for them from time to time. Hemorrhagic cystitis is a significant risk from amphetamines, presumably due to effects on the trigonal area of the bladder. Urologists are the ones who are death on amphetamines.

DR. DUGGER: Because of the peculiarities of the local law,* dextroamphetamine is often the first drug to try, whereas in Michigan I was rather enamored with Ritalin because of the much more cooperative teacher situation. However, I find that quite frequently dextroamphetamine brings on crying jags in children.

DR. CONNERS: That is a fairly well-documented finding which people tend to ignore. Ounstead (1955) in his study of amphetamine with epileptics reported that only 9 percent

* When teachers may not give medication to the children at noon, long-acting drugs given in the morning are sometimes used to obviate the legal problem [L. T.].

showed the classic improvement picture and something like 42 percent became depressed, had crying jags, and so on. We often refer to this as instant superego, because the children in addition to becoming sad and weepy become very sensitive to criticism and very sensitive to doing wrong.

DR. REYNOLDS: Is this the effect of the medication or the effect of its wearing off?

DR. DUGGER: That's a good point. It usually happens after school.

DR. REYNOLDS: Isn't a rebound depression to be expected of the amphetamines?

DR. RICHANBACH: This takes us to what Dr. Clements was saying about measuring the effects of drugs. In discussing medication I would like to stick to methylphenidate (Ritalin) and amphetamines for the moment.

In giving small doses the first thing I look for is no effect at all. If there is no effect, I think I'm on the right track. In general if a child gets the usual stimulant effect, particularly from amphetamine in small doses, it will make him jittery, and the more jittery he gets, the more you know you are doing the wrong thing.

If a child gets a beneficial effect, fine. The symptoms of overdosage in my experience are those of depression almost to the point of paranoia. So a child who becomes depressed and worried and sluggish is getting too much medication. Some children are remarkably sensitive to it; very small doses may be adequate. One of my colleagues has been dealing with hyperkinetic children under the age of 2. He finds a milligram or less may have a dramatic effect on such small children.

Depression is a common symptom of overdosage, and simply reducing the dosage is all that one needs to do. The drug that I use basically is methamphetamine, and I use the Desoxyn Gradumet, which is the sustained-release tablet. Costwise with the sustained-release tablet the patient does just as well on proprietary drugs as on the generic, because the generic drugs are diffi-

cult to get. Five-milligram tablets of dextroamphetamine are
available. Then the druggist can order beyond that. So even
though the proprietary drugs are more expensive, by the time
you get into big doses, the cost factor becomes insignificant.

In the late afternoon some children on amphetamines will
come home very upset. I don't know how to explain this. There
may be children who need repeat dosages during the day.

DR. DUGGER: Have you tried them on another dose?

DR. RICHANBACH: Yes, except that the amphetamines are
predictable in terms of how long they last. I have 1 patient of
8 or 9 who takes 15 mg in the morning, at noon, and at dinner,
but still goes to sleep like a stone at night. There is tremendous
variation.

Ritalin is much more likely to wear off in the afternoon and
because of this, in spite of my prejudices, I sometimes give a
number of doses during the day.

DR. REYNOLDS: It seems that your choice of amphetamines is
based primarily on the fact that it is available in sustained-action
form, as there are then no problems of giving medications in
school. I'm not sure I'm in agreement on that. I have done an
about-face. I used to use amphetamines in a fair amount, but I
have certainly been using more methylphenidate (Ritalin) in
the last three years. I often find it is not an insurmountable
problem to have the child take his medication in school, himself.

DR. DUGGER: I find we play the game according to the school
rule. The school rule says the teacher or nurse cannot give children medication, so send the medication with the child and have
the teacher remind him to take it.

DR. WHITSELL: I think this rule has been changed in the last
year by California legislation.

DR. REYNOLDS: This is the difference between *giving* the
pill, and the school nurse or the teacher *making the pill available* to the child.

CHAIRMAN TARNOPOL: Has anyone had experience with children who showed no symptoms of hyperactivity or short attention span, but who had a learning disability of some kind, with whom medication was used effectively?

DR. PETERS: On children of this type I have used it in small doses, mainly for a bit of sharpening of the attention span, and principally with younger children, not with adolescents.

DR. CONNERS: I have been doing some studies on these children, and I would like to suggest that this is probably a neglected group in terms of drug treatment. Unfortunately we don't know all the mechanisms whereby a child will develop reading disorders. But Bradley's early studies (1937–1938), which I think deserve rereading because of their careful clinical observations, noted that there were a number of children who seemed to have primarily learning problems, who did very well on medication, and he attributed this to the fact that the drug—Benzedrine in that case—had the effect of changing the child's interest in his environment. He described the children as becoming more zestful, more interested in the external world. They became more euphoric and he felt that the change in emotional attitude, the change in the feeling of happiness, had a lot to do with their ability to progress in school.

Interestingly enough, he found that the most likely area of change in school was arithmetic. Spelling didn't show much improvement, and reading was variable. Some children did make large gains in reading, although the net effect across the group was not very impressive.

I have found that there are children in whom one can eliminate practically every other source of difficulty except a reading problem, who suddenly do much better with drugs. The source of this change is still enigmatic. In one study we used a large battery of tests in a school population who were referred specifically for learning difficulties and not behavior problems. The cluster of tests that showed the change had to do with a sort of zest for accomplishment and interest in life.

There are adult studies that are interesting in this respect. There is one study by Wayne Evans (1964) that measures "need for achievement" by McClelland's technique; the study shows in adults on drugs an increased need for achievement. Also more risk-taking, more ability to gamble, have been documented; these might be changes having to do with a slight euphoria, a more optimistic appreciation of the external environment. Such drugs may have positive effects in some children who are inhibited and depressed.

I think we are some distance from being able to say that this particular kind of reading disorder will profit from drugs and that another one won't. But in view of the safety of the stimulants that we are talking about, I would be inclined to err on the side of giving the drug rather than on the side of not giving it, in a case where a child is experiencing severe reading difficulties.

DR. PETERS: Didn't you and Eisenberg (1967) find that when you gave dextroamphetamine (Dexedrine) to normal, non-troubled children, that there was an improvement in some?

DR. CONNERS: Yes. We didn't call these normal children, but they were about as normal a sample as we have had access to, and they did in general improve, particularly on the whole issue of working on a task.

DR. PETERS: I think Conners and Eisenberg's research gives a base line and a perspective. In children with a specific reading disability, mild or severe, and *without* hyperactivity, I would still give Dexedrine or Ritalin in small doses; i.e., where a specific skill is dissonant with the general level of intelligence and with the reasonable expectancies of his family and school. As Dr. Conners said, it somehow gives him zest for his tasks, and it appears to focus attention and make for better integrated thinking. In some of these children I have seen remarkable improvement in attitude and accomplishment. However, I like to give any of these drugs, to this kind of child or to hyperactives, in an improved setting wherein his actual level of skill functioning is accepted and he is taught *at his level* and where, if needed, the family will accept counseling. Unless the school and family are favorable and cooperative, the gains to be expected are not usually remarkable. There are some exceptions, of course.

Dr. GOFMAN: How small a dose do you mean?

Dr. PETERS: About 5 or 2½ mg.

Dr. REYNOLDS: To do this you would have to be in a developmental center. The child who has only a reading disability isn't likely to be taken to the physician for advice.

Dr. RICHANBACH: We are talking about two different things. Many hyperkinetics do not lack a zest for living, so we are after almost a paradoxical effect. When you are talking about this nonspecific effect of increasing activity and interest, this is what one would ordinarily expect from an amphetamine-type drug. In studies such as the one you are talking about, I question whether or not these children were carefully evaluated for subtleties of function in school performance.

Dr. CONNERS: Every child had a physical and neurological examination as a prerequisite of being in the study. That was a requirement of the school. A child psychiatrist carried those out. Every day for ten days we administered tests; there were over a hundred from a large battery Cattell developed. I think we have more information on those students than is usually the case.
   Since these were very deprived children, there was a large amount of depression and poor motivation in the group. As I said, I think most of the effect was due to the change in drive and optimism, and probably some direct antidepressant effect as well.

Dr. RICHANBACH: I think we could all agree that poor attention span and distractibility may also occur in a hypoactive child. So I think we need a history of the child's behavior.

Dr. PETERS: My attention was directed in the last discussion to the treatment of pure dyslexia without hyperactivity.

Dr. RICHANBACH: Just paying attention to kids and special educational adventures are useful. Hyperkinetic children are often hyperkinetic because the other kids are doing something they can't. The analogy I use with parents is this: If you are playing baseball with Willie Mays, pretty soon you say, "Look, Willie, you play baseball. I will go and run around the track." If they are given something appropriate to their needs and achieve some degree of success, I think even the hyperkinetic children in a school environmental situation calm down and learn, and this makes it very difficult to evaluate the drug. Unless there is some other behavior indication, I have not attempted to give medicine to a student who is purely dyslexic.

DR. CONNERS: I would like to suggest not that it be given as a routine treatment for dyslexia, but that it is an important area for study. There is another interesting group that usually gets written off in terms of drug therapy, and that is the so-called psychopathic-sociopathic delinquent or predelinquent child. It's fairly clear from research that many of these children do in fact have some central nervous system problems.

DR. DUGGER: Some 35 percent of them are dyslexic and hyperkinetic.

CHAIRMAN TARNOPOL: In our study (1970) of 100 delinquents from lower socioeconomic minority groups, we found that there appeared to be a relatively high incidence of neurological dysfunction and reading disability. For example, 28 percent of these 17- to 22-year-old males were reading below the fourth-grade level and their average reading level was about fifth grade. On the Bender Visual Motor Gestalt Test only one-third scored in the normal range. This finding is significant because the Bender is one of the best predictors of reading failure among children.

DR. CONNERS: Exactly. The incidence of learning disorder is high. I know of only two studies, one we did (1967) and one Korey (1944) did in the National Training School for Boys, where Benzedrine was used. Both of those studies on adolescent juvenile offenders seemed to show fairly substantial improvement, and again I consider it related to this issue of mood, because those kids are generally very depressed, regardless of their overt behavior. Even for a child who comes from a very disorganized slum environment and who has been acting delinquent, a small part of the overall plan for treatment might well include drugs. It is certainly worth considering doing some large-scale research.

We had one very striking case of a boy who was diagnosed as a sociopath. He was stealing, lying, doing all the classic things, a very antisocial boy who made a very remarkable personality change. This may have been an idiosyncratic form of response; Lauretta Bender describes one of these. He really did change personalities and became a good child all of a sudden. I am not generally very impressed with clinical anecdotes, but I think the controlled study also suggests we might pay attention to this group as a possibility for treatment.

DR. RICHANBACH: The effects of amphetamines can be spectacular. Just to observe the remarkable changes in a child who is troubled, and the way it is possible for him to have a better-organized personality after medication, can be an immensely impressive thing.

DR. REYNOLDS: Are you talking about the adolescent?

DR. RICHANBACH: I have had less experience with adolescents, but younger children by the time they get to be adolescents can be extremely screwed up. They are at a tremendous risk of delinquency simply on the basis of their failure. This is why they are described more often as neurotic. Adolescents, who have been grating on society for years, have been viewed as a problem for a long time. They view themselves that way and act it.

One of the neurologists we worked with in our study is also connected with the hospital for the criminally insane at Atascadero. He insists that a tremendous number of people institutionalized at Atascadero must have been neurologically handicapped as children.

DR. REYNOLDS: I agree. Our organization is certainly concerned with this because many of our members are going through it firsthand with their own children. The California Association for Neurologically Handicapped Children (CANHC) has two committees that have been meeting for several years, concerned with the adolescent NH (neurologically handicapped) child, and the NH child and the law. I think most of us take it for granted that delinquent or antisocial behavior is going to come for many if they are not recognized and medically treated and helped educationally.

But to backtrack, we are now talking specifically about the adolescent. My limited experience has been that, with medication beyond age 12 or 13, I am not impressed that it does very much. I anticipate more positive effects between the ages of 5 and 8.

DR. LASTER: Let's consider three major groups of children with learning problems. First, there is the more or less constantly hyperactive or so-called organically hyperactive. Second, there is the child who is not hyperactive but has a short attention span and may or may not be withdrawn. The third group is the intermittently very hyperactive, depending often on his situation and environment.

My own experience is that the best results of drugs are seen in the organically hyperactive. Ninety percent of these are preadolescents. Where beneficial results are seen in the other groups, drug therapy has usually been combined with a fairly active school program to correct academic deficits. Unless this scholastic help is available, I usually don't see much effect from drugs. I wonder if this is a common experience.

DR. PETERS: This tends to be our experience. I am reluctant to give the drug unless I have some kind of cooperation from the school.

DR. CONNERS: There is a paper by Conrad (1967) which attempted to look at both these issues, that is, the role of organicity and the role of environmental support. Briefly what was found is exactly what you said, namely, *the best results occur with children under age 7 or 8 who tend to be more organic by medical history and current testing, and whose parents are supportive and cooperative in the treatment program.*

The poorest results came from the nonorganic type over the

age of 8 with disorganized families. These are general trends, and of course within each group are notable exceptions. But I think it calls attention to the fact that when talking about the use of drugs, we probably ought to think about some of the non-drug variables which may be crucial in determining the outcome.

CHAIRMAN TARNOPOL: This brings us to the question of the concurrent therapies and environmental factors that are helpful and should be considered along with medication.

DR. DUGGER: I think it is always necessary to get more than one source of feedback on the effects of drugs. We had a teacher who had 30 of these children in a nongraded primary class. She was not aware that one child was any different on medication until his father asked, "Does he still crawl under everybody's desk?" She said, "No, as a matter of fact, he stopped that."

DR. RICHANBACH: It depends who gets asked as to what is going on. One of the most hyperactive kids I have ever seen was part of our original pilot study. He was kicked out of school in the third grade and was taking "lethal" doses of amphetamine to stay reasonably calm. I was never able to get the family to admit he was anything but a model child. The parents were both over 40 or 50. This child was a doll to them; he was no problem. But he was wild. He was brilliant enough so that in the fifth grade he was doing nothing but high school work in a special class. Nobody had the impression he ever paid any attention, and his IQ scores were in the 70's. But this was a bright kid and immensely hyperkinetic.

Many families don't notice any change. And I wonder if the children may not change at home because their patterns are so set and their relationships with the family are such that the effect of the medication has no impact. But if they are getting special attention in school and are carefully watched, you get an effect in school that can be used.

DR. LASTER: But you wouldn't want to give drugs with hyperactivity just because there is hyperactivity. There are hyperactives who can control themselves or who can be effectively channeled by others.

Before medicating a child, I address two questions to teachers through the parents. First, "Is this child one of the most active in this class?" And I have rarely found any teacher who did not understand that question. Second, "If he were less active, do you think he could learn more effectively?" Sometimes the answer is surprising. The teacher might say, "Yes, he is active, but I can control him. I may use him in certain activities. I have him open the windows in the morning or knock the erasers together, and by doing such things I can employ his energy usefully."

DR. RICHANBACH: But by trying a drug you might permit the kid to slow down and do his schoolwork instead of opening windows and beating erasers.

DR. LASTER: This way he is providing his own controls and I think this is much more natural and less complicated than using a drug.

DR. REYNOLDS: You get a reliable feedback on a child who has a dramatic response. How do you evaluate the feedback from the teacher of the child who doesn't have such a startling response?

DR. CONNERS: One of the things that I think is probably essential, if you have any doubts, is some form of measurement. For example, schools almost always have achievement tests and I would be much more inclined to be impressed with the fact that the child has gained six months in reading over the last month of treatment, regardless of what the teacher said. I think there are simple measurements that can be instituted on a regular basis. If you are treating an outpatient population of school children, one of the things you can do is use a standardized report from the teacher. That helps to focus her observations. Another is to use either some tests in your office or have the teacher administer some tests. They are usually familiar with the standard educational tests.

DR. GOFMAN: Do you know of any studies to test the effect of, say, amphetamines and the child's response to failure? So many of the hyperactive children with learning problems have been sensitized by failure experiences. On testing we often note that difficult behavior, including hyperactivity in response to failure, often disappears when the child experiences success. We've been impressed with the overreaction of these children to failure and frustration. Have there been any studies to see how amphetamines might affect the threshold for failure? Could the child fail "more gracefully" with the help of medication?

DR. CONNERS: Unfortunately, I don't think there are any studies, although that is a perfectly fascinating question. Our people who have tested these children often say in their notes, "He seems to shrug it off more easily when he fails." However, this may reflect a sense of optimism and euphoria that might be present.

DR. DUGGER: Do you see any appreciable change in their performance on these tests whether they are on or off medication? There are child psychologists who insist the child go off medication for several days before they test him, saying, "Don't give the medicine because we want to test him the way he really is."

DR. CONNERS: I think that is rather an absurd approach when what you are trying to do is reorganize the child.

DR. DUGGER: Particularly if you are trying to find out whether it is one of the language functions he is having difficulty with.

CHAIRMAN TARNOPOL: I think that is an important point. The question involved here is the child's true potential. By true potential we mean the potential which he is capable of exhibiting under the best conditions which we can arrange for him. And if that includes medication, he should remain on medication unless the purpose of testing is to observe the differential effect, in which case testing should be done under both conditions. Often more than one intelligence test is administered to a child because they may tap different aspects of intelligence. As a rule, the Wechsler Intelligence Scale for Children (WISC) should be given to children with learning disorders rather than the Stanford-Binet Intelligence Test. This is because the WISC gives a Full Scale IQ, a Verbal IQ, and a Performance IQ, as well as ten subscale scores, all of which may have important diagnostic value.

DR. RICHANBACH: One of the purposes of testing is to determine the child's potentials, so the high scores are more valid than the low scores. Generally, even though an IQ score may be low, you may go on the basis of the psychologist's opinion that the child has better potential than indicated by his IQ score of, for example, 70 or 80.

DR. REYNOLDS: How do you test the child on whom you are trying four or five medications in succession? Aren't you going to have invalid test results simply by repetition?

DR. CONNERS: There are various answers. In a study you can counterbalance the testing sequence. For an individual child, one would look for a test with alternate forms. For example, Porteus Mazes is a good, drug-sensitive intellectual measure and has three alternate forms which are designed to minimize practice. Most intelligence tests have two forms. You may have to use measures which are not standardized, but which have face validity for the function you are interested in.

CHAIRMAN TARNOPOL: I think we are getting into the area of some fundamental questions. What we want to know is, which type of child goes with which type of medication, and how do we determine this? How do we know when we are getting results? How do we differentiate the effects on the different types of children of the different medications?

DR. CLEMENTS: Would everybody agree with these two points to get this started? For these children with whom we are concerned, hopefully medication would do two major things: First, the medication would be useful for the control of a wide range of "negative" symptoms which are disturbing factors in this child's environment. And second, the use of medication would somehow enhance the learning process itself.

DR. CONNERS: Might you want to add change of mood? The unhappiness of the child may not be disturbing to others and may not really interfere with his learning.

DR. CLEMENTS: I am thinking about our clinic in the process of evaluating a child. They say, "He is climbing the walls. We have got to put him on medication." At this point they are thinking that this child must be very difficult to manage in a classroom situation and at home the same thing applies. If you give his parents some relief and give the teacher some relief and the other children in that class some relief, medication is indicated for the hyperactivity. Also we hope that the medication would somehow, if this is a child with learning disabilities, enhance the learning process.

DR. DUGGER: If the child has some hyperkinetic problem, is not learning, and so forth, it is easy to give medicines to reduce his hyperkinesis. The question is whether or not it enhances an intracerebral process that makes it possible for this child to organize and perform better apart from his attention. If it is true, then I would give it to a child with dyslexia who had no problem otherwise.

CHAIRMAN TARNOPOL: Dr. Conners, do you have some data relating medication to auditory learning?

DR. CONNERS: Dextroamphetamine has about a 35 percent improvement effect on performance of auditory synthesis. This is a test in which the child is presented with words that are broken up into phonemes, and he has to identify the word. I suspect that like many other perceptual functions, this ability is cut across by the function of attending to the task, and what we may be seeing is improved attention to the task.

CHAIRMAN TARNOPOL: You could separate these variables by statistical or other methods.

DR. CONNERS: One of the deficiencies in the studies of these children is the failure to separate out some of these variables and to examine the drug effects separately. It is quite possible that the degree of hyperactivity is a function of their impaired attention.

DR. GOFMAN: So motor activity alone is not enough of a criterion.

DR. CONNERS: Millichap and Boldrey (1967) showed in the children they treated with methylphenidate (Ritalin) that there was an increase in the actometer level measure of activity. At the same time the children were doing better because there was a more organized motor performance.

CHAIRMAN TARNOPOL: Their motor activity had actually increased, as measured objectively by an actometer, but their activity became focused.

DR. CONNERS: They became more organized in the use of their motor activity. That is in line with what Elinor Maccoby (1965) found in some studies of hyperactive boys. She studied them with the actometer and some tests of motor inhibition, and she found that the hyperactive child tended to have about the same level of gross motor activity as the so-called nonhyperactive child. But when one looked at the specific capacity to inhibit the motor activity in certain tasks they were much poorer, suggesting that a large part of what we see as hyperactivity is really misdirected or poorly channeled activity.

DR. DUGGER: We were talking about hyperkinesis as that which we are treating, and I don't think we are. I think it may be the outcome of the problem. Among the descriptions given these children are distractibility, obligatory response, and background-foreground problems. This is what I think we are treating with our stimulants. There are studies that show, as you mention, that there is no great change in the total amount of muscular activity or movement of the children, yet obviously the teachers are delighted with the difference because the activity is channeled into more acceptable goals.

From this study, one would think that giving stimulants to children does not change their activity and they are just as jumpy or just as bouncy. But I think any of us who has treated these children has seen those who got too much, and who sat and looked at the wall for two hours. Such a child is *not* moving as much as he used to. So there is more than one effect, as emphasized by the child who when given too much sits and looks at the wall, but as we reduce the dose he regains some of his normal activity. To deduce from these few papers that there is *no* change in their overall activity is misleading.

DR. CONNERS: Of course many of these phenomena are dose-related, and it is quite possible that we have a U-shaped curve. If you look at the effect of amphetamine on the simple conditioning process and, say, motor speed, you will see it is indeed a stimulant. I think it speeds up the ability to make rapid responses. But what is interesting with these children is that if you look at a task in which they have to make rapid responses, overall they do become more rapid. But when there is a critical stimulus, they become slower and make more correct responses. So they are more selective in their ability to control their activity, not just more energized. And I think that's a critical variable.

You also mentioned some other things that would suggest to the pediatrician the kinds of things he ought to ask about and measure, for example, the foreground-background problem. I think that's an important aspect of the process of attention. One has to attend to one thing and selectively ignore other things. There are tests that can measure foreground and background problems. And perhaps we ought to use them as one of our measures.

DR. GOFMAN: Can you name these tests?

DR. CONNERS: For example, Frostig's Test of Developmental Perception.

DR. DUGGER: As mentioned, the child on medication seems better able to ignore distracting input. Clay Lafferty has a beautiful demonstration. When he is talking to parents, he turns his back to them and says, "Now you have been looking at me for an hour. What color is my tie?" Hardly anyone can tell him, but they have been listening and watching for an hour. They have been able to focus on the important parts of the input. They don't pay attention to the color of his tie or the cars going by. These children are distractible and it is distractibility we are treating.

CHAIRMAN TARNOPOL: Conditioning is sometimes discussed as being related to learning. Has anyone done research on the effects of various medications on conditioning in children?

DR. CONNERS: Generally children do condition more rapidly and they make discriminations more rapidly, which partially accounts for the relation of conditioning to learning. It is interesting to note that drugs sometimes widely used with these children, such as chlorpromazine (Thorazine), tend to inhibit conditioning except in situations where the subject is highly anxious and the drug is calming him down to a point where he can engage in a task.

Most of the reviews of work on the phenothiazines seem to indicate that with children they have a detrimental effect on learning. I think even though this drug controls behavior, it might not be worth the price of interfering with the learning process unless it is an absolute therapeutic necessity. In studies of the retarded, these drugs are used as chemical camisoles to calm the children, probably at the price of blocking out what little cognitive resources they have left.

DR. WHITSELL: What about qualitative differences among the phenothiazines? There is a group of so-called activating, stimulating phenothiazines—the ones like Stelazine and Prolixin, to name a couple. I question a sweeping statement about the effect of these when there are so many factors that enter into a child's ability to learn.

DR. CONNERS: Right. I was talking more about chlorpromazine than anything else. On the other hand there are no controlled studies that I know of with those drugs regarding learning, so I would leave it as an open question.

DR. WHITSELL: I could mention several instances in which one of the activating phenothiazines has been highly successful in contrast to either amphetamine or methylphenidate in an individual child.

CHAIRMAN TARNOPOL: Highly successful for what purpose?

DR. WHITSELL: For controlling the child's overactivity, apparently for improving his attention span and allowing learning to proceed better.

DR. REYNOLDS: What about the side effects of the phenothiazines?

DR. WHITSELL: I am very worried about them and children getting these drugs have to be watched closely.

DR. CONNERS: I think this area has sorely required attention by physicians, because in the published research on these drugs —Stelazine, for example—many people have commented they are extremely useful for the type of child described by Barbara Fish and the group at Bellevue (1966), especially autistic, hyperexcitable children.

On the other hand, the one well-controlled study I know of that considers the use of Stelazine with some other drugs on an autistic child, studied over a 2½-year period in a careful way, shows absolutely no positive effects of the phenothiazine but very dramatic effects of the anticonvulsant (Sultiame) they happened to be using.

DR. WHITSELL: One of the greatest problems about all this is the heterogeneity of each of the populations with each label that we have so far. There is such a difference in children selected for hyperactivity. There is a great difference among individual children with paroxysms or almost any other diagnostic label.

DR. RICHANBACH: There is evidence that if amphetamine is given during an EEG that shows an abnormality, the EEG will change. Some people have suggested amphetamines as a tool in diagnosing hyperkinetics.

DR. CONNERS: Cutts and Jasper (1939) and also Lindsley and Henry (1941) did some EEG studies, and they found a disassociation between EEG and behavior. In other words children often improved with no real changes in the EEG. However, the large-amplitude 4- to 6-cycle waves seemed to be predictive of who would respond. The children that had 4- to 6-cycle waves seemed to have the larger percentages of improvement.

It is interesting that in adults this is precisely the effect of amphetamines on EEG's, to reduce these 4- to 6-cycle, large-amplitude waves. But in general the drug does not affect the EEG concomitantly with the behavior change. Behavior may or may not change, regardless of the EEG pattern.

DR. WHITSELL: There is a recent report of a statistical study of a group of children who were given dextroamphetamine. The children with normal EEG tracings had a much higher incidence of improvement than the group with abnormal EEG findings.

DR. CONNERS: Burke (1964), I think, reported that. But the study is so sloppy, it is hard to tell what the results show. It is a question again of the heterogeneity of hyperkinesis.

The literature is very divided as to whether or not EEG's have anything to do with hyperkinesis. About 60 percent are reported to have abnormal EEG's among hyperkinetics. But when Ellingson (1954) reviewed this literature, he said the estimates went from 2 to 80 percent. That doesn't give one a lot of confidence in the information.

DR. RICHANBACH: Would somebody briefly comment on the value of an electroencephalogram in diagnosing learning disorders? This is one of the problems we have in this state where the laws govern admission programs to classes for the educationally handicapped. Children get EEG's to tell whether they have neurological dysfunction along with their learning problems.

DR. LASTER: I find the EEG a useful tool in a backhanded way. The schools tend to be impressed by the results of a machine. Since you can often find nonspecific abnormalities in many of these children, I note that if the EEG is reported as borderline or mildly abnormal, the school comes to attention and you can do some manipulation of your own. This is the main use I find. And since it is a painless, harmless test, when it is free I do it.

DR. DUGGER: I find EEG's useful in order not to miss a case of petit mal. The pediatrician's basic function is a negative one, determining that the child isn't hypothyroid, gets enough sleep, and is well nourished. Include an EEG if you think it's necessary according to the history. That's the extent of the pediatrician's function in the beginning phase of the diagnostic study.

DR. LASTER: In the Stanford Clinic, I can think of 2 children in the last two years who really had no overt signs of neurological dysfunction but who were having significant problems in school with learning and behavior, and in whom we got rather typical patterns of paroxysmal sharp waves on the EEG. Had we not done the EEG, we might have tried Ritalin or amphetamines, but instead, by treating one with Dilantin and the other with Dilantin and subsequently Mysoline, we were able to modify their behavior and performance significantly. So for 2 out of a thousand children, it was well worth doing the EEG.

CHAIRMAN TARNOPOL: Has anything new been learned by programing the EEG so that the waves are not individually studied but are added together and studied after they have been summed to produce averaged potentials?

DR. CONNERS: I would like to comment on the average EEG's or cortical evoked responses which we are working on now. I have been particularly interested in the possibility that the average EEG might give us some indication about the central nervous system dysfunctions in these children. We have completed three studies in three samples of children, two of which were specifically learning disability samples, one of which was an outpatient clinic population. There is enough similarity in the findings so that I think the technique may show some real promise.

One finding is that there are two late waves in this averaged-evoked potential which seem to be very strongly related to reading and spelling disorders. It is possible of course that these are effects of some functional disorder, but I think they are suggestive.

Another finding is that increased amplitudes on the left side of the head, where presumably most of these children have their speech and language dominance, makes for poor performance. A large discrepancy between the hemispheres makes for good performance, particularly if it is low amplitude left and high amplitude right. This is suggestive because of some developmental findings that others have determined, that as one grows older there is a tendency for larger discrepancies between the hemispheres in the amplitudes of the waves.

We are now trying to screen the children into much more select groups. For example, match pure dyslexics against learning disorders of another kind and see whether these effects hold true. In one study we did, that's exactly what we found. The children with primarily language disorders had a very striking difference in the amplitudes on the left side.

There also appears to be a relationship to intelligence. In general it appears from our preliminary data to be opposite that found with adults. That is, children with slower latencies of the visual evoked response tend to be brighter and have better performance levels on tests. In adults faster latencies of the evoked response have been shown to correlate with higher intelligence levels. However, the evoked response is a complex wave form and the results may depend on which portion of that curve one is inspecting.

As far as medication is concerned, we have one study that is partially complete that shows interesting differential effects between Ritalin and Dexedrine. The Ritalin produced a pronounced speeding-up of these latencies, whereas the Dexedrine didn't change it. In one study we found that Dilantin had a significantly slowing effect, making latencies longer. This was a group of children with violent temper outbursts with whom we thought anticonvulsive therapy might be used.

CHAIRMAN TARNOPOL: You talked about the waves being averaged. Are the waves actually averaged or is this a summation?

DR. CONNERS: It is a summation. When you have a signal-to-noise ratio, the ratio increases as the square root of the number of times you repeat the signal. So you repeat the signal one hundred times and the signal becomes ten times larger relative to the noise. What the computer is doing is simply storing the signal and then giving you much better amplification of the signal-to-noise ratio.

DR. DUGGER: Did you say the background is random?

DR. CONNERS: Right. The background is random and averages to zero. The signal is nonrandom and tends to summate.

DR. DUGGER: I think one of the first objectives of this meeting is to help pediatricians concerning giving medication. If they are to read this transcript and get anything from it, I think how to use methylphenidate and dextroamphetamine is one of the things they might get. As to the function of the pediatrician, in the beginning he tells what the child doesn't have; subsequently he may wish to follow the child and prescribe medicine.

DR. WHITSELL: Can I go back to one of the indications for an EEG, an indication which perhaps ought to be mentioned here for learning disorders? The possibility of precipitating seizures with phenothiazine or a tricyclic compound or deanol, for instance, should be considered. In prescribing these drugs I would have a safer feeling to have obtained an EEG that is reasonably normal and shows no suspicious preseizure activity or anything that would suggest a proneness to seizures. I have had to medicate despite this in some cases and I felt a little better for having the EEG and knowing that I was going to have to proceed more carefully.

DR. GOFMAN: I find that many times physicians get confused if the parents don't have much of a complaint about the child but the school does. As this child is seen in the office, he may not strike the physician as being hyperactive at all. So no use of medication is made.

DR. LASTER: What conclusions do you draw initially when you hear that story?

DR. GOFMAN: Often in a one-to-one situation as in a doctor's office, we may not see the same behavior as demonstrated in a stressful situation in a classroom. Also the family may be able to tolerate hyperactivity, but at school, where greater conformity is required, such activity may be intolerable.

DR. RICHANBACH: This was brought home to me last night. I got a call from Jerry Mednick who is a pediatric neurologist here at Children's Hospital. He had just seen a patient of mine with hyperkinetic behavior that was driving the mother clean out of her skull. I had also seen the child not too long ago. The mother was disgusted with my failure to intervene. Apparently the child in my office did not bother me too much and the mother had not tried to impress upon me how badly this child was behaving. She went to see Dr. Mednick and he got the story, and he could see it was an obvious case for medication. It depends on how they come to you.

DR. CONNERS: I have seen so many children who had been described as veritable dynamos but who were perfectly calm during the testing.

CHAIRMAN TARNOPOL: Does this also suggest something about the fact that a general question such as, "What is your complaint? Why are you here?" may not always elicit the information you need? You have to have a series of questions which will bring out what you need to know. You pointed out that many people feel the child is just fine. But they don't recognize the things that you are looking for and so they can't tell you what you need to know. You have to have the right questions to elicit the information. We may have to start listing the type of questions that pediatricians and others should be asking the parents and teachers.

REFERENCES

Bradley, C.   The behavior of children receiving Benzedrine. *American Journal of Psychiatry* 94:577, 1937.

Burke, H. F.   Effects of amphetamine therapy on hyperkinetic children. *Archives of General Psychiatry* (Chicago) 11:604, 1964.

Conners, C. K., Eisenberg, L., and Barcai, A.   Effect of dextroamphetamine on children. *Archives of General Psychiatry* (Chicago) 17:478, 1967.

Conrad, W. G.   Anticipating the response to amphetamine therapy in the treatment of hyperkinetic children. *Pediatrics* 40:96, 1967.

Cutts, K., and Jasper, H.   Effects of Benzedrine Sulfate and Phenobarbital on behavior problem children with abnormal electroencephalograms. *Archives of Neurology and Psychiatry* 41:1138, 1939.

Eisenberg, L., Lachman, R., Molling, P. A., Lockner, A., Mizelle, J. D., and Conners, C. K.   A psychopharmacologic experiment in a training school for delinquent boys. *American Journal of Orthopsychiatry* 33:431, 1963.

Ellingson, R. J.   The incidence of EEG abnormality among patients with mental disorders of apparently nonorganic origin: A critical review. *American Journal of Psychiatry* 111:263, 1954.

Emory University Alumni Magazine, 1969.   Drug side effects found dangerous.

Evans, W., and Smith, R.   Some effects of morphine and amphetamine on intellectual functions and mood. *Psychopharmacologia* 6:49, 1964.

Fish, B., Shapiro, T., and Campbell, M.   Long-term prognosis and the response of schizophrenic children to drug therapy: A controlled study of trifluoperazine. *American Journal of Psychiatry* 123:32, 1966.

Gofman, H.   The Physician's Role in Early Diagnosis and Management of Learning Difficulties. In L. Tarnopol (Ed.), *Learning Disabilities: Introduction to Educational and Medical Management.* Springfield, Ill.: Thomas, 1969.

Korey, S. R.   The effects of Benzedrine Sulfate on the behavior of psychopathic and neurotic juvenile delinquents. *Psychiatric Quarterly* 18:127, 1944.

Krakowski, A. J.   Amitriptyline in treatment of hyperkinetic children: A double-blind study. *Psychosomatics* 6:355, 1965.

Lindsley, D. B., and Henry, C. E.   The effect of drugs on behavior and the electroencephalograms of children with behavior disorders. *Psychosomatic Medicine* 4:140, 1942.

Maccoby, E., et al.   Activity level and intellectual functioning in normal preschool children. *Child Development* 36:761, 1965.

Millichap, J. G., and Boldrey, E. E.   Studies in hyperkinetic behavior. *Neurology* 17:467, 1967.

Neill, A. S.   *Summerhill: A Radical Approach to Child Rearing.* New York: Hart, 1960.

Ounstead, C.   The hyperkinetic syndrome in epileptic children. *Lancet* 2:303, 1955.

Rapoport, J.   Childhood behavior and learning problems treated with imipramine. *International Journal of Neuropsychiatry* 1:635, 1965.

Shirkey, H. C.   Editorial comment: Identification of prescribed drugs on the label of the container. *Journal of Pediatrics* 71:592, 1967.

Splitter, S. R., and Kaufman, M.   A new treatment for underachieving adolescents: Psychotherapy combined with nortriptyline medication. *Psychosomatics* 1:171, 1966.

Tarnopol, L.   Delinquency and minimal brain dysfunction. *Journal of Learning Disabilities* 3:200, 1970.

5 Proceedings of the Panel on Medication

Medicating Children with Learning Disabilities

Part II

SAM D. CLEMENTS, C. KEITH CONNERS,
JAMES A. DUGGER, HELEN GOFMAN,
JAMES P. LASTER, JOHN E. PETERS,
JOHN REYNOLDS, HENRY S. RICHANBACH,
LESTER TARNOPOL, AND
LEON J. WHITSELL

CHAIRMAN TARNOPOL: I think we should begin to focus the discussion.

DR. DUGGER: Dr. Clements posed some pertinent questions. How do you pick out children for medication, and what are your criteria for various approaches? I didn't notice any eagerness to attempt to deal with these questions.

CHAIRMAN TARNOPOL: Would you like to start with the first item? How do you select children? On what basis do you determine which children will receive which medication?

DR. GOFMAN: Since this is for the average pediatrician or practitioner, could we list the questions you would ask of the parents and questions you would ask of the teacher?

DR. DUGGER: I have in the past been struck by some wonderful questions used by various people who were doing so well with their particular group of people that I incorporated their questions in my review, and got back nothing.

A case in point was a doctor who always asked the mother, "How does he get along with his dad?" And he got reams of information that were beautifully useful in performing his function.

So I tried the question, and I got nothing, whereas I have other successful questions. The questions he might ask both the teacher and the parent might or might not be meaningful to other persons. You might change the question and ask, "What information do you need to work with?"

CHAIRMAN TARNOPOL: That's a good suggestion. It probably will also help to have items which can be selected and tried. You have to try different things and see if they work.

DR. DUGGER: In a pediatric practice you can pick some of these children at the age of 2 if you ask certain questions, which are essentially: "Is this child driving you crazy? Is he this way all the time? Is he always on the go?" You will very quickly get from the mother what you need to know. On the other hand, the school sends the older child for a checkup because they think he is educationally handicapped and they need a physician's statement so he can be screened into a special class.

DR. RICHANBACH: I have a ritual I go through to start. Basically, there are three parts to the history. First I ask them why they have come to me. As mentioned earlier, in my practice I sometimes miss people because I don't ask the right question, or they don't come with the appropriate complaint. I ask people, "Why are you here?" Were they referred by a school psychologist or another physician? If the teacher says he is in trouble at school, that is a good clue that there is a problem.

As a pediatrician I go through the regular history and physical and family history, birth history, and so on. There is a long list of behavioral characteristics that I look for. I ask about hyperactivity. I ask about the child's attention span, and again you may have to phrase it in different ways, depending upon the sophistication of the people. Some of them have read more of the literature than I have so I have to be careful how I couch the question about compulsiveness and organization. Is he neat? What age are his playmates? What about his concepts of time? His memory? Often this gives you a good idea.

They may say, "He is fine at home, but at school they tell me he can't pay attention." They almost all say about hyperkinetic children, "The school says he is immature." *Immature* is what the teachers almost invariably label these children. Then I also take a school history, or if they say that the child's behavior is a problem, I ask, "When did it begin?" "Well, he was fine until he started school."

"What was he like in kindergarten? What did that teacher say?" If there was no trouble in kindergarten, I ask, "What happened in first grade? Did he learn to read in first grade? Was he a problem? How did he behave?" I go chronologically through the grades. The child who does fine for the first two or three grades and blows in the fifth or sixth, I am inclined to think may have some emotional problem if he suddenly hit the fan at 10 or 11 and was not some kind of problem before that.

CHAIRMAN TARNOPOL: Sometimes evidence of neurological dysfunction may not appear until the child reaches the fourth to sixth grade if his problem is primarily in the area of concept formation.

DR. RICHANBACH: You can also ask the child, "How do you get along in school?" You have to try to get the child to talk about it, particularly if you have other sources of information. "Well, don't you have a little trouble sitting in class? Could you do better work if you weren't quite so active?" Or, depending on the child, "Do you get up and walk around the class a little bit?"

"Maybe a little."

"Does the teacher like it?"

"Oh, no, she doesn't like it."

Children are a remarkably good source of information if you can get them to talk. But often you have to confront them with information you get from other sources. And I think getting the child's recognition that he has adjustment problems in school is an essential part of how you manage him when you give him drugs, because if he will verbalize the problem and if he changes, you have established a communication that is one of your better sources of information.

DR. DUGGER: It is helpful to encourage the physician to recognize that it is not a single diagnostic group. There are all kinds of children, kind of a motley crew. There is no single diagnostic guide. You get all the information you can get and keep digging for more.

DR. RICHANBACH: From what was said earlier, these drugs may have a tremendous effect on the child. And to give such a pharmacological agent to a child without having an understanding with the family and the child, and a way of observing it, could be harmful. We don't want to transmit the concept that once you identify a hyperkinetic child, you know he is going to respond to drug therapy.

DR. REYNOLDS: Looking at it from a different point of view, we are trying to determine how to choose a child for medication. I think a practical problem is how parents find the right physician, one who will prescribe medication when the child ought to be receiving medication. I think there is a great deal of reluctance among many physicians to prescribe it.

DR. DUGGER: I have a corollary. Suppose the school recognized the problem and the doctor does nothing about it by way of medication. What does the school do?

DR. REYNOLDS: It is a common situation, and it puts the school in the area of the practice of medicine again. I think the physician on the Admission Committee for Special Education can have a great deal of influence. But I still think there is a great deal of conservatism built in, especially about medicating children.

DR. CLEMENTS: I wonder if we couldn't change the emphasis slightly from the problem of the pediatrician vis-à-vis the school and go back to what I think was the starting point. What sort of plan should the pediatrician have for evaluating the child?

I would like to propose the following. In order to make sure that the pediatrician is detecting all the children who need his services and not simply focusing on one kind of obvious syndrome, which we ourselves seem to have focused on, namely the hyperkinetic syndrome, we should have in mind some principles of evaluation with which we are all familiar but which pediatricians sometimes ignore. I would suggest that, in addition to a careful developmental history in which he pays attention to a number of factors of normal growth and development, he concern himself with the following three items.

First, there is the behavioral status of the child vis-à-vis peers, school, and parents. This would include not only disruptive behavior but failure to relate or failure to be in contact with an appropriate number of people. This includes a list of behavior symptoms. For example, I would be as concerned about daydreaming, shyness, clinging, dependency, and immature behavior as I would about disruptive, aggressive behavior.

Second, the physician ought to know something about the cognitive abilities of the child, because even though the child may be relatively intelligent on superficial examination, an item of concern should be, Is he doing more poorly than his brightness indicates?

There is also such a thing as an overachievement problem, in which children begin to suffer in other areas because they are striving (overcompensating) beyond their bounds in some area. Then there is the extremely bright child who is doing about average work. Sometimes it is found that he ought to be doing superior work. Thus he qualifies as learning-disabled because he is achieving far below his potential.

Cognitive assessment is probably a very weak part of pediatrics and general practice. There are simple techniques which a physician should be apprised of. For example, it helps to know that the drawing of a man can give a rough estimate of mental development, or that there is a useful one-minute vocabulary test. Better still, one might get a psychologist's evaluation with more sophisticated approaches.

Third, a physican should learn something about the effects of the emotional aspect of this child's life, not only as perceived by the parents and teachers, but as revealed in the examination of the child. Here perhaps the psychiatrist has something to offer in terms of sensitivity, of the way the child relates to the doctor, whether he is happy or sad, preoccupied, and so on. The emotional area is important because if the child, for example, is achieving but unhappy, that may be just as bad as if he is not achieving and unhappy, or not achieving and happy.

Thus behavioral assessment, cognitive assessment, and more effective emotional assessment would be the broadest outline of what ought to be done.

CHAIRMAN TARNOPOL: Dr. Clements' three suggestions are most important and I hope they will be further elaborated in the discussion. It was also stated that when you see a child who has gone through four to six grades and who has apparently gone along normally and then begins to fail, that he would not be considered in the category of the neurogenic learning disabilities child. I would like to hear some other experience.

DR. LASTER: I think this may depend on the type of learning situations in a particular school district. In our area, for example, I may see a child who did fairly well during the first three grades and then poorly in the fourth. This may be due to the fact that in the first three grades the child spends most of his time with one teacher. Also it seems that the educational hurdle from third to fourth grade is a significant jump.

DR. DUGGER: That's where they stop teaching reading and make demands for content in reading. It makes demands on some children which they can't meet.

DR. CONNERS: Particularly where abstraction and abstract reasoning are concerned. Piaget (1954) has shown that the pre-adolescent age from 11 to 14 is when hypothetical, deductive reasoning capacities are first developed. And that is when schools begin to teach abstract concepts. There are learning disability children who have these deficiencies and who do well until they get to abstract concepts.

DR. RICHANBACH: In some cases you will find they haven't really kept up, but they got a general pass. They haven't acquired the basic academic skills, and by third grade their failure became apparent when they had to perform.

DR. DUGGER: I have a couple of points I would like to add to the previous discussion, when we talked about the difficulty of finding a physician who will do a good job and cooperate with the schools. The law could help us a good deal. In the other forms of special education (orthopedic, blind and deaf, et cetera) the law says a certified specialist in this particular area must certify the child into the program. The law for this disorder could be helpful by specifying that persons examining and certifying the children into the program should be established as competent in this field. Then the school could have a list of physicians in the area they know are competent in this field from which to draw.

DR. RICHANBACH: I would make several comments on that. I think there are inherent dangers in stamping or labeling a child as cerebral palsied, orthopedically handicapped, or with any of the various categories of disorders. In a properly monitored program, if enough material can be collected on a child to determine not only what his diagnosis is but what his needs are in relation to what the school has to offer, I think a committee decision on an individual basis is better than certification. There is also a medical-political problem which arises from having certified specialists.

DR. CONNERS: The pediatrician is the man who is most likely to come in first contact with these disorders and have the opportunity to recognize them early if he is attuned to them. He sees the child shortly after birth, and he sees him through the preschool years. These disorders clearly involve several disci-

plines. Most psychologists are not competent to deal fully with
these problems and are not educated by their training to recognize and treat them. The same is true of pediatricians. Pediatric
neurologists may be more so but sometimes are not. I think what
we are talking about is a problem which engages the competen-
cies of several disciplines. And one of the things that each of the
disciplines has to do is learn something about the others.

A psychologist has to learn something about the neurological
indications that he might pick up in his own behavioral observations during testing. The pediatrician probably needs to learn
something about mental development and the indications of
cognitive growth in children, and so on. Maybe he ought to have
a little standard checklist which includes things which he
wouldn't normally think of, such as, can the child copy a design
appropriate to his age.

DR. DUGGER: Suppose you select young children with learning disabilities. What is the school going to do about it?

DR. LASTER: There are several possible things which could
be done. A child could be placed in a situation with a designated
teacher who knows something of the problem and is able to keep
him under closer observation. Also the size of the kindergarten
class could be reduced, which might circumvent many of the
problems the child faces in a group situation.

DR. GOFMAN: And certainly, help the parents.

DR. RICHANBACH: The City of San Mateo has a developmental program with the first two or three grades almost unclas-
sified. They may keep them two years in the first grade, or they
may have an ungraded primary.

DR. CONNERS: I wonder if it isn't the responsibility of the
medical profession to make physicians aware of the fact that
these disorders are as disabling, if not more so, than the kind of
diseases they ordinarily treat, so that it becomes a requirement
of postgraduate education that they get some training.

CHAIRMAN TARNOPOL: Dr. Gofman teaches this field not only to postgraduate but also to senior medical students in pediatrics at the University of California Medical School.

DR. WHITSELL: Could I reintroduce a topic that has been raised several times and then lost with various other important considerations? And that is the question we have all asked. What are the indications for the use of drugs in learning disorders? I would like to propose possible choices of medication and some rough indication for each.

My first choice for learning disorders when there is difficulty with concentration or attention span, some type of hyperactivity, and mood variability, impulsivity, or variability of motor performance is either methylphenidate or dextroamphetamine.

If the child already has a history of poor appetite, my first choice is methylphenidate. If the child is overweight and has also been relatively hypokinetic, I think my first choice would be dextroamphetamine. Then the question arises, if either of these first agents failed, would one try the other? I would prefer to do this than to go on to the second choices. There are statements in various articles to the effect that there isn't much difference expected in the results from methylphenidate and dextroamphetamine. I don't think this is necessarily true just because it is stated in print. Certainly there are gastric intolerances to either drug and there may be stimulation of the cardiovascular system with either drug. A rash occasionally occurs with methylphenidate. I think it is much rarer with dextroamphetamine.

These I think are the safest class of drugs and we have the longest experience with them. Certainly with amphetamines it is well over thirty years. Our experience with methylphenidate has not been as long, but on a theoretical basis it should have a very closely related long-term safety.

DR. DUGGER: Have you found, as I have, that a child might not do well on one and will on the other?

DR. WHITSELL: Yes.

DR. CONNERS: Have you had any experience with amphetamine (Benzedrine)?

DR. WHITSELL: Yes, and I think there are subtle qualitative differences from dextroamphetamine, especially in the gastrointestinal and cardiovascular effects. This brings up another point, the possibility of using another amphetamine entirely, namely, methamphetamine. This might have great advantages over the other two but it has a bad name as "Speed." We have to face the fact that this is a problem. In Sweden the amphetamines have been banned entirely. They are not allowed to be prescribed on any conditions. Amphetamine is not available for prescription, and I understand methylphenidate was also withdrawn from the market there some time ago. A similar situation also exists in Japan.

Formerly, my second choice as to low toxicity would have been deanol acetamidobenzoate (Deaner). But now I have it way down the list, since it is apparently difficult to predict on which children it will have a positive effect. I have had a couple of outstanding successes with it where nothing else seemed to work, and it seems to be nontoxic although there are many side effects with higher doses, and it is often not well tolerated. It may have some value in improving the appetite in a child who has a very poor one.

My second choice would be one of the major tranquilizers of the phenothiazine series for hyperkinetic behavior, if there were complete failure of dextroamphetamine and methylphenidate. The other main indication for use of a phenothiazine would be such symptoms as bizarre behavior, a tendency to withdrawal, assaultiveness, or a serious estrangement from the peer group. For symptoms of these and other more clear-cut autistic or schizophrenic trends, a phenothiazine compound might well be the first choice.

The decision about which one of these compounds to use would depend on whether to choose a more sedative agent, such as chlorpromazine (Thorazine) or thioridazine (Mellaril), or one of the more stimulating drugs such as trifluoperazine (Stelazine) or fluphenazine (Prolixin, Permitil). The sedative drugs such as chlorpromazine are much less likely to create basal ganglion stimulation in children seen as tremor, rigidity, or dystonia, especially in small doses, but these may have other more dangerous reactions.

DR. LASTER: Could you define "complete failure," especially with respect to dosage? I was interested in your comment that children might respond to small doses of dextroamphetamine or methylphenidate.

DR. WHITSELL: I think that the whole range of dosage ought to be tried if necessary because of gastric intolerance or impairment of appetite. Once in a while one sees very severe hyperactivity produced by a single dose and it can be alarming.

DR. LASTER: What do you do about that?

DR. WHITSELL: My tendency has been to withdraw the drug temporarily and probably later try a very much lighter dose.

DR. LASTER: In many of these children I have urged the parents to hang on and go five or ten days, and then it subsides.

DR. WHITSELL: I am talking about a case where a mother and child are up all night with one dose. I have pleaded with mothers to stay with it when the child gets overactive and over-stimulated.

There is a definite place here for a trial of the stimulating phenothiazines. These sometimes give impressive results with some children in whom there is no response to methylphenidate or dextroamphetamine. In these situations the child's response to the medication may have significant diagnostic implications.

DR. CONNERS: I would like to put in the record that there are some frightening reports about the long-lasting effects of phenothiazines on young children. And this, I think, is where a physician certainly needs to use caution in prescribing, which is not always being done. There is a report, for example, of perma-

nent infertility in children treated before puberty with chlorpromazine. I don't know if this applies to the other drugs because nobody has looked.

DR. WHITSELL: I think this would be a very serious consideration. We are all acquainted with the fact that thioridazine,
for instance, sometimes has a profound temporary effect on gen-
ital functioning. What would long, continued use of this type of
drug possibly do to an immature child?

DR. PETERS: But has this been reported as being long-lasting
after the drug is removed from adults?

DR. WHITSELL: Not as far as I know.

DR. PETERS: It is a temporary effect.

DR. DUGGER: You might point out the toxicity of the tricyclics with dextroamphetamines.

DR. WHITSELL: We have to worry especially about the effect
of these drugs on the immature brain as contrasted with a mature brain. There is a question of whether some important
phase of maturation might be inhibited or altered by the use of
a drug which has a chronic high concentration in some area that
is very closely connected with the hypothalamic-pituitary axis.
This is a real worry and I don't think it has been worked out.
    I am also concerned about other effects such as the occurrence
of pigment deposits with long-term use of phenothiazines; pigmentation of the cornea, conjunctiva, lens, and even more the
retina, as well as the skin and some of the inner organs. We all
have to be concerned about this because these potent drugs are
being used by pediatricians and general practitioners for children. I think that these drugs are sometimes used indiscrimi-
nately, with no thought that there is any more potential hazard
than, say, with phenobarbital. Some medical practitioners are
apparently not adequately prepared to be concerned about all

these points. Here the need for continuing education is a vital issue in medicine.

My third choice of medications would be the tricyclic antidepressant drugs. The one specific indication that would make me think of using one of these first in a child with a learning disorder would be the coexisting condition of enuresis. When a child with a learning disorder comes in and has coincidental enuresis, my first thought would be to try one of these, with the same concern about how long are we going to have to continue this drug, and what is going to be the long-term effect of a relatively new agent? In an adolescent who has a rather clear-cut depressive trend, this would tend to be my first choice. I would not hesitate to use methylphenidate or an amphetamine as a sort of coagent with a phenothiazine or tricyclic drug if it seemed to be indicated in a severe case. But I don't think we should mix too many medications for milder cases.

DR. REYNOLDS: I thought someone was concerned about cardiac effects, from what was said earlier, in mixing tricyclics with amphetamine. With hyperactivity it could be disastrous.

DR. WHITSELL: It is also well known that a hypotensive crisis may occasionally occur. This happens particularly in adults, in such conditions as diabetes with an autonomic neuropathy and a previous tendency toward orthostatic hypotension. A serious hypotensive crisis can be induced with very small doses of phenothiazine or iminodibenzyl compounds in such cases. These are relatively rare reactions in children.

DR. LASTER: Dr. Whitsell, could you tell me the highest doses of methylphenidate (Ritalin) and dextroamphetamine (Dexedrine) that you have seen to be effective?

DR. WHITSELL: Methylphenidate, 80 mg daily, divided into 20-mg doses four times a day.

DR. LASTER: Seventy didn't work, then you got a breakthrough at 80 mg?

DR. WHITSELL: I didn't go up that gradually. I went from 60 to 80.

DR. DUGGER: I have seen 20 a day not work and 40 a day not work and 60 a day work.

DR. WHITSELL: I have heard of people using twice that much and I am scared of that.

DR. RICHANBACH: The higher dosage comes, I think, from the repeated dosages during the day. I have gotten up to 30 mg in one dose in the morning. This is the highest I have reached in a single dose, and repetitions during the day would depend on the circumstances in which the child lives.

DR. WHITSELL: I was talking about total daily dose. The largest I have used was 20 mg four times a day for methylphenidate. For dextroamphetamine and the other amphetamines my highest dose would be about 40 mg a day, but I know higher doses have been used.

DR. CONNERS: We had one child who didn't respond to anything until we got to 50 mg of dextroamphetamine. That was the highest we tried.

DR. WHITSELL: I don't think I would hesitate to go to 60, or even higher, if there were no indication of gastric intolerance or other problems.
I think we also have to be concerned about the habituation effects. The reputation of methylphenidate is that it is far less habituating than the amphetamines. I am not sure this is true. I don't recall hearing of any serious problem cases of this sort. We also should be concerned about larger doses of amphetamines as possibly inducing toxic psychoses and paranoid or schizophrenic reactions.

DR. GOFMAN: Could we come back to observing increased hyperactivity and sleeplessness and persisting with medication for several days? Because this is something I think the pediatrician is often reluctant to do.

DR. LASTER: I warn the parents before starting the drug that this is a possible reaction, but to hold on and call me if things really get out of hand. It is the parent who is unprepared for the reaction who tends to get panicky. A number of parents have told me they just lived through this phase and then suddenly there was a calm, smooth period.

DR. GOFMAN: How many do this, and how many continue to be hyperactive and do not respond?

DR. LASTER: I don't think one out of ten continues to be hyperactive.

DR. WHITSELL: I think one has to be guided by his own experiences, which tend to prejudice one. When the physician has been kept up all night with the parents and child, it gets to be very disturbing.

DR. DUGGER: What do you do if a child gets very overstimulated with his initial dose? Calm him with chlordiazepoxide (Librium) or diphenhydramine (Benadryl)?

This happened to a patient of mine on a dose of 10 mg of dextroamphetamine. The child went home and said, "I have had the most wonderful day I have ever had." She proceeded to mop the kitchen floor, bake some bread, and so on. The mother got alarmed. She happened to have some diphenhydramine in the house. So I told her to give her that.

DR. WHITSELL: Yes, I think that's what I would order if they had it on hand. Chlorpromazine or phenobarbital or meprobamate might also be used as an antidote.

We haven't discussed the possible use of diazepam (Valium) in learning disorders. I think there might be a place for the occasional use of this, particularly if the child has a considerable degree of athetosis or even a tendency toward choreo-athetoid symptoms.

CHAIRMAN TARNOPOL: Dr. Whitsell, would you care to comment on the use of anticonvulsants?

DR. WHITSELL: I have a very strong prejudice against regarding an abnormal EEG by itself as an indication for treatment. This is, however, often being done, I believe. When a child has any EEG abnormality, some physicians would probably use diphenylhydantoin (Dilantin) as first choice. With many children there is a bad reaction because of an increase in preexisting ataxia or just an intolerance to a relatively small dose. Hyperactivity would be made worse by such a reaction.

DR. CONNERS: Are there children, regardless of the EEG, for whom you would consider using diphenylhydantoin?

DR. WHITSELL: I realize this is something I should be considering. I saw a note that Dr. Archie Silver does this and that he has had a number of successes, and he is a person I respect. He has had very wide experience. But I have not personally had much experience with it. I have used it on children with seizures but it is not entirely a nontoxic drug. It has many possible hazards.

DR. DUGGER: I have seen several teen-agers who needed help in school, where the case histories sufficiently coincided with temporal epilepsy or psychomotor seizure in the presence of a normal EEG, where I have tried diphenylhydantoin with a good deal of success.

DR. WHITSELL: If I had a strong suspicion of epilepsy, I would go ahead.

DR. CONNERS: How about ethosuximide (Zarontin) or other anti-petit mal medications?

DR. WHITSELL: Yes, if I had a suspicion of petit mal, but there is usually an indication in the EEG.

DR. DUGGER: There is a difference in the age groups to be considered. In the younger school child I would be tempted to use ethosuximide if I thought he had some deep centrencephalic problem. But with the older children in junior high school, much of their acting-out is socially determined or hostility determined. Giving them either a stimulant like dextro-amphetamine or one of the anticonvulsants like methsuximide (Celontin) may bring out very gross hostility, and then they start being combative, destructive, and abusive, based on the reaction to the drug.

DR. WHITSELL: I would like to suggest two more possible choices to complete this list, since the anticonvulsants have been brought up. We ought to mention the diphenylmethanes, particularly diphenhydramine (Benadryl), and possibly hydroxyzine (Atarax, Vistaril). I say "possibly" because of the contradictory reports. I have had no great personal success with either of these, except to use one or the other as an antihistamine or as a sleep-inducing agent on an occasional child.

There has been trouble with children who had been given one of these drugs. Their *hyperactivity has often been increased by the sedative effect during the daytime. That has also been my usual experience with phenobarbital and with some of the other minor tranquilizers, such as meprobamate.* I think there might be a place for these in an occasional case of hyperkinetic behavior. But aside from one case, where I think it might have been a placebo reaction, I have not had any striking success with them.

DR. RICHANBACH: Diphenhydramine (Benadryl) is useful where a child gets a desirable effect during the day from other medication but is unable to sleep at night. This has been most reliable as a sedative.

DR. PETERS: This is exactly the pattern I have found.
I have some concern about a pediatrician starting drug treat-

ment of children, perhaps on the basis of having read an article, and then not engaging in the kind of follow-up that seems to me very necessary. For instance, he may just start off on a fixed dose of dextroamphetamine. This might go on for a year or two without his ever following the child to check the results. I have seen this kind of thing happen. It seems to me it should be very clear that pediatricians and general practitioners who are going to engage in this sort of treatment need to become well informed, and preferably to have taken postgraduate courses.

CHAIRMAN TARNOPOL: I see general agreement among us on this issue.

DR. RICHANBACH: I will suggest my routine for starting medication. I have a drawer full of samples. So I give the children their initial dosage from among my samples, usually. I have them come back in one or two weeks, usually two weeks. The instruction to the child is that he, himself, must improve. The medicine may help. I give the parents a letter to the teacher, which I write in longhand, and which I probably should mimeograph. I might say that this child has been started on medication in the hope it will improve his behavior and performance. It is a private matter not to be discussed, and I would appreciate hearing any of her impressions, pro or con.

I don't get a 100 percent response, but I do get a good many phone calls. I get some feedback and often there is a good communication with the teacher, the school psychologist, or the principal. When the child comes back I often have an impression of what has happened in class, without defining what I am looking for in advance. Sometimes the effect is dramatic, or the teacher may note that he is a little quieter.

I may keep the dose the same or I may increase it, depending on the effects of this first trial dose. Or I may start with a morning dose one-half hour before breakfast and another dose before lunch if it happens to be methylphenidate. I see the child every week or two for several visits until I arrive at optimum results. If the child has all his important classes in the morning, he may not need it in the afternoon. You don't need to repeat the dose. If the teacher says he is fine, you might find that a larger dose would be even better, but I don't increase it. I will see the child again after three to six months. I don't prescribe medication for children I am not seeing every three or six months. I feel I have to follow each child's progress. Maybe at six months I will do another physical examination.

CHAIRMAN TARNOPOL: You say you send a note to the teacher saying you are putting the child on medication and you expect him to improve. Do you sometimes alternate this procedure with a placebo? How do you know you are getting an effect from the medication?

DR. DUGGER: I give the child methylphenidate or dextro-amphetamine and tell his mother to tell him it is vitamins, not to discuss it with anybody, specifically not to tell the teacher. A week later I contact the teacher or have the mother contact the teacher and say, "Have you seen any difference in this child?"

DR. REYNOLDS: This is what I do. I usually see these children for months and years, and if it is purely a placebo effect, the effect will disappear. I am interested in having some benefit come from my having acted as his physician. One value of following the children arises when the school situation, or the family situation, or other things are not reinforcing or helping what you are trying to do with the drugs. If the family is divorcing, or a parent is going to the mental hospital, the pills just aren't able to overcome the effects of the imposed stress. Here other supplementary therapy may be indicated.

DR. PETERS: You have grown up in this work, and you have been in it a good many years. But how about the pediatricians who are just starting? Is it to be recommended that they take some kind of postgraduate course first?

DR. DUGGER: There is hardly a journal issue that doesn't have an article about it, or a meeting where it isn't discussed. But I submit that these articles and symposia are on *recognizing* these children. There are thousands of physicians who now admit there is such a problem, and they admit that medication helps. Now we have to go the next step and tell them how to select the medication.

DR. LASTER: I agree that you may do the child a disservice by medicating him without good observers. Maybe there is a certain placebo effect in telling the teacher but I find most of them fairly reliable in what they see. I also may be getting an effect which has nothing to do with the drug, but certainly it is good for the child. That is, the teacher now perhaps gives him a little more attention and focuses on him.

I work through the parents, telling them to inform the teacher. Two weeks after starting the drug, the parents contact the teacher again to learn what has been observed. That, together with the parents' experiences at home on weekends and after school, is then relayed to me. I have avoided personal contacts with the teacher unless they are on paper because of the possibility of misunderstandings. The teacher may say one thing to me and something slightly different to the parents, or there may be a different understanding of the same verbal statement. There is an educational process with the teachers just as with the parents that this is a child with a problem.

DR. DUGGER: I think a parallel to this which I have noticed occurs when emotionally disturbed children are brought in. Immediately there is an improvement at school simply because the parent cared enough to bring the child to the doctor. I personally feel that telling the teacher during the initial week deprives me of a good piece of objective observation—not that I won't eventually tell her.

DR. RICHANBACH: Any drug this active, that can change a child this much, should be given the child with some warning. You have to be honest with him. You don't have to tell him everything.

DR. LASTER: A frequent question from a mother is, "What do I tell Johnny as to why he is taking this pill?" How do you reply?

DR. RICHANBACH: It will help him function better. I may say to the child, "You have got to control yourself better, and the pill will help. You are taking the pill for me. I am prescribing it. Your mother is not giving it to you. The school is not giving it to you. If you find things go better for you let's keep up the medicine for a while."

DR. CONNERS: There appears to be a certain conflict of interest between the need for objective, unbiased observation of the effect of the pure pharmacological action and the clinical responsibility and obligation to the patient. It is possible that social attitudes may color teachers' observations of whatever positive effects the drug might have. So you, in a sense, deprive the child if the teacher doesn't know, but on the other side you introduce the possibility of bias and the Hawthorne effect.

One of the things we have been trying to do religiously in our studies, which are research studies, is to send out, before the child gets into the initial stages of our work-up, a standardized teacher report form which has a place for a free-response description of the child and his problem, his previous testing, academic performance, and behavior in the classroom with peers and teacher. No mention of drugs is made, but a cover letter states that this child is being seen for evaluation in our clinic and would you kindly give us this information since this is an essential part of our treatment. Then after the child has been on medication for the length of time prescribed, a similar form, which has been labeled as follow-up, is sent to the teachers with most of the items identical except for the background information which we already have. We have worked with this form enough to be able to segregate the answers into clusters, so that we can get a profile of changes in behavior from the teacher who is neither specifically informed, nor not informed. That is, we don't know whether the parent chooses to tell the teacher or if the child tells the teacher.

Sometimes it is quite obvious because the child has to take the pill in school. I worry about these effects from a purely scientific point of view because you don't know what part of the behavior variance is due to nondrug factors. But as a form of measurement and as a clinical follow-up, I think this is a useful, simple thing to do. One thing it does is engage the teacher in the whole process because you make her feel, which is quite true, that what you are doing cannot be done adequately without her involvement. And I think this is usually rewarding to her, although occasionally she may not give you follow-up information.

DR. PETERS: Would you be willing to include this form in the material?

DR. CONNERS: Dr. Tarnopol has copies of this material and a Parent Questionnaire.* The Teacher Questionnaire* has the virtue that it has been factor-analyzed, and it can be shortened and have clusters of symptoms scored by using a scoring key to get a measure of changes in different areas of behavior. I might mention what the findings are because I think they are pertinent to the issue of classification of these children.

The first factor which emerges is a trouble-making conduct or a behavior problem factor in which there is a strong component of aggressiveness. This is a trouble-making, hyperactive child.

The second factor is an emotional disturbance factor which involves anxiety symptoms, shyness, withdrawn, and immature behavior.

The third factor is an interesting one in that it involves all the hyperactivity symptoms such as short attention span, lack of concentration, and restlessness, but is totally lacking in any of the aggressive components. This is a child who might be described as liked by his peers, is a friendly and cooperative child, but has inattention, cognitive symptoms, and restlessness.

I think that the distinction between the aggressive hyperactive and the good-tempered hyperactive child is an important one. What we are doing now is looking at the way these children can be handled. It is our guess that the distinction may be a function of how the parents have reacted to the hyperactivity in the form of external control. If they punish the child, he tends to become a mean hyperactive child. If they try to set limits, without being too punitive, he may become a nice hyperactive child.

* See Charts 5-1 and 5-2 respectively at end of chapter.

DR. PETERS: I see this as a function of natural temperament rather than a reaction to parental controls.

CHAIRMAN TARNOPOL: Is this distinction being made from empirical data?

DR. CONNERS: No, I am saying this is something I would like to investigate.

DR. RICHANBACH: There may be a fourth category for girls. We did a study in the Belmont, California, schools. We found just as much psychometric abnormality and just as much hard-and-soft neurological abnormality amongst the girls as the boys, but the girls were generally doing fine.

DR. DUGGER: That may be because schools are created for little girls and run by big girls. The corollary is that boys learn in different ways from girls.

CHAIRMAN TARNOPOL: I agree. We should perhaps also note that girls do evidence the hyperkinetic and hypokinetic syndromes and they may also have social and learning disabilities. In our survey of 450 such children, the ratio was 4 boys to each girl. When a girl has social problems, it is particularly devastating. Girls cannot afford to be as eccentric as boys in our society since it affects their social lives adversely.

DR. CONNERS: There are two other factors which emerge and I am not quite so clear about what they mean, but I think the general principle could be successfully applied to both clinical and research purposes. These symptoms do tend to cluster into broad categories.

If you look at the research in which behaviors of children vis-à-vis parents, or deviant behaviors in a training school, have been studied, and an attempt has been made to correlate them, generally two very broad, distinct factors have been revealed. I think these may represent separate causal factors that reflect basic temperamental dimensions. One cluster of items is the behavior-conduct disorders, and the other cluster is personality disturbance or emotional problems. I think it is very useful diagnostically to think of this as a two-by-two table in which a child can have any combination (high or low) of these characteristics.

In other words, a hyperactive child can quite independently have a neurotic disturbance. A neurotic child can be hyperactive, and this we may tend to overlook. A child can be low on both. He can be essentially normal or he can be high on both. This classification I find very useful in communicating with parents to give them the idea that there are trends in development which are somewhat independent: "Your child may have a temperament which leads him to be impulsive and restless. He may also have a predisposition which makes him sensitive, fearful, and anxious."

From a measurement point of view, it is essential to distinguish between these, because you may want to affect or treat some pattern of these symptoms selectively.

Dr. Peters has done work on temperamental typing in dogs. The types I have described are very clearly present in animals. And anybody that works with them is familiar with the fact that in the same breed, but more particularly between breeds, there are differences in temperamental characteristics.

We are talking not only about a spectrum of developmental deviations, but about a range of temperamental characteristics. If you bring this out to parents, it helps their understanding and often leads to progress with them. That is, if you can tell them, "You haven't been an abnormal parent, but you happen to be a person whose personality doesn't necessarily mesh with that of your child. You are a person who likes to be orderly, and that is fine. Your child happens to have a temperament which disposes him in the opposite direction." That is sometimes a very surprising insight for parents because most literature has failed to consider this possibility. Instead parents have generally been presumed to be guilty of failing to understand their children and to handle them properly. Thus, they say things like, "Well, I always had the feeling that it couldn't be all my fault that he behaves this way but everybody has always *told* me it is my fault."

CHAIRMAN TARNOPOL: They are surprised because both the literature and professionals iterate over and over again that the child is the product of his environment and the parent is the controlling factor in the environment. Relieving parents of such guilt feelings tends to permit them to function more intelligently in their child's best interest.

DR. RICHANBACH: This is what Thomas, Chess, and Birch, (1968) are talking about.

DR. WHITSELL: I would like to bring up something else that we ought to cover. What is the expected duration of the use of medication for a child with a learning disorder? What period of time should one consider using a drug?

Traditionally the amphetamines are supposed to be discontinued when there is no longer a need as the child approaches adolescence. This is a statement that is very often found in the literature. I think someone indicated that this is not always true. There may be an indication for continued use and there may even be greater indication for use in some adolescents, discounting the problem of drug abuse.

There is also the question of drug use during vacation periods and during weekends. With many children who have hyperactivity at school or a short attention span, there may be no apparent problem at home on weekends and during vacations. On the other hand, several times parents have called and asked if they might have the child continue to take the drug during vacation since they had stopped it and he was obviously not doing so well. They hadn't realized things had been so much better at home. But probably more often the drug may be stopped during vacation when there is no exposure to the specific situation which induces the most distressing symptoms for the child, namely, the pressures in the classroom.

There are also cases where drugs may help learning difficulties and behavior in which the child's behavior is quite all right in the classroom, but the parents complain of hyperactivity at home and of their inability to get the child to pay attention to his homework and the child's lack of cooperation with household chores and just general disorganized behavior. In these cases I think there would be more indication for continuing to use the drug over weekends and vacations. It also depends on the type of medication that is being used and what the target symptoms are. If one of the symptoms is enuresis, then the situation would be different from the use of a medication primarily aimed at controlling classroom distractibility. It would be a drug you would want to continue until there has been a long period of freedom from enuresis, assuming it has been successful.

The question of using drugs on into adolescence and early adulthood, when they have been started in childhood, is one that probably has to be individualized. Last year I started three college students on medication (methylphenidate) because of their great difficulty in note-taking and auditory attention. They had managed to cover up their difficulties fairly adequately during high school but were breaking down under the pressures in college. In each instance there was evidence of long-standing learning disability of a minor degree.

Here is a situation where we are in a new field of medical practice, where the physician is responsible for the continued care of the patients and their families over a period of many years and has to be concerned.

CHAIRMAN TARNOPOL: You didn't state what results you achieved with the three college students.

DR. WHITSELL: In all three instances there was a very satisfactory effect.

DR. RICHANBACH: I agree with everything you said. I would add one additional variable, and that is the physician. Dr. Dugger and I have different approaches, and what is appropriate for him may not be appropriate for me. I have different ways of dealing with people.

In terms of adolescence my experience is that the children change through the years. Some of the original group that we saw nine years ago I still see as 17- and 18-year-olds. Many are off medication; a few still take it. There appears to be no change that I can relate to puberty. Some may take it between 6 and 9 and drop it between 10 and 11 before they have entered puberty. Some children change in their neurological findings, we have observed, after five years. The Babinski sign is absent, chorea is gone, and their ability to distinguish parts of their bodies has improved. One of the original group is now on the pole-vaulting team in high school, which requires very fine coordination. Yet he was clumsy when he was young.

DR. CONNERS: I think there are two considerations, the short-term management of drugs and the long-term.

DR. DUGGER: With the child without any complications whose prime problem is drivenness, I find two years of medication almost always is sufficient because they have, among other things, been able to learn control over their impulsivity with the help of the medicine. Many opportunities come up for a mother to forget a dose, so that in two years it is pretty obvious which patients can stop medication because the mothers take them off. If they miss two or three doses and the child doesn't fall apart, then they find he doesn't need it.

DR. REYNOLDS: I have had cases where the mother on weekends and summer vacations has discovered that the child did need medication. I usually take them off during the summer and do not reinstate it when school starts until there is a recurrence of the problem. At some point in time, some of these children go back to school and they don't need to keep taking a pill. Usually I suggest they try being off medication for the summer and the first month of school. However, you must get a teacher's report after that first month, otherwise you find children lapsing into difficulty again unbeknown to the doctor.

DR. WHITSELL: There is one other matter I would like to stress, the source of information about the drug's effect. In addition to the parents and the teacher and our own clinical observations as a source of information, the child's own appraisal may be a very significant one, and I think at times better than anybody else's, especially when his main difficulty is an inner symptom such as loss of control about paying attention or listening. Many children get the idea the drug helps them *listen* to the teacher better. They cannot *hear* any better but they are able to follow what is said and get their thoughts organized better.

DR. REYNOLDS: Don't you sometimes run across children who recognize a need for the medication?

DR. RICHANBACH: Yes, I write on the chart the quotes from the children. This is part of management. It is hard to evaluate scientifically, but they have to be a part of knowing they are behaving better. They may say, "I don't get mad anymore." "I get all my work done." Often they are very aware of the effect, but not always. You can use their change of behavior to point out to them what they were like before intervention. You may say, "You know you got into trouble."

"Because the kid next to me is mean and he kept hitting me all the time."

Then later on you find they are not getting into fights any more. "Maybe he was hitting you because you were bugging him."

He might say, "I am quieter now. Maybe that's why I don't bother people anymore." He may develop insight.

DR. CONNERS: I wonder if it would be possible to spend a few minutes on some of the issues involved in the science of drug therapy, as opposed to the art. We have spent a fair amount of time on the assumption that what is being done with the drug is effective and usually useful; in a sense we are preaching to the converted. I think it might be worth interjecting some note of caution.

We have perhaps slightly underplayed the role of the placebo phenomenon. There is data to show that you can get very dramatic placebo effects, depending upon the mental set of the person at the time the placebo was given and the role of the doctor, his authority, et cetera. In adult drug studies on outpatients, when you look at the sizable, well-controlled research, you see that nondrug variables such as expectations, the instructions of the physician, the type of personality, and the type of patient tend to contribute more to the total variance than the drug phenomenon. The drug phenomenon in adult outpatient neurotics contributes only a small part of the total variation in the symptomatology. So I would like to suggest that, although we are dealing with somewhat more dramatic effects in children than in adult neurotics, we consider several issues.

How does a physician in practice set up his procedures so that they become self-correcting and he begins to accumulate useful knowledge, so that he doesn't fall into a stereotyped pattern of treatment with built-in errors? I think it is quite possible, for example, to get some dramatic successes which may tend to be overwhelming and produce a halo effect in the whole area of drug treatment. If this goes too far, you may get the phenomenon where every patient is treated with a drug and every patient is a success.

The course of research on drugs seems to show a clear pattern ever since the phenothiazines were introduced in the fifties. First a drug comes out and is wildly applauded in clinical reports. Then there are some doubts about it from various people. And then there are some extremely negative reports in which the clinicians say, "What they said isn't true at all."

Then there are some controlled studies. Controlled studies almost always show less improvement than the noncontrolled studies. These results are partly a function of poor research design. So-called controlled research may be unscientific in the sense that, for example, if you take a large population of patients and divide them randomly into a placebo and control group, measure them before and after, *you may get no improvement as a result of the fact that within the group are both improvers and nonimprovers who cancel out the total effect.* And I must admit that some of my own research tends to fall into that type. I have become disenchanted with classic experimental designs, since what the clinicians have done is sometimes more scientific. They have a base line observation, a change induced by medication, withdrawal of medication, rebound, perhaps a placebo, and so on.

DR. REYNOLDS: This off-and-on design is an important part of handling children on medication. The parents may not be convinced the medication is helping or a teacher may not be convinced. Stop it for a week or two and very soon there may be a reversion to the undesired traits. This convinces many people.

Dr. CONNERS: The second thing one needs to think about is multiple measurement procedures. We have the observations from parents, clinical observations, and objective tests which alone may not be too useful. For a satisfactory documentation of drug effects one requires multiple measurement procedures, where you are using the observations of others, observations of the child, and some independent objective test procedures. My feeling is that without all three of these you really don't get a satisfactory documentation. You may get a nice improvement in ratings from parents or teachers because of a halo phenomenon in which they see something happening, and they know that the child is supposed to be getting better. Ergo, he is better all around. This is not so much a problem with a very dramatic drug effect with a simple drug. But I think with other drugs that might be of interest these effects are somewhat questionable. Where we have a complicated symptomatic picture, I think these issues really need to be observed. As an example, I have met physicians who swear by hydroxyzine (Atarax, Vistaril). Where you are using dextroamphetamine, Atarax works beautifully, or diazepam (Valium), or deanol, and so on.

Dr. WHITSELL: The most careful survey of research on psychotropic drugs in children that has been done that I know of is by Roger Freeman. He has recently expanded it to be published as a chapter in Menolascino's new volume on mental retardation (1969). This study by Freeman seems to indicate that there is no single drug that we have for use in treating learning disorders which has had fully acceptable proof of being an effective agent.

Dr. CONNERS: I don't know about Freeman's recent version, but the earlier one has some defects in it. He managed to overlook a few of the better controlled studies and perhaps some of the better clinical work. But in substance I think he is correct. The state of the field scientifically is pretty tenuous.

There are two studies I have seen which I think are models for research. One is by Hutt (1961), a two-and-a-half-year study of an autistic child. They put the child into a room every day for twelve minutes and this room had a fixed number of objects.

Each time they would put in one new object. They filmed the first two minutes and the last two minutes of this twelve-minute period and later scored for such things as amount of locomotion, exploration, curiosity, amount of visualization, and so on. And they tried several drugs in a predetermined sequence.

The other kind of study which is newer, and I think worth thinking about, is a study in which one gets away from a global rating method to a time-sampling observation system. That is, you take a fixed amount of time, say in a classroom, and count the occurrence of certain behaviors in which you are interested. Attention, for example, can be broken down into whether a child is looking at his book or looking at the wall or is up and out of his seat. John Werry and his group (1970) did a very nice study of methylphenidate, phenobarbital, and placebo, and showed quite a bit of improvement in attention behaviors in the group treated with methylphenidate. This sort of study gives one much more confidence that we are dealing with real phenomena.

DR. DUGGER: I find most parents are interested in whether or not something can be done for their child, not only at school but in my office. It is not difficult to throw a little hope their way that this medication may have a beneficial effect. I find it necessary to explain all the side effects that may appear, principally in my own self-defense so I won't have to talk on the phone many, many times and answer questions. I don't tell them the specific, desired effect, like "This is going to quiet your child down." The message is, "This is a medicine which often helps, and we will give it a try. It may or may not help, but if it doesn't, we will continue to try." And then I list all the toxic side effects I want them to know about.

DR. WHITSELL: I would like to put in a word here for being certain that the use of the medication is put in the proper frame of reference as far as the parents are concerned—that we do not regard the medication as specific for the learning disability. Rather it is being used as one means of helping, as part of a total program with due emphasis on the need for special help with the educational problem, which presumably is being individualized for the child's needs along with whatever other help the child may require in the way of psychotherapy, parent counseling, and so on. It is very important for the parents to realize that the medication is not going to take the place of changing their own ways of handling the child if changes are needed.

Medication is not going to substitute for making every effort to secure the right placement of the child in school. There is a tendency on the part of some practitioners to regard medicine as the main therapy. When the mother complains that the child is failing in school and he is hyperactive and she can't control him, the pediatrician may write a prescription for chlorpromazine (Thorazine) or for hydroxyzine (Atarax, Vistaril). If the next time he sees the child is when the next cold comes or there is some accident, this is not fulfilling his obligation as a physician.

In the same way, it would be inappropriate to embark on a long program of psychotherapy as the main treatment, because of symptoms of anxiety and hyperactivity and so on, without recognizing the need of the child for special educational programs, home management, and the very high potential of controlling some symptoms with medication.

DR. DUGGER: I completely agree with you. And again to emphasize my position, we use every modality at our command to give every attention possible.

DR. REYNOLDS: I think we should make it clear, too, that we are dealing with different populations of children with different needs. Probably each of you is dealing with children more involved behaviorally or neurologically, or both, than most of the children I see in general practice who are brought to me by parents with a request for medication because a disturbance has cropped up at home or at school. These are children who are getting along up to a point in the regular school environment. They are children usually without any apparent neurological involvement. These are children who are reaching a point of decompensation in the regular school environment.

I may overmedicate in terms of your individual experience, but I have seen many a child who has functioned more effectively and has been a happier child and has been maintained in the mainstream at school because of medication. That child, without this assistance, I think might well have been out of the mainstream. There are those who do need a special school and home environment who may need psychotherapy, or who may need counseling, but these are certainly a very small percentage of the children I have on medication currently.

CHAIRMAN TARNOPOL: Dr. Reynolds, what sorts of things do you tell the parent when you start the child on medication?

DR. REYNOLDS: I must overcome not only the resistance— possibly of a father, or both parents—to medication, but also the resistance of one or both parents to the fact that the child even has a problem. Some of these children are referred not because the parents think they are troublesome but because the teacher does. Usually it is the mother who brings the child to me, and one problem I may have is overcoming resistance to medicating the child. I accomplish this, I think as much as anything, through referral to our sponsoring group here, the California Association for Neurologically Handicapped Children, which has a great deal of literature that can be understood by anybody of average intelligence.

Then I attempt to assure them that I will be giving the child only medications which are not going to be damaging, though they may obviously cause some bothersome side effects. Depending again on the intelligence of the parents, I may tell them what to look for, especially if appetite may be affected. I try not to suggest that we are doing anything other than trying to help this child function more effectively and more happily. This drug may not work, and there are other things we can try; maybe several other medications. It may go beyond the area of medication to include tutoring in a special class and psychiatric counseling for the entire family. My experience has been that with more than 50 percent of the children, medication makes the difference between staying in the mainstream and dropping out.

DR. DUGGER: I believe the parents need to know a great deal to act intelligently. I have a minimum of five meetings with people in the family and three of these are with the mother, before treatment is started, after treatment is started, and a final summation. There is a standard block of time devoted to this problem.

DR. REYNOLDS: Here again you are meeting with a different population. In my practice of general medicine I am occasionally surprised to have brought to me a child whom I have delivered, in a family with whom I have worked for many years. Suddenly I am made aware that this child, in second or third grade is about to be dumped out of school. Often I start out with a tremendous working knowledge of the family, and this facilitates the prescription of medication. The biggest problem is to get parents to recognize that physicians can help in behavioral and educational problems. These people rely on my judgment and I don't have as much resistance to overcome.

DR. GOFMAN: We find, as I know all of you have, that parents of the child with deviant behavior or deviant learning from this culture's "norm" are often made to feel guilty. This is especially true for the parents of the hyperactive child—the child we have been describing who stands out as different at a very young age in his restlessness, distractibility, short attention span, and overreaction to stress, frustration, or excitement (even pleasurable). Many of these children show cyclic behavior, mood swings, being charming and pleasing one day and difficult and impossible the next. Their behavior is often unpredictable. They may react intensely, often with extreme acting-out anger to disappointments and delayed gratifications. Their responses to failure experiences may increase this undesirable behavior.

Their parents usually have received *much* criticism from their relatives and neighbors and sometimes from teachers and physicians for their child's unruly behavior. Thus they tend to be sensitive to possible criticism and fear the horrible scenes accompanying the frustration from their attempts to impose limits. Many of these parents state they feel as if they are "walking on eggs" when they are with this child, or that they must "handle him with kid gloves." As a result many of these children are not given much practice in learning to accept limits and to deal with disappointments or with delayed gratifications. Thus these children, who need more practice because this is harder for them to learn, usually get less.

These parents need a lot of understanding and support from the physician. They are often defensive and demanding because they feel so helpless and bewildered. Their child's behavior makes them feel they are failures as parents. This is demoralizing. Many of them are praying for a magical cure and are repeatedly disappointed because the physician doesn't give the medication in sufficient dosage, for a long enough trial, doesn't use the appropriate medication, or more often because too much is expected of the "magic pill." I think most of these families need some counseling help in managing these children at the same time medication is being tried. We find seeing the whole family together gives us much information about family communications, especially regarding feelings. Many of these children tend to keep their worries and their failures to themselves, which may result in their expression as destructive acting-out behavior.

One of the questions we have found helpful is, "How can you tell when your child is upset, worried, or has had a hard time at school?" Often the parents can tell only by the child's facial expression, his slamming into his room or picking on siblings. Seldom does he tell them in words what is troubling him. The result is that he expresses these unhappy feelings in ways that often result in more anger, criticism, and unhappiness for him.

Another helpful question is, "What do you do that makes your father or mother proud of you?" Many of these children experience little success and have great difficulty answering this question. Some will say, "I don't do anything that makes them proud." This is often an eye-opener for the parents, who have been unable to give this child much praise or recognition.

Exploring these areas may open the door for further counseling help, especially if the parents are helped to see that their child is more difficult to manage partly on the basis of his nervous system dysfunction. Most parents seem to be able to grasp the concept of a "more sensitive" or "more irritable" nervous system which overreacts to certain situations. If the parents have described specific situations, these can be used in making this explanation. The concept of being unable to sort out irrelevant stimuli is usually understood if you can have the parents imagine the state of their minds if they responded equally to the noises, movements, and visual stimuli in a busy office or clinic.

I think it is important to explore the parents' previous experiences with psychotropic medications. Have they known any other children who have been on medication? What was the effect? What expectations or fears do they have about medication for their own child?

We have found that sometimes with medication these children calm down and begin to talk more about things that bother them; often they cry more. Parents may misinterpret this verbalization of feelings as suggesting their child is becoming more morose, more unhappy. Such verbal expression may be very desirable and the parents may need counseling to understand and handle this new mode of expressing unhappiness and disappointment.

CHAIRMAN TARNOPOL: I certainly agree with Dr. Gofman's excellent description of the counseling needs of many parents.

Another area which requires consideration by the panel members is the function of medication in diagnosis. Who has some experience to contribute here?

DR. WHITSELL: The use of medication has a diagnostic value also. There are several potential ways, and one of them is that the child may be able to face some of his difficulties and start talking about them better. Another one is that there may be a pathological family configuration in which there is a need for the child to have an identity as pseudostupid or ill, and the whole program is sabotaged.

Sometimes the parents' resistance to the use of medication may be the initial harbinger of a dangerous situation. Awareness of this on the part of the physician is helpful when he is starting to prescribe medication. The initial resistance of the parents, the initial types of statements that parents make, or their questions, ought to be filed away as part of one's diagnostic data to be reconsidered later, because the diagnostic process in neuropsychiatry is a long-term affair. There is no such thing as a complete examination. The examination goes on and on in the sense that there are elaborations on our knowledge of what is happening.

There may be a psychotic parent for whom social adaptation or adjustment is kept going by a family pattern that conspires to permit this. Something else might bring the child to the doctor's attention, and in such a case the treatment program may be resisted.

DR. GOFMAN: I think it would be very helpful if you could include the father, too, in the work-up. We didn't do this previously but now we insist on it. We get the father and it has made a world of difference. It would be even better to include the whole family.

DR. DUGGER: Fathers so often reject the fact that there can be anything wrong with their son. It is rejecting their own image.

DR. WHITSELL: Sometimes the father brings the child in, and the mother is the sick one.

DR. DUGGER: I noticed on the suggested agenda a question, "How about tachyphylaxis?" This is not a problem that I have noticed—that after a while the drug doesn't work any more when resistance builds up, and then the dose has to be increased.

DR. LASTER: I have seen it with methylphenidate.

DR. WHITSELL: I think you can see it with almost any agent. I think you see it with iminodibenzyl compounds or phenothiazines in adults. Here it is necessary to switch either to a slightly different agent or out of that class of medications.

DR. LASTER: I get initial prolonged results.

CHAIRMAN TARNOPOL: I think what we are asking is, if you get an effect, and after a few weeks of the drug it appears to be ineffective and you then increase the dosage, does it then become effective as a rule?

DR. LASTER: As a rule, yes.

CHAIRMAN TARNOPOL: What is your experience with habituation?

DR. RICHANBACH: I don't think I have observed or would be concerned about habituation or dependency on amphetamines. I think this is largely a phenomenon of excessive doses. But I have had no trouble continuing children on amphetamine, even after several years.

DR. WHITSELL: I haven't had trouble either when it has been used for this specific purpose. The cases I have run into are mainly certain adults who have been taking it for weight reduction and got quite dependent on it. They have acquired a tolerance for amphetamines of up to 150 mg a day and are becoming psychotic. I don't think this has been much observed with children.

DR. CONNERS: There are a few reports.

DR. WHITSELL: But not very many of them.

DR. RICHANBACH: In the population I have seen, the children want to quit as a rule.

DR. WHITSELL: But there have been reports of occasional psychotic episodes.

DR. CONNERS: It is an idiosyncratic reaction, and there is one case report, I think, of a paranoid reaction from amphetamine in small doses.

DR. RICHANBACH: Would it be an acute episode or prolonged treatment?

DR. CONNERS: An acute episode which disappeared with removal of the drug and reappeared with readministration.

DR. RICHANBACH: That can come from marijuana, alcohol, and all kinds of things.

DR. CONNERS: But this is a dose-related phenomenon.

CHAIRMAN TARNOPOL: Have any of you seen anything like this in your practice?

DR. CONNERS: We have 1 case, a methylphenidate-induced paranoid reaction. That is the only one I know of.

DR. WHITSELL: I saw a couple of children who were coming close to that. Also I want to mention a recent report of 4 cases (including 1 adult) of basal ganglion stimulation syndromes with dyskinesias, torsion spasm, and other similar reactions, to dextroamphetamine (Mattson and Calverley 1968).

DR. DUGGER: I think another phase of drug abuse is the need to know who else is in this home. If there are teen-agers, ask the druggist not to label the bottle, so the teen-ager doesn't pick up the child's medicine and make off with it.

DR. WHITSELL: In some of the higher economic groups, I think even with the smaller children these drugs have reputations. It is a matter of concern. I would like to disagree with the use of spansules. I appreciate that this type of preparation has a long action. On the other hand, I think there are occasional instances to be found in which the absorption is apparently erratic, and the maximal effect is at 1 A.M. to 3 A.M., with violent tachycardia from a single 8 A.M. dose. A long-acting form of a drug also makes it difficult to determine a child's optimal dose initially. In titrating the dosage in a child it is a great advantage to use a short-acting drug.

When I do use a long-acting phenothiazine, Stelazine or Prolixin, I feel very cautious about the approach because of the lack of immediate reversibility, or the longer duration of a bad reaction if it does occur.

DR. DUGGER: As one familiar with the inner workings of drug companies, I can assure you they don't know the absorption pattern of any extended absorption formulation. It is impossible to devise one that is truly reliable.

CHAIRMAN TARNOPOL: A most important area which has not been sufficiently discussed is physician training. Both the University of Arkansas and the University of California medical schools are engaged in training physicians in this field. Perhaps Dr. Gofman would like to tell about her teaching program.

DR. GOFMAN: Those concerned with medical education have the responsibility of making the medical profession aware of the serious short-term and long-term implications for the child who is experiencing language or behavior difficulties, or both, in school. Over the past six years we have developed a teaching program that attempts to do this for our senior medical students and pediatric house-staff.*

I find that most of our pediatric house-staff coming from other medical schools have had little or no exposure to the evaluation of children's learning and behavior problems. Even though many of our medical students will not be specializing in pediatrics, the majority of them will be seeing children in their practices. In general practice they will certainly be asked to help with these problems. As ophthalmologists they may be the "first port of call" medically for the child who can't see the difference between *b* and *d*. The otolaryngologist will be (or should be) concerned with children's communication problems, with the child who "doesn't seem to listen," and with the child who shows delayed or deviant speech or language development.

Children under pressure may attempt to defend their egos by the use of physical symptoms such as headaches, vague joint pains, nausea, vomiting, and abdominal pain. Some of these children have even had exploratory laparotomies (abdominal incisions). A child with a chronic illness, such as asthma, may react to school difficulty with increased symptomatology leading to a vicious cycle of school absence, more school failure, increased symptomatology, more school absence, and so forth. It is

* The content of this teaching program is described in more detail in Gofman (1969).

evident that many specialists should be aware of the serious implications for children who have difficulty in school adjustment and learning.

We feel that many of these future physicians will be influential citizens in their communities. It is important for them to have some understanding of the need for early recognition and treatment of children with school difficulties so that they can support improved school programs designed to meet the individual needs of children. And the children we are discussing today certainly do have individual needs which, if not met, can sometimes almost destroy the child, his classroom, and his family.

We have found that we can best engage these young physicians' interests in such chief complaints as school behavior problems or reading difficulty (which at first impress them as being "nonmedical" complaints) by assigning them as the primary physician to a child presenting with such a problem. On the basis of information requested from both the school and the child's local physician, appropriate consultations are prearranged over a four-day period. Following an orientation regarding the importance of school problems, the environmental and neurophysiological functions related to learning problems, and the approaches helpful in their evaluation, the physician-trainee sees the child for a medical history and physical examination. He then accompanies the child through the prearranged consultations in order to learn the usefulness of these other disciplines in such an evaluation and to become acquainted with some of the terminology used by them. Until this experience, much of the terminology used by psychologists and language and educational consultants is as mysterious to the physician as his terminology may be to them. These consultations usually include psychological testing, neurological evaluation, and a family interview, including the child, parents, and sometimes siblings, conducted by one of our Child Study Unit staff (trained pediatrician or psychiatric social worker) who serves as the trainee's consultant for this four-day study.

During the trainee's contact with the child and his family, we try to stress the usefulness of assessing the strengths and weaknesses in the child's neurophysiological functioning, and the skills required for the task he is being asked to do—usually learning to read, write, and spell. We are also interested in assessing the strengths and weaknesses in the family which may aid or interfere in helping the child with his difficulty. The trainee has the opportunity to observe the child in different settings. Many times the trainee is impressed with the difference in the child's behavior in relationship to such factors as anxiety, stress, fear of failure, success, positive recognition, or even the time of day. The child and his family may appear quite different to the student after he has got to know them and has become more aware of some of the defenses the child may be using to cope with stress and failure. A child who is restricted and relatively quiet in the doctor's office may "climb the walls" in the stress of academic testing. The "wall climber" in the office may be quiet and attentive when coping with a task successfully.

The trainee has the responsibility of presenting the findings of these studies at a staffing conference attended by all the consultants. We try to arrive at some consensus regarding the child's difficulties and make recommendations for changes in management at home and at school. Following this staffing the student and his consultant meet with the family to explain our findings and help them plan ways of helping the child which may include a trial of medication, ongoing family therapy, and counseling. We then contact the school, either by a visit or telephone and by a written report.

CHAIRMAN TARNOPOL: Thank you very much, Dr. Gofman. I can see there is no doubt the discussion could go on quite a while longer, and we haven't covered as much of the subject as we would like to have covered. But at this time we will have to terminate the session, and I have prevailed upon Dr. Conners to summarize for us.

DR. CONNERS: First I would like to thank the Chairman for this privilege of giving my distortion of other people's distortions of the subject at hand.

I think we covered roughly three areas. First, we seem to have focused largely on the issues of diagnosis, recognition, and classification. Here I think we all agreed that there are a wide variety of disorders that we are discussing and that no single classification is appropriate.

We did emphasize that there are certain categories of children who are likely to be overlooked because they are less troublesome. We discussed the presenting picture for various kinds of neurological disorders, the temperamental problems, the purely educational problems, and there was some discussion about the appropriateness of medication for each of these classifications.

The impression I got from the discussion was that the recognition of the problems is not a great issue; that there are clear enough indicators, if one is sensitized to the problem—that it is not a terribly subtle problem. But we did emphasize the fact that there are children who will be overlooked, who do need drug treatment, and who could profit from it.

We had some discussion of formal techniques for classification. Generally the impression I got is that classifications that we are relying on are combinations of several levels of observation, social history, the observations of parents, and a very strong emphasis on the observations of teachers to guide us as to whether this child has a learning disability or behavior problem.

Most of the discussion has concerned the details of management and therapeutics. Here I think there are two subclassifications that we focused upon. First was the issue of the specific drugs that are useful and ways in which these are administered, with some attention to the issue of side effects.

Dr. Whitsell gave us an outline which didn't seem to be violently objected to, which placed the stimulants methylphenidate and dextroamphetamine probably first on the list, in terms of efficacy and general safety. These are drugs of first choice for children with the hyperkinetic behavior syndrome or problems of distractibility and concentration.

Next on the list were drugs appropriate for children who are schizoid, with some loss of reality contact, some bizarre behavior and, I assume, some hypermotility. Here some of the phenothiazines were thought to be appropriate.

It seemed to me that the list reconfirmed the general opinion which Dr. Whitsell quoted from Eisenberg in his outline, namely, that older drugs are to be preferred to newer drugs, and the more familiar ones with the fewer side effects are preferred to the newer ones with more toxic effects.

There are a number of details of drug management which were discussed that I think are important from a practical point of view, such as the dosage of these drugs, which usually seemed to be underestimated in the hands of the nonexperienced practitioner.

The issue of drug holidays, when and how often children should be relieved of the obligation to ingest the drugs, the issue of timing with regard to the onset of adolescence, and the complication of addiction that might ensue following prolonged administration were discussed.

A second aspect of the drug management problem that received considerable emphasis, and which highlights the broad context in which drugs are useful, is that of the psychosocial, family context in which the drugs are given. Here I think a number of variables were pointed to that seem to be important. The way in which the family perceives the drug; the way the child perceives it; the teacher's attitude; the role of the child in the family vis-à-vis his parents; the expectations that they have regarding the importance of this as contrasted with other therapies, such as educational therapy.

The basic point on which everyone agreed was that drug therapy is an important, sometimes essential, but never sufficient form of management. That it has to be given in cooperation with a number of other agencies and persons concerned in the care of children and that probably its best effects result in a situation in which there is a multidisciplinary solution, or attempted solution, of the child's learning problem. So the whole psychosocial context becomes part of the treatment problem.

A third area which we touched on from time to time was what might be called the evaluation or measurement or scientific aspect of drug treatment. And here we had some discussion of the kind of experimental design which would be appropriate, some questions about measurement, and some issues about the kinds of follow-up and the kind of assessment which are useful.

We talked a little about office instruments or office measurements that could be used and some kind of practical, feasible method that can be used for evaluating drugs. This is an area we did not highlight very much, although I think the whole discussion took place within the context of the assumption that everything that is said about drugs needs to be rather critically reviewed and is not to be accepted without careful evaluation of all of the factors which enter into drug treatment.

CHART 5-1. *Parent Questionnaire*

Child's Name: Date:
Your Name: Relationship:
Instructions: Please check *every* item in every group. Put your check under
the column heading (not at all, just a little, pretty much, very much) that
is most true of *your* child.

	HOW TRUE IS THIS OF YOUR CHILD?			
	Not at All	Just a Little	Pretty Much	Very Much
I. PROBLEMS OF EATING				
1. Picky and finicky	—	—	—	—
2. Will not eat enough	—	—	—	—
3. Overweight	—	—	—	—
II. PROBLEMS OF SLEEP				
4. Restless	—	—	—	—
5. Nightmares	—	—	—	—
6. Awakens at night	—	—	—	—
7. Cannot fall asleep	—	—	—	—
III. FEARS AND WORRIES				
8. Afraid of new situations	—	—	—	—
9. Afraid of people	—	—	—	—
10. Afraid of being alone	—	—	—	—
11. Worries about illness and death	—	—	—	—
IV. MUSCULAR TENSION				
12. Gets stiff and rigid	—	—	—	—
13. Twitches, jerks, etc.	—	—	—	—
14. Shakes	—	—	—	—
V. SPEECH PROBLEMS				
15. Stuttering	—	—	—	—
16. Hard to understand	—	—	—	—
VI. WETTING				
17. Bed-wetting	—	—	—	—
18. Runs to bathroom constantly	—	—	—	—
VII. BOWEL PROBLEMS				
19. Soiling self	—	—	—	—
20. Holds back bowel movements	—	—	—	—
VIII. COMPLAINS OF THE FOLLOWING SYMPTOMS EVEN WHEN THE DOCTOR CAN FIND NOTHING WRONG				
21. Headaches	—	—	—	—
22. Stomach aches	—	—	—	—
23. Vomiting	—	—	—	—
24. Aches and pains	—	—	—	—
25. Loose bowels	—	—	—	—

	Not at All	Just a Little	Pretty Much	Very Much
IX. PROBLEMS OF SUCK-ING, CHEWING, PICKING				
26. Sucks thumb	—	—	—	—
27. Bites or picks nails	—	—	—	—
28. Chews on clothes, blanket, or others	—	—	—	—
29. Picks at things such as hair, clothing, etc.	—	—	—	—
X. CHILDISH OR IMMATURE				
30. Does not act his age	—	—	—	—
31. Cries easily	—	—	—	—
32. Wants help on things he should do alone	—	—	—	—
33. Clings to parents or other adults	—	—	—	—
34. Baby talk	—	—	—	—
XI. TROUBLE WITH FEELINGS				
35. Keeps anger to himself	—	—	—	—
36. Lets himself get pushed around by other children	—	—	—	—
37. Unhappy	—	—	—	—
38. Carries a chip on his shoulder	—	—	—	—
XII. OVERASSERTS HIMSELF				
39. Bullying	—	—	—	—
40. Bragging and boasting	—	—	—	—
41. Sassy to grown-ups	—	—	—	—
XIII. PROBLEMS MAKING FRIENDS				
42. Shy	—	—	—	—
43. Afraid they don't like him	—	—	—	—
44. Feelings easily hurt	—	—	—	—
45. Has no friends	—	—	—	—
XIV. PROBLEMS WITH BROTHERS & SISTERS				
46. Feels cheated	—	—	—	—
47. Mean	—	—	—	—
48. Fights constantly	—	—	—	—
XV. PROBLEMS KEEPING FRIENDS				
49. Hits or kicks other children	—	—	—	—
50. Wants to run things	—	—	—	—
51. Picks on other children	—	—	—	—

	Not at All	Just a Little	Pretty Much	Very Much
XVI. RESTLESS				
52. Can't keep still	—	—	—	—
53. Always into things	—	—	—	—
54. Fails to finish things he starts	—	—	—	—
XVII. TEMPER				
55. Stands there screaming	—	—	—	—
56. Throws himself around	—	—	—	—
57. Throws and breaks things	—	—	—	—
58. Pouts and sulks	—	—	—	—
XVIII. SEX				
59. Plays with own sex organs	—	—	—	—
60. Involved with sex play with others	—	—	—	—
61. Modest about his body	—	—	—	—
XIX. PROBLEMS IN SCHOOL				
62. Isn't learning	—	—	—	—
63. Doesn't like to go to school	—	—	—	—
64. Is afraid to go to school	—	—	—	—
65. Daydreams	—	—	—	—
66. Truancy	—	—	—	—
67. Won't obey school rules	—	—	—	—
XX. LYING				
68. Denies having done wrong	—	—	—	—
69. Blames others for his mistakes	—	—	—	—
70. Tells stories which did not happen	—	—	—	—
XXI. STEALING				
71. From parents	—	—	—	—
72. At school	—	—	—	—
73. From stores and other places	—	—	—	—
XXII. TROUBLE WITH POLICE				
74. Why?				
XXIII. FIRE-SETTING				
75. Describe:				
XXIV. PERFECTIONISM				
76. Everything must be just so	—	—	—	—
77. Things must be done same way every time	—	—	—	—
78. Sets too-high goals	—	—	—	—

	Not at All	Just a Little	Pretty Much	Very Much
XXV. ADDITIONAL PROBLEMS				
79. Runs rather than walks	—	—	—	—
80. Can't watch TV for long	—	—	—	—
81. Can't be left alone	—	—	—	—
82. Always climbing	—	—	—	—
83. A very early riser	—	—	—	—
84. Runs around between mouthfuls	—	—	—	—
85. His demands must be met immediately	—	—	—	—
86. Can't stand too much excitement	—	—	—	—
87. Laces and zippers are always open	—	—	—	—
88. Is depressed and saddened	—	—	—	—
89. Acts as if driven by a motor	—	—	—	—
90. Unable to stop a repetitive activity	—	—	—	—
91. Mood changes quickly and drastically	—	—	—	—
92. Poorly aware of surroundings or time of day	—	—	—	—
93. Still can't tie his shoelaces	—	—	—	—

XXVI. PLEASE ADD ANY
OTHER PROBLEMS
YOU HAVE.

_____

_____

_____

_____

_____

XXVII. HOW BAD DO YOU THINK YOUR CHILD'S PROBLEMS ARE?
(Check one)
Not at all _____ a little _____ bad _____ very bad _____

SOURCE: C. K. Conners. Symptom patterns in hyperkinetic, neurotic, and normal children. *Child Development* 41:667, 1970.

CHART 5-2. *Teacher Questionnaire*

I. IDENTIFYING INFORMATION
   Child's Name: School:
   Grade: How long have you known this child?
II. In your own words briefly describe the child's main problem.

III. STANDARDIZED TEST RESULTS
   1. Intelligence tests
      Name of Test   *Date*   *C.A.*   *M.A.*   *IQ*

   2. Most recent achievement tests
            Grade When Tested   *Achievement Grade Level*

      Reading
      Spelling
      Arithmetic
IV. ACHIEVEMENT IN SCHOOL SUBJECTS (list subjects)
   Subject   *Very Good*   *Average*   *Barely Passing*   *Failing*

   What special placement or help has he had? (Underline below)
   Ungraded, sight-saving, special class, remedial reading, speech correction, tutoring
   Other (specify) _____

   Please check for *every* item the one that is most true of this child.

	Not at All	Just a Little	Pretty Much	Very Much
V. BEHAVIOR OF CHILD				
1. Sits fiddling with small objects	—	—	—	—
2. Hums and makes other odd noises	—	—	—	—
3. Falls apart under stress of examination	—	—	—	—
4. Coordination poor	—	—	—	—
5. Restless or overactive	—	—	—	—
6. Excitable	—	—	—	—
7. Inattentive	—	—	—	—
8. Difficulty in concentrating	—	—	—	—
9. Oversensitive	—	—	—	—
10. Overly serious or sad	—	—	—	—
11. Daydreams	—	—	—	—
12. Sullen or sulky	—	—	—	—
13. Selfish				
14. Disturbs other children	—	—	—	—
15. Quarrelsome	—	—	—	—
16. Tattles	—	—	—	—
17. Acts "smart"	—	—	—	—
18. Destructive	—	—	—	—
19. Steals	—	—	—	—
20. Lies	—	—	—	—
21. Temper outbursts	—	—	—	—

	Not at All	Just a Little	Pretty Much	Very Much
VI. GROUP PARTICIPATION				
1. Isolates himself from other children	—	—	—	—
2. Appears to be unaccepted by group	—	—	—	—
3. Appears to be easily led	—	—	—	—
4. No sense of fair play	—	—	—	—
5. Appears to lack leadership	—	—	—	—
6. Does not get along with opposite sex	—	—	—	—
7. Does not get along with same sex	—	—	—	—
8. Teases other children or interferes with their activities	—	—	—	—
VII. ATTITUDE TOWARD AUTHORITY				
1. Submissive	—	—	—	—
2. Defiant	—	—	—	—
3. Impudent	—	—	—	—
4. Shy	—	—	—	—
5. Fearful	—	—	—	—
6. Excessive demands for teacher's attention	—	—	—	—
7. Stubborn	—	—	—	—
8. Overly anxious	—	—	—	—
9. Uncooperative	—	—	—	—
10. Attendance problem	—	—	—	—

VIII. FAMILY

1. Do other children in the family attending your school present problems? (Amplify)

2. Please add information about this child's home or family relationships which might have bearing on his attitudes and behavior, and add any suggestions for improvement of his behavior and adjustment.

Signature:
Title:
Date:

Name of Principal:
Name of school:
Address of school:

SOURCE: C. K. Conners. A teacher rating scale for use in drug studies with children. *American Journal of Psychiatry* 126: 152, 1969.

REFERENCES

Gofman, H.   The Physician's Role in Early Diagnosis and Management of Learning Difficulties. In L. Tarnopol (Ed.), *Learning Disabilities: Introduction to Educational and Medical Management.* Springfield, Ill.: Thomas, 1969.

Hutt, C., Jackson, P., and Level, M.   Behavioral parameters and drug effects: A study of a hyperkinetic epileptic child. *Epilepsia* 7:250, 1961.

Mattson, R. H., and Calverley, J. R.   Dextroamphetamine-Sulfate-Induced Dyskinesias. *Journal of the American Medical Association* 204(5):400–401, 1968.

Menolascino, F. (Ed.).   *Psychiatric Approaches to Mental Retardation in Childhood.* New York: Basic Books, 1969.

Piaget, J.   *The Construction of Reality in the Child.* New York: Basic Books, 1954.

Sprague, R. L., Barnes, K. R., and Werry, J. S.   Methylphenidate and thioridazine: Learning, reaction time, activity, and classroom behavior in disturbed children. *American Journal of Orthopsychiatry* 40:615, 1970.

Thomas, A., Chess, S., and Birch, H.   *Temperament and Behavior Disorders in Children.* New York: New York University Press, 1968.

6

The Neurology of
Learning Disabilities

PHILIP R. CALANCHINI AND
SUSAN STRUVE TROUT

LANGUAGE AND LEARNING are biological phenom-
ena, the result of anatomical, physiological, and biochemical
processes within the human nervous system. The understanding
of these phenomena has been continuously advancing through
effort in several disciplines—neurology, psychology, linguistics,
education. Each field has used its own research techniques, language, and orientation to advance knowledge. These different
frames of reference have resulted in a lack of communication
between and among the disciplines. Although each has made
unique contributions, the need for effective interdisciplinary
effort has become increasingly apparent. The value of the interdisciplinary approach has been well demonstrated by several investigators including Luria (1966), Geschwind (1965), Schuell
(1964), and Penfield (1959), who have studied disruption of
language in adults suffering from cerebral damage. Interdisciplinary communication has yielded more definitive diagnostic
analyses, wiser selections of therapeutic methods, and more
fruitful research than would have been possible had investigators been working alone.

Application of knowledge from many disciplines to the problems of children who cannot learn certain language tasks due to
brain dysfunction has unlimited possibilities. For example, if a
child can read but not write, it is theoretically possible to pool

information from several disciplines and devise a specific training program related directly to that child's brain function and educational needs. This program could help him learn to write despite his brain inefficiencies.

If more were known about the learning patterns of normal children, educators could design programs which would capitalize on a specific child's unique way of learning. As Guilford (1967) has stated, not only would there be fewer teaching failures but the innate creative talents of a child could more efficiently be channeled into vocations for which the child's learning style was best suited.

This chapter was written to propose a theoretical basis upon which knowledge of brain function might be advantageously integrated with what is known psychologically and educationally about children with specific learning disabilities. We are aware of the hazards of trying to relate clinical problems to experimental findings in lower animals. We have tried to align clinical and experimental findings, without trying to close the gap between them, and we recognize that these attempts risk being incorrect or incomplete. We hope that by bringing into focus the relationship of the brain and learning disabilities we may suggest new areas of exploration.

The thesis proposed is that learning disabilities are cortical in origin and primarily a result of poor function in the phylogenetically and ontogenetically newest and most complex areas of the brain. These areas, the prefrontal, inferior parietal, and inferior temporal regions, are the last to mature in the developing brain (Fig. 6-1). According to this thesis, learning disabilities are a result of inefficient function in these or adjacent cortical areas. The inefficiency is more often an imperfection of nature than a result of actual insult to the brain. Just as the relatively fixed nearsightedness due to an imperfect eye can be compensated for by corrective lenses, so can the learning disability due to an imperfect brain be compensated for by properly selected teaching methods and learning habits.

HISTORICAL VIEWS OF BRAIN FUNCTION

In the past, attempts to understand higher cortical functions* have fallen into two supposedly opposite schools of thought. One school, at its extreme, claimed that each aspect of behavior was the responsibility of a localized group of brain cells. The other school asserted that behavior was indivisible, a function of the brain as a whole.

Despite their divergent views, each school made notable contributions toward the understanding of brain function—those who believed in localization by stressing the highly organized differentiation of brain function, and those who held a holistic view by emphasizing that the brain functions as a whole, yet has a hierarchical organization and is an adaptable organ. Both failed in the attempt to relate behavior directly to brain structure, as they did not first adequately determine the biological or psychophysiological components of behavioral phenomena.

Kleist (1934), one of the strong proponents of localization, published a chart that directly related behavioral phenomena to specific areas of the brain. Functions such as counting and number recognition were attributed to area 19 and efficiency of thought to area 46 (see Fig. 6-2). Lashley (1929), one of the most outstanding proponents of the holistic view, suggested that different parts of the brain were equipotential for complex behavioral functions, and that such functions as counting and number recognition were not localizable to a specific area.

Geschwind (1964) and others have pointed out that localization versus antilocalization is an oversimplification. The major premises of these older points of view have been coordinated to form a more cohesive concept of brain functioning (Geschwind 1965, Luria 1966).

The subtle anatomical differences between cortical areas (see Fig. 6-3) may justify the conclusion that there are as many different functional units as there are anatomical units. The function of each unit is not an observable one, in terms of gross

---

* Function may be defined physiologically as (1) the activity of a cell type, cell group, tissue, or organ, or behaviorally as (2) the end product of complex brain activity such as writing, calculation, and so on.

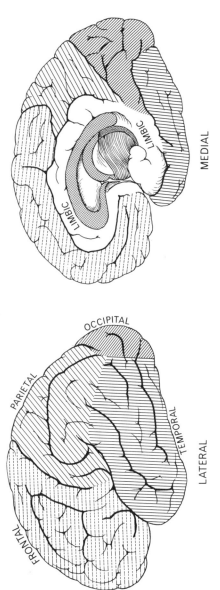

FIGURE 6-1. *Human cerebral hemisphere, lateral and medial views, showing lobes of the brain.*

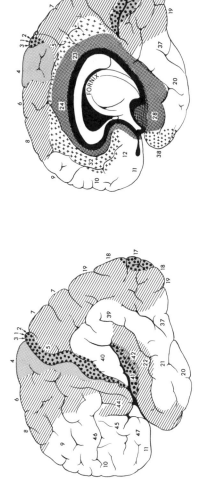

FIGURE 6-2. *Cytoarchitectural map of human cerebral cortex. Areas with large dots, primary receptive cortex; diagonal lines, primary association cortex; white areas, phylogenetically new secondary association cortex; small dots, motor cortex; stippled area, limbic system. (Modified from Brodmann 1909.)*

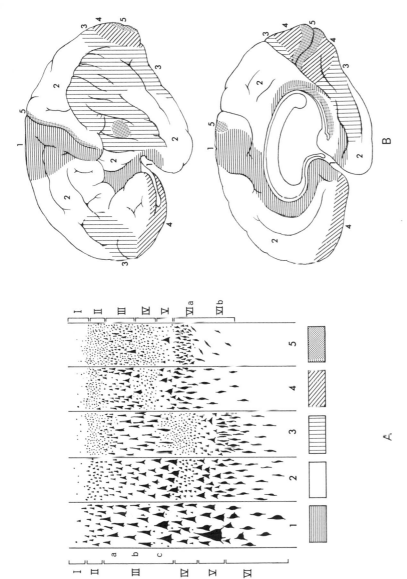

FIGURE 6-3. (A) The five fundamental structural types of cerebral cortex, and (B) their distribution. 1 = agranular; 2 = frontal; 3 = parietal (homotypical); 4 = polar; 5 = granular ("koniocortex"). (After von Economo, The Cytoarchitectonics of the Human Cerebral Cortex, Oxford University Press, 1929; modified from Peele, T., The Neuroanatomic Basis for Clinical Neurology (2d ed.), New York: McGraw-Hill, 1961. With permission.)

211

behavior. Rather the function of each unit is very specific; for example, the cells of the unit may be activated or inhibited by a specific stimulus. Complex function of the brain such as speaking, reading, or writing is the product of multiple units in various areas of the brain working together in a temporary relationship to analyze and integrate external and internal environmental stimuli in order to produce behavior. Many parts of the brain may be involved in a single behavioral act. Later the same units may be involved in a different behavioral act.

To try to understand behavioral acts in terms of brain activity, Luria (1966) further developed an approach termed *dynamic localization* of cortical functions. According to this approach a specific brain function is the end product of sequences of brain activities that involve many widespread units acting in temporary combination. The process is a dynamic one and depends upon the orderly performance of the various units. In relating brain structure and physiology to a behavioral act Luria requires that each component part of the behavior be determined. For example, the act of singing might be separated into discrimination of pitch, changes in pitch direction, sequential analysis of pitch patterns, timbre, control of muscle movements, breathing, and so on. Luria refers to the process of relating component parts of behavior to brain structure as *psychophysiological analysis*.

A disturbance in any one of the many units or links results in impairment of the optimum performance of all the functions for which the disturbed unit is a necessary part. Thus failure to discriminate changes in pitch may affect not only singing ability but also speech and reading. If a disturbance involves several units, the impairment in several functions may be severe or even complete.

The concept of dynamic localization of function is relatively new, but already has been fruitful. An excellent example of the contribution of psychophysiological analysis to understanding the dynamic localization of function is provided by Luria (1966a) for the act of writing. First the sounds of speech must be analyzed so that the discrete phonemes (which make up words) can be identified. This requires an audioarticulatory mechanism. The identified sounds must then be recoded into graphemes (visual signs) which must be distinguishably different from each other and spatially organized. This requires visual and visual-spatial analysis. The visual signs must then be recoded into a system of muscle movements which lead to the accurate movement of the writing instrument. This requires accurate innervation and complementary inhibition of various muscles in a smooth "kinetic melody." The muscle movements are aided by constant visual and proprioceptive (impulses from receptors in muscles, tendons, joints) feedback as a means of monitoring the act of writing. The muscle movements of writing, the visual analysis, the monitoring, and the identification of the consecutive series of sounds to be recorded (auditory analysis) occur at the same time.

This particular psychophysiological analysis is no doubt incomplete, but it illustrates that much of the brain is involved in the writing act though the many units and their linkages are located in different, localized areas of the brain.

BRAIN FUNCTION AND LEARNING DISABILITIES

Unlike the gross functional disabilities of brain-injured adults, the neurological learning disabilities in children are not necessarily the result of brain injury; some may be genetic, many are the result of just an "imperfection of nature," some are due, perhaps, to a maturational lag; some no doubt are the result of actual brain injury. So-called normal variation in the mental abilities of individuals may also account for some learning disabilities. Some persons of good intelligence are "tone deaf" or cannot sustain rhythm or pitch; others cannot draw in perspective or have a poor sense of direction. Different levels of ability in an individual probably exist because his brain does not have equal potential in all of its processes. Individuals with these variabilities may be thought of as having brain inefficiencies of certain functions which result in an inability to learn readily and subsequently to perform a particular activity (Quadfasel and Goodglass 1968).

To have certain brain inefficiencies may be no great problem in our society. One can avoid singing or drawing or depend on others to find one's way. It is a true disadvantage in our society, however, to have brain inefficiencies in the component units necessary to master language skills and academic learning. A person in our culture is dependent upon the ability to read for warning purposes and for most employment; he is dependent upon writing for completing forms and upon arithmetic for calculating bank accounts and tax reports.

Whether or not a child's neurological learning disability is due to a genetic or an acquired cause, a better understanding of his disability will result from knowledge of brain anatomy and physiology as it relates to the dynamic localization of brain function. Much of this knowledge has come through the study of adult brain-injury problems. A better understanding of learning disabilities in children will be gained by applying a similar approach to children.

Even at this early stage of knowledge it is possible to relate the neurology of learning to diagnostic appraisal and educational remediation of children with neurological learning disabilities. What is known about the brain and learning can be incorporated in the selection of a diagnostic test battery, in outlining guidelines for the interpretation of test data and behavior, and in determining the selection of remediation materials and techniques.

This chapter will discuss how the nervous system handles sensory information within the three major sensory modalities of vision, audition, and somesthesis. These sensory modalities may function independently or in conjunction with the other systems. Knowing that each of the auditory, visual, and somesthetic systems within the brain receives, categorizes, stores, and recalls information in conjunction with other parts of the brain helps explain why inefficiencies can occur which interfere with expected functions of some or all of these systems.

It is well established that neurological learning disabilities in children vary widely, and that an inefficiency in the brain can disturb the function of one or more systems without fundamentally disturbing others. This is why some children, for example, have problems in auditory discrimination, auditory analysis-synthesis, and auditory memory without equivalent involvement of these abilities in the visual system. Some children can comprehend the spoken word, integrate and recall it, but not transduce the auditory signals into their motor-kinesthetic equivalents for speech. Still other children may be able to learn what letters sound like but not what sounds look like when printed. Others can receive information through the senses but not be able to interpret what is seen, heard, or touched.

Variations of brain inefficiencies can also occur when information received through one sensory avenue impedes that received through another. This may be seen in the child who has to look away from a stimulus so he can comprehend more efficiently what is said about that stimulus. A child may also disintegrate behaviorally when presented with multiple sensory stimuli or when he is required to integrate complex functions.

To determine a child's learning inefficiencies and efficiencies, observations must be made of how he solves tasks which vary in type of sensory information presented and type of response required. Tasks which include both formal and informal tests are selected to tap learning within each sensory system, between two or more systems, and when a motor response is or is not required. The test battery necessary to evaluate fully a child's learning disabilities must also be selected and designed to measure various functions of the brain at various levels of experience. Hierarchical levels of experiences, sensation, perception, imagery, symbolization, and conceptualization exist within each system (Johnson and Myklebust 1967).

Although it is not the purpose of this chapter to discuss the specific rationale for the selection of each test category nor to outline guidelines for how the tests should be interpreted, the test categories are listed at the top of Figure 6-4. The test categories are grouped under the three major sensory modalities for learning and labeled according to the functions they primarily measure. The section labeled "Academic" is viewed as the result or effect of disruption within one or more of these systems.

CASE ILLUSTRATION

J. M., whose learning profile is shown in Figure 6-4, is able to function well as long as he is presented auditory or sensorimotor tasks. His performance deteriorates whenever he must interpret,

LEARNING PROFILE

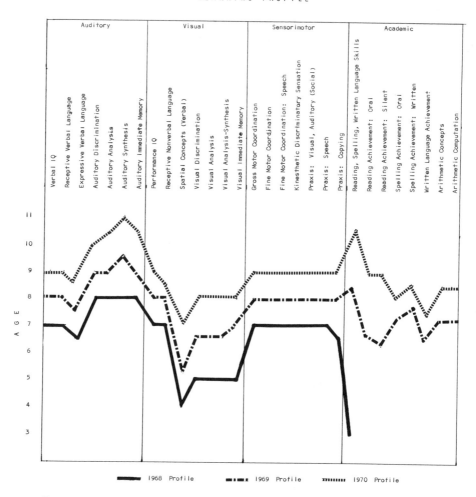

FIGURE 6-4. *Test categories used in determining the 1968, 1969, 1970 learning profiles of J. M. Remedial intervention began in 1968.*

categorize, store, and recall visual stimuli. When first evaluated in the middle of first grade (age 6 years, 10 months), he was unable to read, copy, or perform simple numerical tasks. The underlying reason for the lack of success in these academic areas was the inability to discriminate, analyze and synthesize, retain, and recall the abstract visual symbols well enough to connect them meaningfully to their corresponding sounds. J. M. was therefore unable to give names or sounds to letters, to read numbers accurately, or to discriminate similar visual symbols such as 6 and 9, *b* and *d*. However, because his auditory system was intact, he could identify the *b* and *d* sounds in spoken words. His intact auditory and sensorimotor systems also allowed him to learn to understand spoken words, express his ideas verbally, and engage in fine and gross motor activities. Because he did not understand the structure of the symbols he saw, he could not analyze the various visual symbols and convert them into an integral whole; his attempts to identify whole words for sight reading were therefore impaired. His difficulty with visual structures was also seen in his inability to analyze pictures and designs, and interfered with his ability to copy, draw, or do puzzles.

His motor system appeared to be intact. The disruption of his ability to integrate information from all modalities and thereby learn to read, spell, write, and perform arithmetical tasks was interpreted as a failure in his visual input and integrative systems.

Principles for teaching J. M. were in keeping with what is known about the neurology of learning and what had been learned about J. M.'s unique way of learning. To teach J. M. to read, write, spell, and calculate, the following neurologically based principles were followed:

1. The teaching approach took into account which sensory systems were intact, which were deficient, and which combinations of sensory systems allowed learning to take place. It also took into account which combinations interfered with learning. J. M.'s auditory and sensorimotor systems were intact but deficiencies were present in the visual system; learning would likely take place if material was first presented auditorily, then visually, then in a combination of visual and motor activities.

2. The teaching approach considered at which level of experience learning failed. J. M. could not develop higher levels of visual memory, integration of the visual symbol with the auditory and motor systems, and conceptualization based on visual experience.

3. A child cannot be expected to express himself in motor

output if his brain cannot analyze the sensory input and integrate this input with other sensory information. As J. M.'s learning had been disrupted by deficits in visual input and integration with other modalities, he was not expected to learn to perform the output activities of copying, writing, spelling, and reading aloud.

4. The amount of information presented and its degree of modality integration must be controlled, otherwise the child will become overloaded and his performance will disintegrate. J. M. would be expected to become confused when presented with too many visual symbols at one time or when he was expected to associate these visual symbols with the auditory and somesthetic systems or transfer visual symbols to a motor output.

5. To learn, the brain must successfully integrate information in such a way that it is meaningful to the child. For J. M., integration would take place when what he already knew was used to teach him what he did not know. He would learn most efficiently when what he knew auditorily was presented first, followed by attaching it to what he did not know visually. For example, to learn the meaning of the printed symbol *m,* J. M. first would have to isolate the sound *m-m-,* which he could do easily, and then match this to the visual symbol *m.* He could then transfer to the sensorimotor system and learn to write *m.* Because of his auditory strengths and his visual deficiencies, J. M. would have to guide visual tasks by giving himself verbal directions. To learn how to put a puzzle together, for example, he would have to tell himself verbally how to group the pieces and what to look for in selecting the next piece.

6. Integration rather than the independent development of the deficit or strength should be the goal of teaching. The child must have a meaningful systematic way to approach learning. For J. M., meaning would be basic for his success in learning any task; if he understands what he is to do, he will learn.

Figure 6-4 graphs J. M.'s original and two subsequent evaluations. The figure shows that when J. M. was taught using these neurologically based principles he made remarkable progress. *His learning profile did not alter; the intact and deficient areas remained the same. His method of learning is unique for his brain.* Deviation from this approach will cause him to become confused and to fail to progress. Residual problems remain which reflect his deficits in the visual system. For example, he has learned to read fluently because the visual symbol is stabilized. He has not learned to spell nonphonetic words and he continues to have difficulty with arithmetic; as these tasks rely mainly on visual abilities, J. M. cannot compensate by using auditory meaning.

In summary, the diagnostic tests were used to determine the learning pattern unique to J.M., and the teaching approach was based on what is known about how the brain processes information. Continual changes are being made by the Center staff in their testing procedures and interpretations as more is learned about how the brain functions. Longitudinal studies of children evaluated and taught at the Center are of help in this attempt. The clinical applications of the neurology of learning to J. M. should be viewed, therefore, as a beginning, with changes and modifications forthcoming.

BRAIN ORGANIZATION

The organization of the nervous system can be functionally and anatomically divided into the input, integrative, and output systems. The *input system* collects and transmits environmental information (both external and internal) to the integrative system (see Fig. 6-5). Of the five senses which collect environmental information, three are of prime importance in learning: vision, hearing, and somesthesis (cutaneous and proprioceptive sensation).

The *integrative system* is the most complex and exists at all levels of the central nervous system, including the spinal cord, brainstem, and the cerebral hemispheres. The cerebral cortex is the most complex level of the integrative system and the site of higher cortical functions such as thought processes. The integrative system deals with recognition, selection, integration, storage, and use of information; it is responsible for perception, cognition, memory, intellect, formulation of motor activity, and awareness.

The *output system* is responsible for observable behavior,

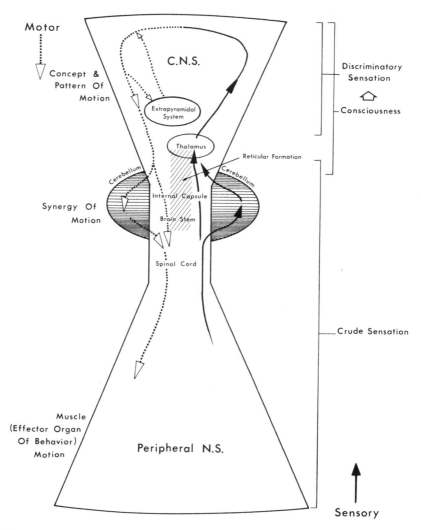

FIGURE 6-5. *Schematic of the nervous system showing input (sensory), integrative, and output (motor) systems. Peripheral and central nervous systems are represented as two funnels with small ends opposed.*

that is, muscle movement and the functioning of the autonomic nervous system. With the exception of the nonobservable processes of thinking and feeling, the only way one can respond to his environment is by muscle movement, as in a gesture, speech, or writing. Even autonomic effects, such as sweating or pallor, and alterations of pupil size are the result of muscle movement.

The output system is responsive to the integrative and input systems. Feedback through the three primary sensory modalities gives the integrative system control over its end product, i.e., its output, and an opportunity to modify it continuously. For example, in describing a movie a person may modify his words as he hears himself speaking aloud, or he may make modifications as he visually recalls a certain scene or as he thinks ahead while speaking. New thoughts occur and lead to further output modifications.

The three systems of the brain are interrelated and interdependent. The smooth functioning of all three requires multiple connections at all levels of the nervous system.

Cortical Organization

Specific brain organization is relevant to language and learning. An understanding of the functional significance of morphological differences is necessary to understand fully the physiology of any part.

The posterior half of the brain has separate cortical areas for each sensory modality. These areas receive the sensory input and are called the *primary receptive* areas. On Brodmann's cytoarchitectural map (Fig. 6-2), area 17 receives visual input, areas 41 and 42 receive auditory input, and areas 1, 2, and 3 receive somesthetic input. These areas (see Fig. 6-3) are called *koniocortex* because of their microscopic dusty appearance. They have a prominent IV layer of granular cells typical of primary sensory receptive areas. Each of these areas has projections from specific thalamic nuclei. Each area is also well defined somatotopically with representation based on function rather than structure (Figs. 6-6–6-8).

Adjacent to each of the sensory receiving areas are the *primary association* areas* which are responsible for further and more complex analysis and synthesis of the information of that

---

* *Association area,* while still in use, is not the term favored by physiologists, who prefer the term *homotypical cortex* (i.e., six-layered granular cortex which has a different cytoarchitecture than the highly granular cortex—koniocortex, Fig. 6-3) or *intrinsic* or *associated areas* (Ruch and Patton 1965, Spinelli and Pribram 1966).

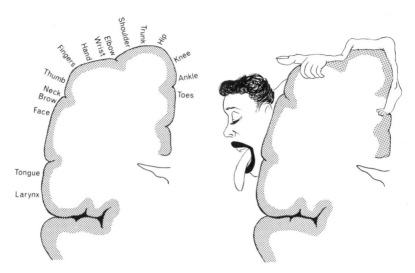

FIGURE 6-6.   *Coronal section in the sensorimotor area of one hemisphere with somatotopic representation of sensory-motor activity in the component parts of the body. (Modified from W. Penfield and T. Rasmussen,* The Cerebral Cortex of Man. *New York: Macmillan, 1950.)*

sensory modality. Areas 18 and 19 are for vision, 42 (in part) and 22 are for audition, and 5 and 7 are for somesthesis (see Fig. 6-2). These areas are homotypical cortex (see Fig. 6-3) with the II and III cell layers predominating. They receive subcortical projections from the integrative or elaborative thalamic nuclei (Peele 1961). The clear somatotopic arrangements found in the primary areas are not found in the association areas.

The primary receptive areas for each sensory modality are cortically connected only with their own primary association areas (Flechsig 1901). They have no direct connections of any note with any other cortical area. Even the analogous area of the opposite hemisphere is not connected. On the other hand, the primary association areas have fairly wide afferent and efferent cortical connections both with the analogous area of the opposite hemisphere and with widespread areas in the same hemisphere. As Luria (1966) says, Pavlov spoke of the sensory cortical areas as analyzers, i.e., the cortex involved in the analysis and integration of complex incoming signals. The first analyzer sys-

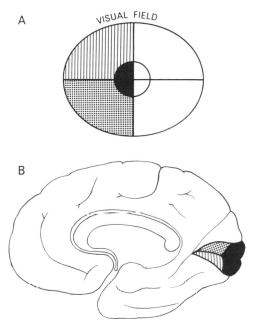

A

VISUAL FIELD

B

FIGURE 6 7.   (A) *Human visual field.* (B) *Medial surface of the right cere-bral hemisphere showing the representation of the left visual field on the striate cortex.*

tem is the primary receptive cortex and the second is the pri-mary association cortex.

The cellular arrangement in these areas, in particular the homotypical cortex (see Fig. 6-3), is in vertical columns of cells involving all six layers of the cortex. Each of these columns serves as an elementary, dynamic unit of cortical function (Pow-ell and Mountcastle 1959, Hubel and Wiesel 1965). The cells in each column have the same peripheral receptive field (e.g., a visual cortex column represents a point on the retina). These cells are responsible for analyzing input received from that field. Any one column of cells may react to only a specific type of in-put from its receptive field (e.g., a bar of light as opposed to a diffuse light). The receptive field is made up of "on" and "off" areas with the "on" areas leading to cortical cell stimulation and the "off" areas to inhibition. Each cell column, then, has its own input and output.

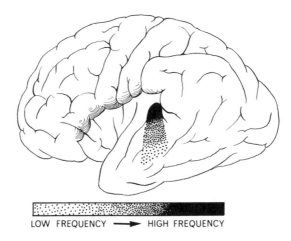

LOW FREQUENCY ───► HIGH FREQUENCY

FIGURE 6-8. *Lateral surface of left cerebral hemisphere with the temporal lobe pulled down to expose Heschl's gyri and show the somatotopic distribution of tone frequencies.*

In the midst of the three sensory fields is a large phylogenetically and ontogenetically recent area of cortex called the *inferior parietal lobule* (areas 39 and 40) and the *inferior temporal region* (areas 20, 21, and 37) (see Fig. 6-2). It is here that the human visual, auditory, and somesthetic analyzers interrelate to each other in a secondary association area. In lower animals only sparse cortical connections exist between these sensory modalities (Myers 1967) and the only firm intermodal connections appear to be through the limbic system.

The limbic system is a more primitive level of the nervous system (see Figs. 6-1 and 6-9). The limbic system mediates between the higher (cortical) and lower (hypothalamic, brainstem) neural areas through abundant connections. Certain specific functions are also localizable to the limbic system; it initiates or controls many types of less complex, repetitive activity of the sort called *automatic.* The pronounced rhythm of popular music and the proximity of the auditory areas to the limbic system may not be a coincidence. The limbic structures also deal with the emotional and visceral brain functions. For example, the olfactory input goes directly into the limbic system; the role of perfume in romance has been known since antiquity.

Sensory-limbic connections are involved in most if not all be-

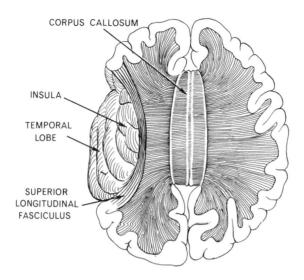

CORPUS CALLOSUM

INSULA

TEMPORAL
LOBE

SUPERIOR
LONGITUDINAL
FASCICULUS

FIGURE 6-9. *Horizontal section of the brain showing fibers of the corpus callosum and the superior longitudinal (arcuate) fasciculus which runs from the lower frontal area into the temporal, parietal, occipital regions.*

havior in animals lower than man, for example, the pleasure of a dog at the sight of his master, his fear at the hiss of a snake. Man also has these sensory-limbic connections, but unlike lower animals, he also has the inferior parietal lobule and inferior temporal region (see Fig. 6-1) where stable intermodal cortical connections can be formed. Most psychologists believe that language, concept formation, abstract reasoning, and the ability to draw logical conclusions, i.e., higher cortical functions, are unique to man. Sensory modality interrelationships which are believed to be the basis for higher cortical functions are probably formed in the secondary association areas. Geschwind (1965) has speculated that man has language because he can form stable sensory intermodal cortical associations; lower animals lack cortical intermodal connections and are capable of forming only sensory-limbic connections.

The anterior half of the brain is commonly known as the *motor half* and has, as one of its principal activities, the formulation and execution (praxis) of motor acts directed to the external world. The three related regions are the primary motor region (area 4); the secondary or premotor region (areas 6, 8, and

44), and the large, phylogenetically recent prefrontal region (areas 9, 10, 11, 45, 46) (see Fig. 6-2).

Area 4, the motor strip, is a somatotopically arranged (see Fig. 6-6) agranular cortex with Betz or giant pyramidal cells in the V layer (see Fig. 6-3). From this motor strip large fibers extend via the pyramidal tract to the motor neurons of the brainstem and spinal cord, which in turn innervate the skeletal muscles. The movements of muscle groups are developed in this area.

Areas 6, 8, and 44, the premotor association areas, are also agranular cortex but with a prominent III layer of pyramidal cells and without Betz cells (see Fig. 6-3). The premotor areas are intimately interconnected with the sensory association areas and through this relationship are able to carry out their principal function, which is formulation of complex motor movements. The only significant cortical connections of area 4—the motor strip—are with the premotor areas and with the primary somesthetic cortex. All these areas have rich subcortical connections which play a vital role in the formulation and modulation of motor activity.

The prefrontal region is mainly granular cortex and, like the secondary sensory association areas, is involved in the most highly integrated types of higher cortical activity. The functions of this area include goal-directed activity and intention but are not well understood.

Connecting the various parts of a hemisphere are long and short fiber systems called *fasciculi*. Connecting the two hemispheres are four commissures of which the largest is the corpus callosum (see Fig. 6-9). Injury to the brain which results in the disconnection of one part of the brain from another can produce striking functional disabilities. Studies of such disabilities have added significantly to the understanding of how the brain functions (Geschwind 1965).

Subcortical Organization

Although the cortical structures effect what is called higher cortical function, the subcortical structures also play a major role in both the transmission and integration of information.

The specific thalamic nuclei receive and send incoming afferent information to the primary receiving areas of the cortex. Other nuclei in the thalamus and brainstem form the reticular formation which is richly interconnected with the limbic system. These structures together probably form the coordination and executive mechanism in the brain for the control of memory, motivation, reinforcement, development of conditioned reflexes, elaboration of emotions, and other functions (Smythies 1967). Smythies also hypothesized that these subcortical structures, the reticular and limbic systems, and their circuits act as "programers" for the brain's computers, one set of computers being the cortical analyzers. According to Smythies these subcortical structures receive both the external and internal environmental input, respond to it in reflex fashion, and program behavior. They draw upon the specialized functions of the cortical analyzers and program the output through the efferent (output) pathways. These efferent pathways are the hypothalamus for internal output and the motor cortex and subcortical motor system for external output. The central structure is the reticular formation with its rich connections to the input and output systems (see Figs. 6-5 and 6-10).

The traditional view of nervous system organization has been a segmental one, ascending from the spinal cord to the cortex. New views emphasize a vertical organization likened to the form of a cylinder (Weiskrantz 1964). The core of the cylinder is the reticular formation with its extensive connections. Surrounding the reticular formation are centers concerned with vegetative functions (e.g., hypothalamus, amygdala) (see Fig. 6-10). Around these centers are a number of systems and circuits concerned with emotional behavior and the classification of environmental events as attractive or unattractive, pleasurable or painful (hippocampus, amygdala). The outer layer of the cylinder consists of neocortical circuits which perform complex analyses, synthesize incoming information, and program motor movements for the output system.

Memory is important in the synthetic-integrative processes and appears to occur in three stages: short-term memory, new learning (recent memory), and remote (old) memory. Newly arrived input is processed in the sensory cortex and can be held

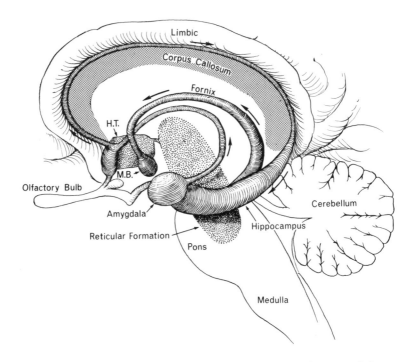

FIGURE 6-10.   *Representation of the limbic system and some of its con-*
nections. Limbic refers to the limbic lobe which has many component parts,
some of which are shown. M.B. = *mammillary body;* H.T. = *hypothalamus.*

at this level in the form of immediate memory, i.e., short-term
memory without storage as in the digit span test. Only a limited
amount can be held in immediate memory, and holding it depends upon continued attention. The continued attention
probably depends upon activity in the thalamic reticular formation which affects the cortex (Smythies 1967).

Unlike short-term memory, new learning or recent memory is
permanently stored in the neocortex, especially the temporal
cortex. The structures involved and the mechanism for this storage are not clear; it seems to be a widespread cortical function.
The hippocampus is necessary for passage of material into storage (recent memory) and has recently been recognized as necessary for both the learning and retrieval of new material, that is,
for the retention or storage and the recall of recent memory
(Symmonds 1966, Russell 1959). Bilateral failure of the hippocampal system or its related circuits, as seen in a patient with

Korsakoff's psychosis or in head injury, explains the ability to perform immediate memory tasks but inability to learn new material or to recall recently learned material. Such patients can, however, recall events or learning from the remote past.

The amygdala plays a role in memory related to emotions. Emotions appear capable of blocking learning as well as vividly imbedding events in memory. Most common emotional events are categorized in such basic terms as reward versus punishment or attractive versus unattractive. Many of the "pain" and "pleasure" centers identified by physiologists are located in the amygdala or in anatomically related temporal lobe and hypothalamic centers. The amygdala in conjunction with the hippocampus probably relates environmental information with emotional or visceral information, a basic factor in the development of conditioned reflex formation (Smythies 1966, 1967).

Interhemispheric Relations

Man has two similar but functionally asymmetrical cerebral hemispheres. The dominant (major) hemisphere, which is almost invariably on the left (Penfield and Roberts 1959), serves the function of verbal language. The other hemisphere is usually considered nondominant or minor, but there is some evidence that this hemisphere may be dominant for nonverbal functions such as spatial relationships and music appreciation. It would be misleading to imply that the two hemispheres are neatly divided in their functions. The specific functions of each hemisphere are not well understood and may vary from individual to individual. For purposes of this discussion it will be assumed that the functions of the two hemispheres are well divided.

The corpus callosum (see Fig. 6-9) connects the cortex of the two hemispheres and is the structure which interrelates the opposite association areas. For sensory information received from one-half of the body to be acted upon by the opposite half, there must be physiological transmission of this information across the corpus callosum from one hemisphere to the other. For example, if a blindfolded person wishes to match a coin in his left hand with a similar coin to be selected by his right hand, there must be interhemispheric transmission of the appropriate somesthetic information. It might be assumed that, since the dominant hemisphere (left) deals with verbal language, information must be transmitted from the left hemisphere to the right in order for the nondominant hemisphere (right) to respond to a verbal command, e.g., "Point the left index finger at the door." That this is so, and that the corpus callosum is the main pathway, was demonstrated by studies of an adult patient by Geschwind and Kaplan (1962). Lesions of the corpus callosum can split the brain and leave all (or, most commonly, part) of one hemisphere incapable of transmitting to or receiving appropriate information from the other hemisphere. In effect, one half of the brain is unaware of what the other half is doing.

Some humans may have a nondominant hemisphere that is capable of comprehending spoken or written language independent of the dominant hemisphere. Gazzangia and Sperry (1967) demonstrated this in their epileptic patients who had undergone division of the corpus callosum and the anterior and hippocampal commissures. In these patients the minor hemisphere could no longer express itself in writing or speech but could express itself nonverbally. For example, with vision and hearing occluded, the minor hemisphere could select an object with the left hand, match it, or show the proper use of it. When allowed to see the object and to hear, the patient could match the object with the printed or spoken word, the latter apparently limited to familiar object nouns. This would indicate that, in some humans, both hemispheres can comprehend spoken and written language, but the ability to express this verbally in writing or speaking is exclusively a function of the dominant hemisphere.

Sperry (1967) concluded that complete transection of the corpus callosum plus the anterior and hippocampal commissures in man demonstrates convincing evidence of two separate consciousnesses. Each half of the brain is able to perform tasks that are contradictory to what the other half is doing; one half can learn material independent of the other half.

The corpus callosum is necessary for one half of the brain to have access to many of the unique functions of the other half. More importantly, it may be primarily responsible for the brain asymmetry that exists. It may prevent bilateralization of learning and memory, especially in the case of language (Sperry 1967), making it complemental and supplemental in design rather than symmetrical.

Some of the learning failures in children may be related to lack of development of brain asymmetry or failure of communication between the two hemispheres (Gooddy and Reinhold 1961). This might, for example, explain why one child when blindfolded repeatedly elected to identify geometric shapes verbally and to place them in a formboard with his right hand, even if to do so he had to change the object from the left to the right hand.

SPECIFIC CORTICAL FUNCTION

From the moment incoming signals reach the sensory end organ (e.g., eye, ear, skin), a process of selection begins and continues at various subcortical levels of the nervous system. By the time the signals reach the primary receptive cortex or first cortical analyzer, certain levels of selection and even perception have occurred. The signals are then ready for the complex analysis and integration which is the function of the cortical analyzers.

One of the processes by which selection occurs is through the inhibition of nonessential signals. Input (ascending) signals from sensory nuclei or receptor cells at lower levels are monitored and nonessential signals are inhibited by descending signals. The distinction between an essential and a nonessential signal is in large part learned and is also culture dependent. That is, the developing brain learns to select and attend to those environmental stimuli which are most meaningful.

Many of the problems seen in children with neurological learning disabilities are related to the manner in which the nervous system handles sensory information, particularly from the three major sensory modalities, vision, audition, and somesthesis. How the nervous system receives and begins to process sensory information has already been discussed. In this section the cortical functions as they pertain to each major sensory modality and the activities of the frontal lobe will be discussed.

The Auditory Analyzer

The location of the primary receptive cortex of the auditory analyzer is designated as area 41 and part of 42 (see Fig. 6-2). This area contains the *transverse temporal gyri of Heschl.* It is so arranged somatotopically that the high tone frequencies are received medially and the low tones laterally (see Fig. 6-8).

The auditory association area is located in the superior temporal gyrus (area 22 and part of 42). From this area numerous projections via the arcuate (superior longitudinal) fasciculus (see Fig. 6-9) extend into the inferior premotor cortex (Broca's area 44) as well as areas 46 and 10. These projections connect the auditory analyzer to the motor areas dealing with synthesis of articulation.

Projections also extend from area 22 to other areas including 8, 18, and 19, which deal with vision, and to areas 21 and 37, the nonauditory temporal cortex which also relates to the limbic and visual analyzer systems.

The function of the cortical analyzers is the complex analysis and synthesis of stimuli, simpler analysis and synthesis having already occurred at subcortical levels. In the auditory system, intensity discrimination and tonal discrimination are accomplished subcortically with tonal discrimination being complete at the subcortical level (Whitfield 1967). The cortical level is concerned with the recognition of temporal patterns of sound (i.e., sequential patterns) and the direction of frequency change. The physiological mechanisms responsible for sound localization are still poorly understood.

Understanding the sounds of human speech is directly related to discrimination of temporal sound patterns and direction of frequency change. Speech sounds consist of a series of tones (vowels) and other sounds (consonants) which may merge with each other without interruption. If there are no discrete sounds which can be interpreted, the speech is as unintelligible as a foreign language (Luria 1966).

Distinct speech sounds are known as *phonemes* and they vary from language to language. Nondistinct sounds are called *variants.* The auditory analyzer in the developing brain is responsible for the child's learning to distinguish the phonemic signs of the language to which he is exposed. Selection of distinguishing speech sounds from the flow of speech, and the sequential analysis of these sounds, leads to the perception of speech. The brain cannot identify specifically each of the many stimuli to which it is exposed, so it uses the incoming signal to select the most probable identification from a limited number of possibilities (Whitfield 1967, Bruner 1957). Since these possibilities are based on past experience they are dependent on memory and retrieval. Whitfield (1967) has stated that "the amount of information necessary to identify a sound is comparatively small. For example, vowel sounds are characterized by the position of two or three formant frequencies. The location of these frequencies is constant for a particular vowel irrespective of the speaker."

Since the central nervous system seems to decide the identity of input signals such as speech sounds on the basis of probability determined by past experience, other input signals could trigger the same probability decision and lead to an erroneous identification. Errors suggestive of this are often seen in children with learning disorders. For example, a child may repeat the word *kite* as *night*, *frog* as *log* or *east* for *each*.

It is the direction of frequency change which is most important in the recognition of speech sounds. Examples of errors of this type are *free* for *three*, *cuff* for *cuss*, and *pet* for *pit*.

The participation of the motor analyzer dealing with articulation is another necessary component to the understanding of speech. Initially a child acquiring speech carries out auditory-articulatory analysis by saying or mouthing the words as he hears them. Only later can he hear speech without the active involvement of the articulatory analyzer. Even adults often use the articulatory analyzer when trying to read a difficult and unfamiliar word; that is, the word must be pronounced aloud in order to be identified.

Auditory-articulatory analysis directly involves the second auditory analyzer (the auditory association cortex) with the motor association cortex. This linkage is through the arcuate fasciculus (see Fig. 6-9). In addition the kinesthetic system contributes essential information.

Past experience is necessary for identification of input signals of speech sounds. This implies that the brain must recognize, discriminate, code, classify, store, and retrieve sounds. Auditory input is recognized and discriminated in the auditory cortex. Then, presumably in conjunction with the limbic system, the information is stored in the cerebral cortex and coded and classified. The storage cortex is most likely the nonauditory temporal cortex. The length of time the hippocampal retrieval mechanism is necessary is not clear. As new material reinforces old, learning becomes more "fixed" in the brain and more easily available. How much the clinical model of memory and retrieval (Smythies 1967, Benson and Geschwind 1967) relates to the acquisition of auditory language is as yet unknown. Presumably memory and retrieval mechanisms are not functioning properly in some children. As a result they are unable to retain a sequence of sounds within words or a sequence of words within sentences. Such memory disabilities may explain why some children cannot develop comprehension or expression of the spoken word and thus have learning disabilities.

As a child develops auditory capacities he initially learns to recognize and identify sounds, then to make sound discrimination. He then learns to identify a word as a synthesized whole. Later he develops the ability to isolate and analyze the components of the whole and place them in proper sequence (auditory analysis-synthesis). Simultaneously he develops auditory memory and the ability to reauditorize (Johnson and Myklebust 1967).

Difficulties in the development of the brain mechanisms responsible for auditory processes lead to problems in language development and in learning. An adult who receives an injury in his already-developed dominant auditory cortex will develop an aphasia; his acquired and mature skills of language formulation will be disrupted. The child with dysfunction in the same regions of the brain, however, poses a different and more complex problem. As he is in the process of acquiring language skills, the effects of the interference with the normal functioning of his brain mechanisms are more subtle (barring the more gross problem of childhood "aphasia"). Furthermore his brain is still in the process of rapid maturation and there is a continual opening up of new potentials. This can lead to subtle forms of compensation for a learning defect.

Many children with learning disabilities have auditory problems. In fact, it may be that auditory involvement is present in most if not all of these children (Zigmond 1969).

Disruption of the development of auditory learning in children may be seen clinically as errors in auditory discrimination, auditory analysis-synthesis, auditory sequential memory, reauditorization, articulation, or some combination of these. The child may have difficulty hearing the difference between such sounds as *f* and *v* or *a* and *e* and therefore may mishear and misarticulate words such as *fine* for *vine* or *land* for *lend*. He may have difficulty understanding that a word is made up of a series of sounds which must be ordered in the correct sequence. Failure to comprehend this may result in his mishearing or mispronouncing multisyllable words such as *spaghetti/pasghetti, animal/aminal, Methodist/Mesothistdist.** He may be unable to blend the sounds *r-u-g* together to form *rug* or realize that *rug* is made up of *r-u-g*. Failure to grasp this may result in a later inability to learn word attack skills in reading and oral and written spelling. A child may also either be unable to store what a sound or word "sounds like" or he may be able to store it but not retrieve it for use. Such a child may be able to recognize a letter visually but have difficulty learning its auditory counterpart, its sound; or he may be able to learn its sound but not recall it for use. The child who cannot recall a sound will recognize it if given choices or some other clue. Reauditorization problems may also affect expressive language and writing; a child may be unable to recall specific words, certain grammatical structures, or certain word orders. As a result, his speech may sound hesitant or contain abundant descriptions of words and use of such terms as *stuffs* and *whatchamacallits*. His written language may show the same kind of errors, for the child will write as he speaks.

As an individual's speech patterns become more stereotyped he relies less on auditory-articulatory analysis to correct his own speech. However, he is always dependent upon this analysis for the ability to write. Interference with a child's phonemic hear-

---

* Speech errors of a child must be examined carefully as they may be due to dysarthria, apraxia, or represent a developmental delay rather than being a result of disruption of the auditory-articulatory learning process.

ing can interfere with his word writing skills but leave intact the ability to copy (Luria 1966). A child may be unable to write a word or a sentence because he cannot first auditorily analyze whole words into their component parts, attach sounds to the visual letters, or remember or reauditorize the sound(s) of the letters within the word, or words within the sentence. His spelling may therefore not be phonetic, but a hodgepodge of letters which show little if any relationship to the sound of the word. His sentence formulation may show errors in grammar, word order, or word preciseness.

The Visual Analyzer

The primary receiving cortex of the visual system is the striate cortex (area 17), the *primary visual analyzer*. This cortex is somatotopically organized, with the macula and quadrants of the retina being represented in a characteristic fashion (see Fig. 6-7).

Immediately anterior to the striate cortex is the visual association cortex (areas 18 and 19), which is called the *secondary visual analyzer*. The main afferent projection is from area 17 to 18 to 19. There are important projections to the lateral and basal temporal cortex (areas 20 and 37) and to prefrontal cortex (area 8) via the superior longitudinal fasciculus. There are also interconnections with other sensory association areas, particularly area 19, with the immediately adjacent area 7 (somesthetic association cortex), as well as areas 39 and 40 (see Fig. 6-2).

While the auditory analyzer must organize incoming stimuli on a temporal basis, the visual analyzer must organize many stimuli spatially and simultaneously. The elegant work of Hubel and Wiesel (1962, 1965, 1968) has added greatly to our understanding of how this organization is accomplished. These investigators have demonstrated that the organization of visual cortex cells is in honeycomb-like columns. Each column acts as a functional unit and responds only to certain stimulus dimensions, such as retinal position, orientation of lines, stimulation of one or both retinae, and to directionality of movement. These many functional units spatially organize many simultaneous stimuli from the retina. Cortical processing of the visual message begins with cells of the striate cortex which are very specific for the particular stimulus position, shape, and orientation. Areas 18 and 19 enhance the stimulus specificity and, to a lesser degree, generalize certain aspects. Impairment of function in areas 18 and 19 results in intact elementary visual function but a disturbance in the development of complex visual differentiation.

The functions of the various sensory analyzers are influenced by other parts of the brain. Spinelli and Pribram (1966, 1967) demonstrated that the inferior temporal cortex (part of the visual association cortex) and the frontal association cortex of monkeys have efferent influences upon the primary visual cortex at both the cortical and subcortical levels. Their studies suggest that the influence of the frontal association cortex improves temporal resolution of visual stimuli. If this function is disturbed, each experimental task interferes with the next.

The feedback from the inferior temporal cortex influences the input system and seems to enhance discrimination and problem-solving ability. Disturbances in this area of cortex lead to deficiencies in searching and sampling alternatives. The result is an inability to identify objects visually, i.e., an agnosia (Spinelli and Pribram 1966). More recently there has been disagreement about Spinelli and Pribram's proposed mechanism of efferent inhibition (Schwartzkroin et al. 1969), but not about the necessity of inferior temporal cortex for normal visual discrimination.

The visual perception of an object requires an active visual examination of the object, a preliminary categorization, a search and identification of its essential cues, a visual integration of these cues, a correction of the initial conclusions, and a final evaluation of the information (Bruner 1957, Luria 1966). The categorizing, cue identification, and final evaluation depend upon past experience, i.e., memory.

Disturbed physiological function of the visual association cortex interferes with visual perception. This poor visual association cortex function may be a result of a local disturbance or interference with more remote influences such as those from the frontal lobe. These disturbances of visual perception in children lead to learning disabilities which include problems in visual discrimination, foreground-background differentiation, part-whole relationships, position in space, spatial relationships, re-visualization, and sequentialization.

Difficulty with temporal resolution of visual stimuli—for example, the inability of a child to perceive more than one object at a time—strongly suggests an interference with the influence of the frontal association cortex upon visual input. Such a child may become confused when presented with a picture containing several persons or objects. Because he can perceive only one object at a time and cannot shift his attention to another object, he attends to an isolated pictured object and fails to gain meaning from the total picture. (See section on prefrontal function.)

Efferent influence from visual association cortex on sensory input has been demonstrated for the visual system; a similar mechanism has been demonstrated for the auditory and somesthetic systems (Spinelli and Pribram 1966, Dewson et al. 1969).

Areas 18 and 19, the visual association cortex, not only are essential for the interpretation of visual impressions and their intermodal integration but, together with area 8, also are concerned with visual optic reflexes. These reflexes are essential for the voluntary and involuntary conjugate movements of the eyes, as in reading and the active visual examination of an object. Presence of eye-tracking problems in learning disability children has been noted by Kephart (1960), Barsch (1967), and Ayres (1965). Whether interference with the visual optic reflexes accounts for some of the eye-tracking problems seen in these children has not been proved. A more likely explanation is that the child fails to interpret the visual symbols accurately or to perceive the object and its parts correctly, and thus he does not learn to move his eye muscles in a meaningful, systematic way.

Lesions of the dominant visual associative areas cause difficulty with the visual recognition of objects. If the impairment is not complete, the patient may attempt to identify objects by selecting one visual cue; then, through the use of verbal logic, try to reach the correct conclusion. Such a patient might see a pencil as something long and guess that it is a toothbrush. Given the opportunity to feel the object or hear a familiar sound associated with it (e.g., a pencil scratching on paper), the patient may quickly identify it. He is able to use other, intact, sensory modalities for identification of tangible objects. A child with learning disabilities may show difficulty in visual recognition of objects and be able to use other intact sensory modalities to overcome his difficulty. Such a child might say that both the objects shown in Fig. 6-11 were "goggles." However, if given tweezers and a pair of goggles to touch and examine, he may quickly identify them correctly and then correctly name the pictures.

The identification of nontangible or abstract qualities and symbols such as colors and the letters of the alphabet poses a more difficult problem. These have only one sensory cue: visual. For verbal identification of colors or letters the visual input must arouse the appropriate auditory associations. In other words, verbal identification of a color can be made only through a visual-auditory association. Impairment in the ability to make this association will lead to a color-naming defect. This defect may be present in a person whose ability to match colors is intact. When a visual-auditory association defect occurs in a brain-injured adult, it is accompanied by difficulty in reading. Geschwind (1965, 1966) has related color-naming defects associated with alexia to a disconnection of the visual regions from the speech regions.

The reading difficulty of some children is due to impairment in the ability to identify abstract symbols or qualities. This difficulty may be related to subtle impairment in the visual associative areas. These children have difficulty associating the printed letters of the alphabet, which are abstract symbols, with the correct sounds. Improper visual cue identification may lead to the misperception of similar but different letters; this in turn leads

FIGURE 6-11. *Modified from L. Dunn,* Peabody Picture Vocabulary Test. *Circle Pines, Minn.: American Guidance Service, Inc., 1959.*

to improper auditory association, and then to the not-infrequent reversals these children show. A child who does not see the slight visual differences between *b* and *d* and therefore cannot associate the *b* sound with *b* and the *d* sound with *d* uses the letters interchangeably when reading or writing, as he does not visually perceive them as different. As Luria (1966) pointed out, when the structure of the visual act is incomplete, the subject cannot synthesize the various visual signals and convert them into an integral whole. His attempts to identify whole words are therefore impaired. Problems of this nature seen in learning disability children include confusions of words with similar whole configurations but with quite different internal detail. Misreading *shook* for *stuck* or *smile* for *small* are examples of errors of this kind.

As it is equally possible that the learning difficulty may be in the auditory association areas, one must analyze the kind of errors made by the child. If the learning problem is basically within the visual system rather than the auditory system, the child will show some or all of the following symptoms (Johnson and Myklebust 1967): (1) confusion of letters or words which appear similar in shape or configuration, (2) reversals of letters or words and inversions of letters, (3) failure to order letters in the right sequence within a word, (4) poor visual memory of objects, details, words, letters, and so on, and (5) poor visual analysis and synthesis.

The Somesthetic Analyzer

The primary somesthetic cortex has functional properties which are related to cytoarchitectural changes. Tactile sensation is primarily represented in areas 1 and 3 and deep sensation in area 2 (Powell and Mountcastle 1959a). Deep sensation, which is a sense of position and passive movement, is developed in a spatial and temporal pattern by the cortical cell columns. Information from deep sensation tells a person the direction of movement and position of his arms and legs as well as other body parts, which is essential for spatial orientation and proper motor activity. Tactile sensation, though perceived at subcortical levels, is developed as discriminatory sensation at the cortical level. The ability to localize tactile stimuli, to discriminate weights, to identify objects and qualities by touch (stereognosis), and to have a somatic sense of space (e.g., two-point discrimination and graphesthesia) are dependent on discriminatory sensation. Both deep and tactile sensation must be analyzed at a cortical level with simultaneous spatial representation. Ayres (1965), working with children with neurological dysfunction, noted somesthetic problems and devised tests for their detection. For example, she tests the child's ability to discriminate objects by touch without vision, to identify simultaneous stimuli to one or two fingers, and to identify designs drawn on the back.

The ability to manipulate an object properly requires—in addition to the adequate function of the somesthetic analyzer—an intimate link with the motor analyzers for the smooth movement of muscles. Feedback from the deep sensors (tendon organs and muscle spindles) is required for continuous monitoring of joint position, movement, and muscle tension.

The Sensorimotor Analyzer

The cortical mechanisms responsible for formulation and production of movement are the most complex of the analyzing and synthesizing mechanisms. These mechanisms bring into play information from all the other analyzers, i.e., the auditory, visual, tactile, and, in particular, the kinesthetic systems. In addition the ontogenetic development of voluntary movements is intimately linked with speech, the speech signals being used to help develop and refine voluntary movements in the child (Luria 1966).

Kinesthetic signals are the most important sensory information involved in motion. These afferent signals furnish the feedback from the joints and muscles which is necessary for the correct development and carrying through of a motor act. This feedback allows the brain to compare what is taking place with what was intended and to correct the movement as necessary. Visual, auditory, and tactile feedback are often involved in motor control, but not as constantly as kinesthesis.

The various afferent signals are brought together in the premotor areas. Here, in conjunction with subcortical structures, a temporal sequence of movements is formed which comprises a single "kinetic melody" (Luria 1966). This "melody" requires a continuing series of smoothly integrated excitatory and inhibitory messages sent to and received from muscles. The interrelationship of the organized afferent information and individual muscles apparently takes place in the motor strip (area 4) where there is somatotopic representation of muscle groups. Area 4 then provides part of the cortical outflow for efferent signals to the motor neurons of the brainstem and spinal cord.

The close functional relationship between the postcentral sensory region and the precentral motor region has led to the use of the term *sensorimotor cortex* (areas 1, 2, 3, 4). These regions constitute the sensorimotor analyzer, which overlaps the somesthetic and the motor analyzers. The somesthetic analyzer may, however, operate separately, as, for example, in tactile localization or two-point discrimination.

The motor analyzer with its rich connections relates spatial, kinesthetic, and language information to motor formulation and movement. The realization that a motor act is not just an efferent phenomenon but is highly dependent upon afferent information from all the major sensory modalities leads to the recognition that the entire brain is involved in movement. *This helps explain why most children with neurological learning disabilities have motor involvement, regardless of what part of the brain is involved.*

In brain-injured patients, impairment of the kinesthetic input to the motor analyzer may produce a gross defect in movement and even an "afferent paresis." In children with the more subtle problem of neurological learning disorders, many of their impaired motor functions may be due to the same disturbance, a kinesthetic-motor disorder. The kinesthetic-motor impairment is reflected in an inability to develop the smooth selection of individual movements needed to manipulate objects, for example, to tie shoelaces, to buckle a belt, or to manipulate small objects such as puzzle pieces. This may be one of the reasons for the so-called small-muscle incoordination and the choreiform-like movements of the fingers of children with neurological learning disabilities.

If the kinesthetic-motor impairment involves speech mechanisms, there will also be difficulty with speech. Luria (1966) states that this impairment affects the selection of individual lingual-dental and labial sounds. Since speech plays a vital role in the development of the neural circuits for reading and writing, impaired kinesthetic analysis and synthesis may well be an underlying cause in the learning problems of some children. A kinesthetic-motor component may also be present in the auditory-articulatory analysis required to read or write. As a result, reading or spelling aloud may be more difficult than silent reading, or written spelling, because of the added necessity to use auditory-articulatory and kinesthetic feedback mechanisms.

Impairment in the premotor areas disturbs the "kinetic melody." Difficulty in carrying out the series of motor acts needed for smooth movements may lead to repetition of movement or failure to inhibit it, i.e., motor perseveration. Examples of this problem are difficulties in copying, tapping rhythmic patterns, alternately touching fingers, or drawing. The child with disturbance of "kinetic melody" may continue tracing over a line or circle long after he has drawn it once. The effects of kinesthetic-motor impairment on speech may even play a role in stuttering.

Prefrontal Function

The prefrontal region is phylogenetically and ontogenetically the most recent part of the brain. It is the last to myelinate and functionally the most difficult to understand. The outer convexity (9, 10, 45, 46 in Fig. 6-2) connected to many parts of the cortex, is related to the motor analyzer and apparently deals primarily with information from the external world. The mediobasal or orbital region (areas 11, 12, 32, 47), on the other hand, is related to the limbic system and hypothalamus and deals with the olfactory sense and information from the internal environment. Luria (1966) gives reasons to believe that the prefrontal regions are responsible for synthesizing the information from the external and internal environments, which is "the means whereby the behavior of the organism is regulated in conformity with the effect produced by its actions."

One of the possible mechanisms by which the frontal-limbic

system influences other parts of the brain has already been mentioned, that is, by inhibiting afferent inhibitory processes to the auditory and visual input systems (Spinelli and Pribram 1967). This opposes the effect of the inferior temporal association cortex which, through efferent fibers, may enhance afferent inhibitory processes influencing auditory and visual input. These two mechanisms demonstrate at least one method by which the brain may control its own input. Experimental injury to the frontal lobe mechanism impairs temporal resolution of auditory and visual inputs. Each experimental trial interferes with the next and is interfered with by its predecessor. The results of these experiments help to clarify the frontal-limbic system's importance in the programing of sequential behavior responses.

Spinelli and Pribram (1966) speculated that the visual association cortex influences the primary visual cortex and lateral geniculate nucleus by slowing the recovery rate of the nerve cells from a stimulus. Repeated input from the same stimulus must, therefore, find a different population of receptive cells. This can be interpreted as increasing the complexity of the visual input, producing more uncertainty and leading to greater attention to alternatives. As mentioned above, injury to the visual association cortex leads to simplification of the input processing and results in an agnosia for external signals.

The prefrontal association cortex probably influences visual input in the opposite way, i.e., by inhibiting the afferent inhibitory process, which leads to an increased recovery rate of the neurons in the primary visual cortex. One result of this influence is the organization and improvement of the temporal resolution of the input code by slowing the reaction to a novel stimulus and allowing spacing for orientation before another novel occurrence affects the system. The result may be either learning the discrimination or being alerted to its presence (Pribram 1969, Spinelli and Pribram 1967).

Injury to the prefrontal system may lead to perseveration or stimulus binding, in which each task interferes with the next and is interfered with by the previous task. Experimentally, Pribram and Tubbs (1967) demonstrated that the prefrontal cortex leads to temporal resolution of input by parsing the stream of stimuli. An example of such parsing is *onmesatabee,* or *on me sat a bee*. These investigators showed that monkeys with the prefrontal cortex removed could not learn the task of finding a peanut hidden alternately under the right and then the left of two identical cups unless there was a 15-second delay between pairs of right-left presentations. These trials indicated that environmental sequential organization can help substitute for the lack of prefrontal cortical function in experimental animals.

Voluntary movement and activity are more highly developed in man than in lower animals because of man's speech. The relationship of speech to voluntary movement and activity begins early in life. Speech helps define the motor activity by indicating the objective toward which the action is directed and formulating a plan of action (Luria 1966). When frontal lobe impairment interferes with the speech-defining mechanism, pathological inertia and difficulty with sequencing will impair motor activities. The inertia manifests itself as an inability to shift motor activities and as perseveration of voluntary movements. In activities requiring sequencing, the initial actions may interfere with the later ones. The difficulty in relating speech to voluntary movements leads to disordered motor function, which may be apraxic (see Geschwind 1965, Part II, for a full discussion of apraxia).

Inability (or impairment) in relating verbal commands to motor activities may be present if a child has difficulty in writing or drawing to command, in tapping rhythms, or in imitating movements and gestures. Problems such as these are seen in children with neurological learning difficulties. For example, some children can hop on the playground but not to a verbal command, some cannot learn gestures to finger plays or nursery songs, others cannot pretend the use of an object, or copy or draw when given verbal instructions. These children may also be unable to learn motor rhythms or movements to songs, yet show good rhythm in free play activities.

Luria (1966) states that frontal lobe involvement produces impairment of speech connections needed in the development of voluntary motor activity and also impairment of the analysis of kinesthetic feedback.

Impairment of voluntary motor functions is also present in eye movements, with a disturbance in active scanning movements of the eyes as well as inertia of gaze. Children with this type of impairment fail to examine more than a small part of a picture or object before drawing conclusions regarding it. A child whose visual investigation is insufficient will have difficulty in interpreting thematic pictures or a connected series of pictures. Such a child fixates his gaze on one aspect of the picture, failing to survey the picture as a whole in order to gain meaning from it.

Spatial Orientation

The brain mechanisms underlying spatial orientation are complex and not well understood. As a result this discussion will be limited in scope and will of necessity align clinical and experimental findings only in a loose manner.

Spatial orientation depends upon bodily awareness as well as environmental orientation. This division into personal and extrapersonal space is seen as clinically valid, and patients may have impairment in personal or extrapersonal spatial orientation or both. The work of Semmes et al. (1963) on stable brain-injured patients has helped to clarify the problem of underlying neural correlates. These investigators found that both personal and extrapersonal spatial orientation have common and independent neural correlates. Their experiments showed that injury in the posterior dominant hemisphere impaired both forms of orientation. Injury in the anterior hemispheres, especially the left, tended to impair personal but not extrapersonal spatial orientation, while right posterior injuries did the opposite. They were also able to demonstrate that spatial orientation in adults was most dependent upon somesthetic function, with vision not playing a significant role. Extrapersonal spatial disorientation seldom occurred without somesthetic involvement. Personal spatial disorientation from anterior lesions seemed to be related to difficulty in shifting from one frame of reference to another in order to maintain correct right-left orientation.

The somesthetic system collects information from both the external and the internal environments, in contrast to the visual and auditory systems which collect information only from the external environment. The somesthetic cortex, together with the mediobasal cortex of the frontal lobes (see earlier section Prefrontal Function), is aware of the internal environment of the organism and can develop a "neuronal model" (Pribram 1969) of this environment. This internal environment is constant and stable compared to the external environment; Pribram (1969) has suggested that this stable base is necessary for new external events to be integrated into the life of the organism. Teuber (1964) speculates that the organism uses its own sensory inputs to provide a continuous distinction between environmental movement related to body movement and actual movement of environmental objects.

Spatial disorientation due to impairment of frontal lobe function may be manifested in a variety of ways. Teuber (1964) characterized four problems related to frontal lobe injury, all of which can be related to spatial organization: a visual searching deficit, difficulty in compensating for a visuopostural conflict, problems with perspective reversals (e.g., the Necker cube, Fig. 6-12), and personal spatial disorientation.

Semmes et al. (1963) found that extrapersonal disorientation was related to a pathological inattention to background characteristics. The patients these investigators described would ignore environmental background features necessary to their successful completion of a task. Problems similar to this are seen in children with neurological learning disabilities, e.g., they appear to be inattentive to their distance from an object. Such children, failing to be aware of their body placement in relationship to objects in their environment, are the clumsy ones who trip over chairs, run into doorways, or back into furniture.

The visual system plays an essential role in the early develop-

FIGURE 6-12. *Necker cube.*

ment of spatial orientation. Because of the complexity of this subject, it will not be covered in this chapter.

CONCLUSIONS

There can be little doubt that neurological learning disabilities will be well understood only when brain development and function are better understood. An attempt has been made in this chapter to provide a neurological base for the types of learning disabilities seen in children. Many areas were not fully explored; some, such as developmental factors, were only mentioned. Nonetheless, what has been said places the phylogenetically most recent areas of the brain into the limelight as probably the areas of greatest inefficiency of brain function in children with learning disabilities. These areas, the prefrontal, inferior parietal, and inferior temporal cortexes, are the cortical areas that tie brain function together.

Careful study of individual cases, each uniquely different, will help us to understand learning disabilities more clearly. In addition it will add greatly to our knowledge of how the brain "learns." This knowledge should provide a basis for a more intelligent approach not only toward education, but also toward many social problems.

REFERENCES

Ayres, A. J.   Patterns of perceptual-motor dysfunction in children: A factor analytic study. *Perceptual and Motor Skills* 20:335, 1965.

Barsch, R. H.   *Achieving Perceptual-motor Efficiency: A Space Oriented Approach to Learning*. Seattle: Special Child Publications, 1967.

Benson, D. F., and Geschwind, N.   Shrinking retrograde amnesia. *Journal of Neurology, Neurosurgery and Psychiatry* 30:539, 1967.

Brodmann, K.   *Vergleichende Lokalisationslehre der Grosshirnrinde in ihren prinzipien Dargestellt auf Grund des Zellenbaues*. Leipzig: Barth, 1909.

Bruner, J. S.   On perceptual readiness. *Psychological Review* 64:123, 1957.

Dewson, J., Pribram, K., and Lynch, J. Effects of ablations of temporal cortex upon speech sound discrimination in the monkey. *Experimental Neurology* 24:579, 1969.

Flechsig, P. Developmental (myelogenetic) localization of the cerebral cortex in the human subject. *Lancet* 2:1027, 1901.

Gazzaniga, M. D., and Sperry, R. W. Language after section of the cerebral commissures. *Brain* 90:131, 1967.

Geschwind, N. The paradoxical position of Kurt Goldstein in the history of aphasia. *Cortex* 1:214, 1964.

Geschwind, N. Disconnexion syndromes in animals and man. Part I. *Brain* 88:237, 1965. Part II. *Brain* 88:585, 1965.

Geschwind, N. Color-naming defects in association with alexia. *Archives of Neurology* (Chicago) 15:137, 1966.

Geschwind, N., and Kaplan, E. A human cerebral deconnection syndrome. *Neurology* 12:675, 1962.

Gooddy, W., and Reinhold, M. Congenital dyslexia and asymmetry of cerebral function. *Brain* 84:231, 1961.

Guilford, J. P. *The Nature of Human Intelligence*. New York: McGraw-Hill, 1967.

Hubel, D. H., and Wiesel, T. N. Receptive fields, binocular interaction and functional architecture in the cat's visual cortex. *Journal of Physiology* (London) 195:215, 1962.

Hubel, D. H., and Wiesel, T. N. Receptive fields and functional architecture in two nonstriate visual areas (18 and 19) of the cat. *Journal of Neurophysiology* 28:229, 1965.

Hubel, D. H., and Wiesel, T. N. Receptive fields and functional architecture of monkey striate cortex. *Journal of Physiology* (London) 195:215, 1968.

Johnson, D. J., and Myklebust, H. R. *Learning Disabilities: Educational Principles and Practices*. New York: Grune & Stratton, 1967.

Jones, E. G., and Powell, T. P. S. Connexions of the somatic sensory cortex of the rhesus monkey: I. Ipsilateral cortical connexions. *Brain* 92:477, 1969.

Kephart, N. C. *The Slow Learner in the Classroom*. Columbus, O.: Merrill, 1960.

Kleist, K. Cited in A. R. Luria, *Higher Cortical Functions in Man*. New York: Basic Books, 1966.

Lashley, K. S. *Brain Mechanisms and Intelligence*. Chicago: University of Chicago Press, 1929.

Luria, A. R. *Higher Cortical Functions in Man*. New York: Basic Books, 1966.

Luria, A. R. *Human Brain and Psychological Processes*. New York: Harper & Row, 1966(a).

Myers, R. E. Cerebral Connectionism and Brain Function. In

C. Millikan and F. Darley (Eds.), *Brain Mechanisms Underlying Speech and Language*. New York: Grune & Stratton, 1967. Pp. 61–72.

Peele, T. *The Neuroanatomic Basis for Clinical Neurology* (2d ed.). New York: McGraw-Hill, 1961.

Penfield, W., and Roberts, L. *Speech and Brain Mechanisms*. Princeton, N.J.: Princeton University Press, 1959.

Powell, T., and Mountcastle, V. The cytoarchitecture of the post-central gyrus of monkey *Macaca mulatta*. *Bulletin of the Johns Hopkins Hospital* 105:108, 1959.

Powell, T., and Mountcastle, V. Some aspects of the functional organization of the cortex of postcentral gyrus of the monkey. *Bulletin of the Johns Hopkins Hospital* 105:133, 1959(a).

Pribram, K. Neural servosystems and the structure of personality. *Journal of Nervous and Mental Disease* 149:30, 1969.

Pribram, K. The primate frontal cortex. *Neuropsychologia* 7:259, 1969(a).

Pribram, K., and Tubbs, W. E. Short term memory, parsing and the primate frontal cortex. *Science* 156:1765, 1967.

Quadfasel, F. A., and Goodglass, H. Specific reading disability and other specific disabilities. *Journal of Learning Disabilities* 1:36, 1968.

Ruch, T., and Patton, H. *Physiology and Biophysics*. Philadelphia: Saunders, 1965.

Russell, W. R. *Brain—Memory—Learning*. London: Oxford University Press, 1959.

Schuell, H., Jenkins, J., and Jimenez-Pabon, E. *Aphasia in Adults*. New York: Harper & Row, 1964.

Schwartzkroin, P. A., Cowey, A., and Gross, C. G. A test of an "Efferent Model" of the function of inferotemporal cortex in visual discrimination. *Electroencephalography and Clinical Neurophysiology* 27:594, 1969.

Semmes, J., Weinstein, S., Ghent, L., and Teuber, H-L. Correlates of impaired orientation in personal and extrapersonal space. *Brain* 86:747, 1963.

Smythies, J. R. *The Neurological Foundations of Psychiatry*. New York: Academic Press, 1966.

Smythies, J. R. Brain mechanisms and behavior. *Brain* 90:697, 1967.

Sperry, R. W. Split Brain Approach to Learning Problems. In G. C. Quarton, T. Melnechuk, and F. O. Schmitt (Eds.), *The Neurosciences*. New York: Rockefeller University Press, 1967.

Spinelli, D. N., and Pribram, K. H. Changes in visual recovery functions produced by temporal lobe stimulation in monkeys. *Electroencephalography and Clinical Neurophysiology* 20:44, 1966.

Spinelli, D. N., and Pribram, K. H.   Changes in visual recovery functions and unit activity produced by frontal and temporal cortex stimulation. *Electroencephalography and Clinical Neurophysiology* 22:143, 1967.

Symmonds, C.   Disorders of memory. *Brain* 89:625, 1966.

Teuber, H-L.   The Riddle of Frontal Lobe Function in Man. In J. M. Warren and K. Akert (Eds.), *The Frontal Granular Cortex and Behavior*. New York: McGraw-Hill, 1964. Pp. 410–444.

Weiskrantz, L.   Neurological studies and animal behavior. *British Medical Bulletin* 20:49, 1964.

Whitfield, I. C.   *The Auditory Pathways*. Baltimore: Williams & Wilkins, 1967.

Zigmond, N. K.   Auditory Processes in Children with Learning Disabilities. In L. Tarnopol (Ed.), *Learning Disabilities*. Springfield, Ill.: Thomas, 1969.

7 Drugs in the Management of Children with Learning Disabilities

C. KEITH CONNERS

DRUGS FOR IMPROVING behavior and learning in children have been available since the 1930's. Much evidence has accumulated that these agents can significantly add to the management of a wide variety of children, provided drug treatment is done with proper diagnosis, careful follow-up, and integration of drug therapy with educational, psychiatric, and pediatric care.

However, the use of pharmacological agents with children for purposes of improving their learning or behavior is still controversial. In 1962 Grant reviewed much of the early literature in the field and generally found it lacking in scientific rigor. Most of the studies did not have placebo controls. When such controls are used they may show as much as 60 percent improvement due to placebo. Grant (1962) noted a number of other methodological flaws in drug research with children, such as inadequate statistical analyses, nonblind ratings, lack of objective indices of improvement, and other factors of scientific control.

Barbara Fish (1968) stated, "Whether drugs can improve learning and intellectual functioning, and, if so, in which types of children is still to be determined." She adds, however, "If appropriate drugs are chosen they can control symptoms that do not respond readily to other measures." In another paper (1968a) she noted that of the 159 studies in child psychopharmacology published in English prior to 1958, only 33 contained "some aspect of experimental design." This conclusion is similar to that reached by Freeman (1966) who reviewed drug studies on learning in children over the previous thirty years. He commented,

The writer maintains that anyone reading the large number of preliminary, uncontrolled, positive reports and then surveying the status of most of these drugs several years later will be dramatically convinced that the "scientific" and "objective" use of these agents has a long way to go. He will find that perhaps the majority of drugs that were initially reported to have few, if any, side-effects were later found to have serious ones, and that a substantial proportion of them have been withdrawn as dangerous. . . . Until better longitudinal studies of children with and without different handicaps are available and more meaningful diagnostic schemes are developed, it remains difficult to draw firm conclusions about the influence of drugs on learning and behavior.

This generally negative attitude of critical reviewers is not shared by other active workers in the field who take a more "clinical" approach. Eveloff (1966) reviewed research with children in the prior five years and found a number of agents to be useful in a wide variety of disorders, from severe mental impairment to mild behavior disorders. The careful review by Millichap and Fowler (1967) found that although there were relatively few studies that met the criteria of scientific acceptability, some drugs consistently produced a high proportion of improvement. Their survey results are shown in Table 7-1.

Even in adult studies where the issues involved in drug assessment are presumably less complex, there is disagreement regarding the action of drugs on behavior. Baker (1968), for example, found that few if any objective measures of drug effect were found in the literature, while DiMascio, Brown, and Kline (in press) reported numerous effects of drugs on cognitive, perceptual, emotional, motor, and other tests.

Drug research with children presents several difficulties not found in work with adults and shares the difficulties of experimentation found in drug research of any kind. The research is always within a clinical treatment context, and therefore some variations of experimental designs may be unfeasible. It is difficult to control by prior selection of cases the heterogeneity of the diagnostic characteristics of the children studied. This often leads to either very small numbers in the sample, or treatment groups in which the diagnostic variance among the children is very large. Control over heterogeneity of samples by matching subjects may be impossible since the relevant parameters for matching may not be known, and prior measures on which patients can be matched may be unobtainable. Unlike the situation with adults, the treatment of children always involves the immediate family, and usually the school as well. There are many other factors that influence research with children, and these must be understood and given careful attention in the evaluation of drug efficacy. These factors may be conveniently discussed in terms of organismic variables, independent variables, dependent variables, and general issues of experimental design.

ORGANISMIC VARIABLES

Organismic variables refers to determinants of behavior that are largely "internal" characteristics, such as the individual's temperament, genetic endowment, physical makeup, developmental status, brain function, and sensory and motor development. These are variables that must be *inferred* from the relations between stimulus and response characteristics in order to understand the behavior in question adequately. In other words these are factors that may be required in an explanatory schema that cannot be reduced to either stimulus inputs or response characteristics.

TABLE 7-1.1 *Trials of Drugs in Behavior Disorders of Childhood*

Author	Year	No. of Patients	Daily Dose (mg)	Weeks of Trial	Double-Blind	Placebo Control	Objective Tests	Improved No.	%	Worse No.	%	Side Effects No.	%
					Methods of Trial			**Results**				**Side Effects**	
								Improved		Worse			
METHYLPHENIDATE													
Lytton & Knobel	1958	20	15–200	8–20	−	−	−	15	75	0	...	3	15
Knobel	1959	31	60–80	...	−	−	−	27	87	0	...	7	22
Knobel	1962	150	40–80	32	−	−	−	135	90	0	...	occasional	...
Conners & Eisenberg	1963	32	20–60	10 days	+	+	+	(+)	...	...	...	22	70
Nichamin & Comly	1964	100	>5–10	26–208	−	−	−	70 (approx.)	...	...	...	15 (approx.)	...
Millichap & Boldrey	1967	4	0.2–0.5 mg/kg	1 day	−	+	+	...	...	(+)	...	0	...
Totals		337						279	83	4	1	47	14
AMPHETAMINES													
Bradley	1937	30	10–20 (B)	1	−	−	−	15	50	1	3	+	...
Bradley	1950	275	10–40 (B)	1–	−	−	−	201	73	30	11	28	10
Bradley	1950	113	5–30	1–	−	−	−	69	61	18	16	6	5
Pasamanick	1951	10	20–35	1–7	−	−	−	4	40	3	30	10	100
Ingram	1956	9	10–30	...	−	−	−	4	44	...	...	...	...

Study	Year	No. of patients	Dosage (mg)	Duration									
Eisenberg et al.	1963	14	5–40	10	+	+	+	(+)	...	...	...	...	+
Zrull et al.	1963	16	10	2	+	+	−	9	57[a]	2	13	...	...
Burks	1964	43	...(B)[b]	...	−	−	−	43	100	0	...	...	...
Nichamin & Comly	1964	100	>2.5–5	26–208	−	−	−	70 (approx.)	...	...	...	...	15 (approx.)
Totals		610						415	69	54	11	59	...
DEANOL													
Oettinger	1958	125	10–200	4–36	−	−	+	84	67	18	14	11	...
Geller	1960	25	100	12	+	+	−	22	88	0	...	0	...
LaVeck et al.	1961	25	75–150	13	+	+	−	0[c]	...	3[c]	12	0	...
Kugel & Alexander	1963	42	100	12	+	+	+	0	...	0	...	0	...
Tapia	1965	12	50–300	8–12	+	+	+	0	...	0	...	1	8
Knobel et al.	1966	10	600–1,000	...	−	+	−	8	80	0	...	2	20
Totals		239						114	47	21	9	17	7
CHLORDIAZEPOXIDE													
Pilkington	1961	6	40–60	8	−	−	−	5	83	1	17	0	...
Peterman & Thomas	1962	38	0.25 mg/kg	72	−	−	−	23	60	0	...	rare	...
Vann	1962	47	5–60	1–8	−	−	−	24	51	0	...	7	15
Zrull et al.	1963	16	20	2	+	+	+	9	54[a]	2	17[a]	17[a]	...

(B) = Benzedrine, remainder Dexedrine; ...(B) = Benzedrine used but no dosage given; + = presence of condition; − = absence of condition; (+) = statistical group evaluation; † = some standard psychological tests, otherwise subjective; [a] results based on total behavior-ratings; [b] drug minus placebo effects; [c] dose larger than usually advised.

TABLE 7-1.1—*Continued*

Author	Year	No. of Patients	Daily Dose (mg)	Weeks of Trial	Methods of Trial			Results				Side Effects	
					Double-Blind	Placebo Control	Objective Tests	Improved		Worse			
								No.	%	No.	%	No.	%
Kraft et al.	1965	130	30–130	var.	−	−	−	82	63	37	28	36	28
Totals		237						143	60	40	17	43	18
MISCELLANEOUS TRANQUILIZERS													
Craft Atarax, Vistaril	1957	13	500[b]	4	+	+	−	0	...	0	...	0	...
Segal & Tansley Atarax, Vistaril	1957	16	20	6	+	+	−	12	75	0	...	...	...
Zier Miltown, Equanil	1959	25	0.6–2.4 gm.	4–32	−	−	−	17	68	1	4	10	40
LaVeck et al. Prolixin	1961	24	0.5–7.5[c]	12	+	+	−	5	21	0	...	4	16
Pilkington Taractan	1961	7	30–60	8	−	−	−	6	86	0	...	0	...
Oettinger Taractan	1962	23	25–200	2–21	−	−	−	10	43	...	...	6	26
Schulman & Clarinda Sparine	1964	6	40–160	8	+	+	+	0	...	0	...	...	...

Study / Drug	Year	N	Dosage	Duration				n	%	n	%	n	%
Millichap Librium analogue (RO5-4556)	1967	7	0.3–0.8 mg/kg	1 day– 7 weeks	–	+	+	6	86	0	...	0	...
ANTICONVULSANTS													
Pasamanick Phenobarbital	1951	6	40–200	4–6	–	–	–	2	33	2	33	0	...
Ingram Phenobarbital	1956	14	30	...	–	–	–	2	14	8	57	...	...
Millichap & Boldrey Phenobarbital	1967	5	2.5 mg/kg	1 day	–	+	+	2	40	3	60	0	...
Pasamanick Dilantin	1951	21	50–600	2–10	–	–	–	1	5	4	20	7	33
Ingram Dilantin	1956	7	...	...	–	–	–	2	28	1	14	...	...
Ingram Mysoline	1956	10	250	<36	–	–	–	7	70	0	...	...	...
Totals		63						16	25	18	28		

(B) = Benzedrine, remainder Dexedrine; ‥(B) = Benzedrine used but no dosage given; + = presence of condition; — = absence of condition; (+) = statistical group evaluation; † = some standard psychological tests, otherwise subjective; [a] results based on total behavior-ratings; [b] drug minus placebo effects; [c] dose larger than usually advised.

TABLE 7-1.1—*Continued*

Author	Year	No. of Patients	Daily Dose (mg)	Weeks of Trial	Methods of Trial			Results				Side Effects	
					Double-Blind	Placebo Control	Objective Tests	Improved		Worse			
								No.	%	No.	%	No.	%
CHLORPROMAZINE													
Freed & Peifer	1956	25	10–250	16–64	−	+	+	16	64	0	...	7	27
Hunt et al.	1956	23	75–300	4	+	+	−	17	74	2	9	8	35
Johnston & Martin	1957	27	100–300	24	−	−	−	13	54	0	...	0	...
Rowley et al.	1959	54	30–800 (50)	var.	−	−	−	31	57	5	9	13	24
Werry et al.	1966	24	106	8	+	+	−	7	31	0	...	10	42b
Totals		153						84	55	7	4	38	25
RESERPINE													
Johnston & Martin	1957	60	1–3	24	−	−	−	26	43	0	...	0	...
Timberlake et al.	1957	45	1	8	+	+	−	31	69	0	...	+	...
Graham et al.	1958	30	1	8–32	+	+	+	0	...	0	...	...	...
Rosenblum et al.	1958	30	1	16	+	+	+	0	...	0	...	2	...
Totals		165						57	34	0	...	2+	1

(B) = Benzedrine, remainder Dexedrine; . . . (B) = Benzedrine used but no dosage given; − = absence of condition; (+) = statistical group evaluation; † = presence of condition; + = some standard psychological tests, otherwise subjective; a results based on total behavior-ratings; b drug minus placebo effects; c dose larger than usually advised.
SOURCE: Modified from Millichap and Fowler (1967).

TABLE 7-1.2. *Drug Selection in Treatment of Hyperkinetic Behavior in Childhood*

Name of Drug[a]		Preparations (mg)	Average Dose Range[b] (mg/day)	Total Patients Tested	Patients Improved (%)	Patients with Side Effects (%)
Generic	Trade					
Methylphenidate	Ritalin	Tabs. 5, 10, 20	5–60	337	83	14
Amphetamine	Dexedrine	Tabs. 5	5–30	610	69	12
Chlordiazepoxide	Librium	Caps. or tabs. 5, 10, 25	5–30	237	60	18
Chlorpromazine	Thorazine	Tabs. 10, 25, 50, 100	10–50	153	55	25
Deanol	Deaner	Tabs. 25, 100	50–150	239	47	7
Reserpine	Serpasil, var.	Tabs. 0.1, 0.5, 1.0	0.25–0.5	165	34	> 1
Totals				1,741	62	12

[a] For this table, drugs are listed in order of choice according to efficacy and toxicity.
[b] Larger doses sometimes employed (see Table 7–1.1).
SOURCE: Modified from Millichap and Fowler (1967).

Cerebral Function

As Laufer (1967) has said, "There are many possible variations. The symptom picture in a given child is the final result of the organically based tendency toward a deviation of function and the way the child adapts to and compensates for this. The latter, in turn, is a composite of the child's ego strength, coping mechanisms, and state of child-parent equilibrium." It is therefore hazardous to infer that a child has "cerebral dysfunction" from the symptom picture alone, or to infer anything regarding etiology from a symptom pattern suggestive of organic involvement (Conners 1967).

TABLE 7-2. *Syndromes of Cerebral Dysfunction*

Area	Clinical Manifestations
Neuromotor	Cerebral palsy
Neurosensory	Central blindness, deafness, anesthesia
Consciousness	Epilepsy
Communication	Dysphasias, aphasias
Intellectual	Mental retardation
Perception, association, conceptualization, expression	Specific learning disabilities
Object relations	Some forms or components of psychoses of childhood
Impulse control, motility	Hyperkinetic impulse disorder

SOURCE: Laufer (1967). (Copyright © 1967, The Williams & Wilkins Co., Baltimore, Md., U.S.A.) Reproduced with permission.

Some of the common syndromes of cerebral dysfunction were summarized by Laufer (1967) (see Table 7-2). All these syndromes may be thought of as varying in severity from mild to gross impairments, and it is usually the milder forms that pose diagnostic problems. Moreover, the syndromes frequently overlap, so that they are best thought of as flexible class names of related phenomena rather than fixed classes each with its own differentiae. The classification of behavior into such syndromes is somewhat arbitrary and primarily of heuristic value to stimulate research rather than of predictive value in drug studies.

However, most clinicians would assert that these classifications, including the dimension of severity, are useful in predicting therapeutic response to drugs.

Very little objective evidence exists, however, to indicate to what extent variations in these syndromes have an effect on drug treatment. In a study of hyperactive children, half of whom had clearly "organic" histories, and half of whom were nonorganic, we found that on *some* measures of drug effect the organic children improved more; on other measures both groups improved more than those showing a placebo effect (Epstein et al. 1968). Conrad (1967) categorized patients on the basis of case history material and found that "organic" children showed a more favorable response to stimulant drug therapy, particularly if they were young and their family relations were good. Others have also claimed that "organic impairment" has important effects on the outcome of drug therapy, but usually it has been unclear what central nervous system states were being referred to, and objective data to support the contentions were usually flimsy or nonexistent.

A more useful way to interpret drug effects and to provide a rational heuristic approach to research on children is to examine the role of organismic variables or functions of general relevance to behavior. Irwin suggested the following:

A major problem in drug assessment or evaluation is what to measure. One can literally list hundreds of facets of behavior of interest, but, pragmatically, one must reduce them to some manageable quantity. This is best achieved, I feel, by attention to those primary or elemental building blocks of behavior ("target functions") that in reality express the physiologic and psychosocial state of the organism . . . e.g., the levels of wakefulness, behavioral arousal, activity and biosocial drives, endurance, set (attitude or expectations), information processing, responsiveness to stimuli, patterns of affective response, and physiologic functioning.*

According to this approach, some understanding of the child's level of arousal (both central and behavioral), physiological activation, activity level, and other such parameters should be

* Reprinted from the *American Journal of Psychiatry*, vol. 124 (February Suppl.), pp. 1–19, 1968. Copyright 1968, the American Psychiatric Association.

understood in order to determine what effects various drugs may have on behavior. Irwin classified the major drug effects of therapeutic relevance as shown in Table 7-3.

TABLE 7-3.   *Major Drug Effects of Therapeutic Relevance*

Psychomotor Stimulants (Amphetamine-like)	Antidepressants (Imipramine-like)

Greatly increase
  arousal—excitability
  wakefulness
  activity drive
  responses to stimuli
  active avoidance—escape
  fighting behavior
  inhibitory control
	Slightly reduce
	  arousal—excitability
	  discouragement, apathy
	Slightly increase
	  responses to stimuli
	  struggle—escape
	  defensive fighting

Major Tranquilizers (Chlorpromazine-like)	*Narcotics (Morphine-like)*

Greatly reduce
  arousal—excitability
  activity drive
  responses to stimuli
  active avoidance—escape
  fighting behavior
	Greatly reduce
	  arousal—excitability
	  activity drive
	  biosocial drives
	  responses to stimuli (pain)
	  active avoidance—escape
	  fighting behavior
	  discouragement, apathy

Minor Tranquilizers (Chlordiazepoxide-like)	*Hallucinogens (LSD-like)*

Slightly reduce
  arousal—excitability
  inhibitory control
  passive avoidance behavior
  fighting behavior
	Greatly increase
	  arousal—excitability
	  activity drive
	  responses to stimuli

Slightly increase
  responses to stimuli
  social approach
  errors of commission
	Greatly impair
	  inhibitory control
	  perception
	  information processing

SOURCE: Irwin (1968). (Reprinted from the *American Journal of Psychiatry*, vol. 124 [February Suppl.], pp. 1–19, 1968. Copyright 1968, the American Psychiatric Association.)

Central Arousal–Activation

As Fish (1968) remarked, a confusing literature has grown up around the question of the effect of stimulant drugs (amphetamines, methylphenidate) on hyperkinesis and behavior disorders in children. While most authors seem to agree that these stimulants are extremely useful for these disorders, dissenting voices are not uncommon (Freeman 1966). One of the more obvious reasons for the confusion is that behavioral *activity* level and central *activation* are not the same thing; behavioral activity level is a final point of expression of a variety of influences on the central nervous system.

Let us assume that there are certain children who have low or erratic central activation levels for a variety of reasons: slow maturation of the arousal mechanisms, damage to cortical or subcortical structures from exogenous trauma during perinatal development, genetic variation, and so on. Behaviorally, such children might appear hypoactive, hyperactive, or normal, depending on the state of compensatory inhibitory mechanisms. Thus a child with essentially normal cortical *inhibitory* capacities, but a low level of central *arousal* (as in early stages of sleep, fatigue, anesthesia, or because of faulty reticular activation function), might appear behaviorally to be excessively overactive, impulsive, or distractible.

The cortex must receive appropriate tonic stimulation from arousal mechanisms before its full inhibitory and regulatory capabilities are functionally available. Thus a stimulant drug, particularly one that selectively enhances function of the reticular activating system, as the amphetamines and methylphenidate are thought to do (Killam and Killam 1958), appears to have a paradoxical effect, since the stimulation of arousal mechanisms enhances general cortical tonus and capacity for selective inhibition. Conversely, sedative drugs that lower the arousal level should produce even more loss of inhibitory control in hyperkinetic children *who have low central arousal levels.*

Several pieces of evidence support the hypothesis of low central arousal level in hyperkinetic children. Satterfield (1969) has reported that hyperkinetic children have less spontaneous GSR (galvanic skin response) activity than matched controls, who in turn have lower levels than normal adults. They also have lower skin conductance levels and longer recovery times to stimulation than controls and adults. It is known that spontaneous GSR activity increases with behavior arousal, and that under alerting conditions the amplitude of the GSR increases in response to stimulation (Silverman, Cohen, and Shmavonian 1959). Fatigue states also result in a decline of nonspecific GSR occurrence. These findings suggest that hyperkinetic children have lower arousal levels than normal children of the same age. Since Satterfield found that these autonomic indices of arousal shifted in the direction of normal following stimulant drug treatment, the evidence strongly suggests that these children are being stimulated to higher arousal levels by the drug. This in turn can be presumed to reduce disinhibited motor and cognitive behavior.

Two studies on children with poor concentration in school (Dureman and Palshammar 1968) also showed that they have significantly lower skin conductance levels and lower respiratory rates during work periods in a simulated driving task, suggesting that they suffer from a lesser degree of task-relevant activation than children with adequate concentration and good endurance capacity for sustained work. Heart rate also responded in these children in a manner suggesting lowered degrees of central activation.

The relation between GSR arousal and overt behavior is a developmental one: the GSR has been reported to occur in children as young as 3 months, and by the time the child is of nursery school age there is a negative relationship between the extent of the GSR and the amount of overt emotional reaction. That is, children who show low GSR activity tend to be excitable, irritable, impulsive, and restless, while children who have high GSR responses are deliberate, constant in mood, and generally inhibited in their behavior (Jones 1950). These findings, then, are consistent with other evidence in suggesting that impulsive behavior patterns and the hyperexcitable state found in so many children with learning disorders are concomitants of low central activation–arousal responses.

The importance of the arousal process for attention, learning, and memory is well documented (Berlyne 1960). Evidence from small circumscribed lesions in the thalamic reticular formation in humans suffering from parkinsonism (Riklan and Levita 1969) shows how a number of the characteristic deficits in attention, perception, cognition, and affect seen in children with learning disabilities may be attributable to defects in these central arousal mechanisms. For example, it is found that while general intelligence is unaffected by these reticular lesions, planning and forethought as required on the Porteus Mazes is severely affected. Speech and language fluency, both symbolic and sensorimotor, may be impaired by subcortical lesions. The ascending reticular system probably plays an important part in focusing attention upon auditory stimuli as well (Roberts 1966). The studies of subcortical surgery indicate that the effects of lesions in subcortical structures on perceptual function (as measured, for instance, by the Bender Visual Motor Gestalt Test) may be quite significant. The same may be said of emotional expression.

In summary, there is evidence to suggest that *hyperkinetic children,* as well as other children who have poor concentration abilities, may suffer from low central arousal levels, and that a wide variety of learning and emotional functions are dependent on adequate activity of the subcortical structures regulating central arousal levels. Whether such children require a stimulant, sedative, or tranquilizing drug for maximal benefit may depend on the initial state of arousal; if it is low, stimulant drugs should be beneficial, but sedatives contraindicated. If arousal level is too high, then a tranquilizer of the phenothiazine class may be indicated.

Age

It is generally recognized that age is a very important factor in determining the kind and degree of response to psychotropic drugs. Fish (1960, 1964) has said that various drugs have different effects before and after puberty, and that psychological changes at age 7 lead to more organized and stable behaviors; such factors must be considered when evaluating therapies such as the use of drugs.

An example of such age-dependent drug effects which is often cited is the effect of diphenhydramine (Benadryl) before and after age 10. Fish (1960) reported that this drug was effective in diminishing nonneurotic aggressive impulsive behavior in children under 10 with IQ's above 70. Thirteen of her patients were followed in continuous treatment before and after the age of 10, and she claimed that there was a marked diminution of effectiveness after the child passed the age of 10. After this age diphenhydramine acted merely as a sedative. She lists this drug as the drug of choice for the hyperactive, immature child under age 10 and as useful for some hyperactive schizophrenic children with IQ's of less than 70. Unfortunately no controlled studies of the supposed age interaction with this drug have been carried out.

In Conrad's study (1967) cited earlier, he found that amphetamine interacted with age, being more effective in the younger children, but the degree of benefit was also dependent on variables of family status and organicity. To our knowledge there have been no satisfactory developmental studies of drug effects. Such studies are difficult because of the problem of varying age without varying other factors such as the length of illness, the severity of the disturbance, and the meaning of the dependent variable measures (e.g., a reading test at age 7 probably measures something different from a reading test at age 11).

Intelligence

Intelligence is both a general property of the human organism and a set of more specific abilities related to complex problem-solving. Intelligence may reflect both biological and social antecedents in the child's development. For instance, children with IQ's below 60 are not only less able to learn than children with higher IQ's but usually have brain damage or neuropathology as well. A low verbal IQ may reflect specific biological deficits in language processing or be a reflection of cultural-educational handicaps. Heterogeneity of sample on this variable, therefore, may well obscure important drug effects, or produce effects which are related to social class or some hidden organismic factors.

In one study it was found that the degree of impact of a stimulant drug on learning ability and planning ability was related to initial level of intelligence (Conners and Eisenberg 1963). Children with low IQ's showed significantly more increment in Porteus Maze Test Quotient than the brighter children.

Another feature of intelligence tests is that they may reflect motivational factors (which in turn may vary as a function of some other factor, such as social class) rather than intellectual factors. Therefore presumed drug effects in children of differing levels of intelligence, or effects of drugs on IQ scores, may reflect drug-motivation interactions rather than drug-intelligence interactions. This is illustrated by a study in which a large battery of performance tests was used with a group of culturally deprived poor learners (Conners, Eisenberg, and Barcai 1967). A factor analysis of the battery showed (once the variance from personality and motivational factors was removed) that the stimulant drug (dextroamphetamine) had its major effect on a motivational factor (need for achievement) and not on intellectual factors.

Another illustration of the importance of controlling for intelligence is seen in a study which compared the effects of dextroamphetamine and thioridazine (Mellaril) on hyperactive children (Alexandris and Lundell 1968). In this well-designed and -analyzed experiment, 7 patients received thioridazine, 6 amphetamine, and 8 placebo, assigned randomly. Ratings were obtained weekly over a six-month period for hyperkinesis, concentration, attention, aggressiveness, sociability, interpersonal relationship, comprehension, mood, work interest, and work capacity. All these categories were significantly improved on the tranquilizer as compared with placebo, but only comprehension and work interest were improved in the dextroamphetamine group compared with placebo (see Figure 7 1). However, the authors failed to relate the effects to IQ. The IQ's were said to range between 55 and 85 (these were institutionalized, hyperactive children). But the small number of subjects in each group allowed for chance assignments of very dull children to one or more of the treatment groups; this cannot be ruled out since the IQ distribution in the three groups was not given.

Many of these dull children might have been mildly brain damaged. Also, the superior effect of the tranquilizer may simply have reflected a global impression of the raters of less troublesome behavior, leading to a "halo" effect in which every symptom was believed to be improved. None of the *objective* measures (reading, spelling, or arithmetic) showed any drug effect. Thus it is difficult to conclude that the tranquilizer was in

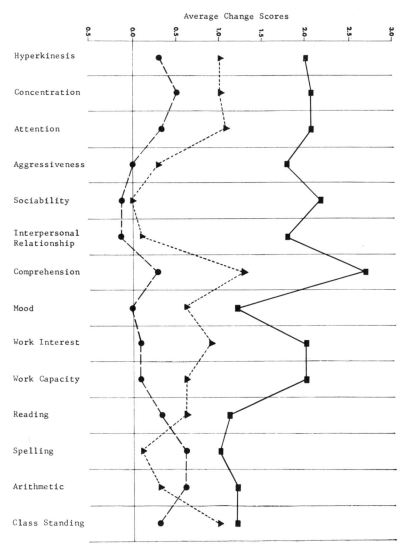

Average Change Scores

FIGURE 7-1. *Effect of thioridazine, dextroamphetamine, and placebo on target symptoms of institutionalized hyperkinetics.* ■———■ *Thiorida-zine (all improvement scores are statistically significant).* ▲-------▲ *Dextro-amphetamine (improvement scores for concentration, attention, comprehen-sion, work interest, reading, and class standing are statistically significant).* ●———● *Placebo (no statistical significance for all improvement scores) (Alexandris and Lundell 1968).*

fact a "better" therapy for these children: they may simply have been pleasing the institutional staff by being sedated and lethargic rather than aggressive and troublesome. Brighter children who actually improved on the stimulant could have been obscured in group results by lack of change in the more retarded patients. It is most important in reporting drug studies, especially with random assignment of small numbers, that IQ *distributions* (not simply means) be given for each treatment group and that the differential effects of the treatment (drug versus placebo) on each child be separated and analyzed.

Biochemical Factors

The role of biochemical factors in learning and behavior disorders, and the possible influence of these factors on the efficacy of psychotropic drugs, is a completely neglected area of research. There is some evidence to suggest that hormone levels may affect intellectual functioning in children. Children with congenital hypothyroidism who are given thyroid replacement therapy before the age of $2\frac{1}{2}$ years have significantly higher IQ's than those treated later (Money and Lewis 1964). Certain genetic anomalies, such as found in Turner's syndrome, may produce difficulties in directional sense, without general impairment of IQ (Alexander, Walker, and Money 1964).

Such factors affecting learning ability not only may occur because of congenital or genetic biological defects, but may *result from* the effects of a stressful environment. The sequence of events from environmental stress, to hormone alterations, to central nervous system (CNS) damage, to intellectual and behavioral deficit is dramatically illustrated by recent studies of hypopituitary dwarfs (Powell, Brasel, and Blizzard 1967; Powell et al. 1967). Thirteen such children with a variety of behavior disorders and intellectual retardation were removed from their very disturbed family environments and began to show immediate behavioral and endocrine alterations without further therapy of any kind. The authors remarked, "We can only postulate that emotional disturbance in these children may have had an adverse effect upon release of pituitary-tropic hormone via the central nervous system." It is therefore conceivable that many learning deficits may reflect changes in the central nervous system due to the impact of stressful environments on endocrine function. How such stress-induced physiological changes may be related to drug therapies has not been investigated.

There may be important organismic variables of a chemical nature involved in drug effects. This is illustrated by a study in which it was found that a group of "organic" hyperactive children excreted more amphetamine than a matched group of "nonorganic" hyperactives, and there were differences in both clinical effects and side effects of the drug on these two groups (Epstein et al. 1968). It is well known that urinary pH affects the metabolism of drugs such as amphetamines, and children vary considerably in normal pH levels. This variable needs to be controlled carefully to avoid concluding that a particular drug is ineffective. Taking the drug before meals rather than after may strongly affect the actual utilization of the drug in the body.

INDEPENDENT VARIABLES

Independent variables refers to factors in an experiment which are manipulated, either statistically or experimentally, and whose effects are to be investigated. Classically, one holds all variables constant except the one whose effects are being investigated and measures changes in the dependent variables as a function of changes in the independent variable. In practice it may be difficult to hold certain factors in the experiment constant, or to achieve the degree of variation in the independent variable that is required. In drug studies the major independent variable is usually the drug itself. The effects of the drug can be studied in several ways: one may compare the results of several dosage levels in a single subject or a group of subjects; one may compare the effects of a fixed dose against no treatment or a placebo, or against both; several drugs may be compared with one another.

There are a number of difficulties encountered in drug studies relating to the issue of varying the amount of the drug and nothing else. The drug blood levels, placebo effects, developmental variations in children, the doctor–patient–family relationship all enter into the final outcome. A number of clinical, ethical, and practical considerations determine how these various factors are managed in a particular study.

Drug Levels

Virtually none of the studies of children attempts to determine the levels of a drug in the blood at the time the effects are measured. Yet it is well known that there are very large individual differences in the obtained levels, for comparable doses of various drugs, in children of the same body weight. Both the child's chronological age and his weight probably affect the amount of drug required to achieve a given blood level. It is quite possible for drug studies to find negative results erroneously because the effective dose of a drug has not been reached. Fish (1968) has noted that many authors have failed to appreciate the fact that children often tolerate much higher dosages of drugs (particularly phenothiazines) for their body weight than adults. Many pediatricians are at first aghast to find that children are receiving as much as 50 mg per day of dextroamphetamine, or 100 mg per day of methylphenidate. Apart from the fact that much of the drugs is excreted unchanged, there are probably different mechanisms of utilization of many psychoactive drugs in children than in adults.

In one study of the anticonvulsant diphenylhydantoin, we found that there was as much as tenfold variation in blood levels of the drug in children given the same dose. It is for this reason that many clinical investigators argue that titration of the dose level to the point of clinical effect or to the point where side effects appear is the best way to proceed. Others prefer fixed dose levels (Sprague, Werry, and Davis 1969).

In some studies it is possible to have the same child tested at several dose levels, or to have separate groups of children, each receiving a different level of the drug. However, most studies have too few children available to make the latter approach feasible. Moreover, it is common experience to find that *a drug exerts its therapeutic effect only at a particular level for a particular child.* In other words, there is some degree of idiosyncratic specificity in the drug response. This means that it probably is highly *unlikely for any child to be assigned the particular dose which is appropriate for him if random assignment of drugs at fixed levels is made.*

The research design will depend on whether repeated measures can be made on the same subjects, thus allowing for systematic investigation of varying dose levels within these subjects. Where general parameters, *not* therapeutic response, are measured, it may be feasible and desirable to establish a dose–response relationship. Such relationships are important for understanding the mechanisms, both behavioral and biochemical, whereby the drugs exert their effects, but they may be irrelevant in a clinically oriented therapeutic study. As pointed out, *manipulating the dosage of a drug does not necessarily mean that an effective manipulation of the state of the central nervous system is taking place.*

Placebo Effects

Placebo effects and other "nonspecific" medication effects are ubiquitous in children taking psychoactive drugs, as well as in the adults who monitor their behavior. It is not uncommon for parents or teachers to report marked improvement in children after the beginning of a drug study, even though the child is receiving an inert substance. However, the use of a placebo does not automatically ensure control over expectations and general set for improvement. The studies of Schachter and Singer (1962) illustrate how the presence of some physiologically detectable effect by a subject interacts with his expectations to produce a change. In their studies, subjects were injected with epinephrine, a naturally occurring hormone which produces a number of physiological actions like that of the sympathetic nervous system. In one group subjects were told the drug would make them feel more angry while another group was told they would feel more happy. The behavior of the subjects tended to be in the direction of the experimenter's suggestions. The interpretation of this finding is that people who experience some physiological effects (autonomic in this case) will tend to behave in a manner consistent with psychological expectations or set that happen to be present at the time. Patients appear to make hypotheses as to what is supposed to happen in an experiment and produce such changes for the sake of the experimenter (and possibly produce changes *against* the hypothesis, depending on the subject's personality, his relationship to the doctor, and his attitude toward the medication).

In this regard one author (Knobel 1962) pointed out that there appear to be "medication-accepting" and "medication-rejecting" families, and that the outcome seems to depend partially on their expectations. Kraft (1968) also noted that the family beliefs and attitudes tend to determine the clinical efficacy of certain drug treatments. Bradley (1950) has pointed out that the powerful therapeutic effects of the amphetamines in the controlled residential treatment environment may be dissipated when the children leave and confront a more disorganized environment. The studies of Conrad (1967) show that the degree of family organization definitely interacts with the drug in determining clinical benefit. Few studies have actually attempted to control or systematically vary such effects with children, though their importance has long been recognized in adult psychopharmacology.

Physician Variables

Little attention is usually given to the impact of the physician's personality and beliefs in the use of medication with children, though from a general psychological point of view one might expect that this factor could be a most important determinant of the treatment benefit. One can only speculate what the differences in outcome might be with an enthusiastic, confident, charismatic physician who delivers the medication with assurances that it will produce certain effects, as opposed to a conservative, even doubtful attitude. One physician, who seriously doubted the value of the analeptic drugs for behavior disorders, seemed to change his opinion when he observed an experienced practitioner deliver these drugs in practice (Freeman 1969).

Social Class

Adult psychopharmacology is replete with examples of differences in drug effects as a function of social class. Very little systematic work with this variable has been reported for children, though there is every reason to believe that social class factors may play an important role in drug effect. Patients' attitudes and beliefs about medication will be affected by their social class. The lower social classes will be more subject to hazards of pregnancy, perinatal trauma, poor nutrition, and other factors likely to produce CNS damage, thus altering some of the organismic variables described above.

In one recent, unpublished study the effects of dextroamphetamine were compared in two samples of different social class, identical in age and referring symptoms (learning disorders, with or without behavior problems). Many more positive effects on objective test measures were found in the lower social class sample, though about the same degree of effect was found on measures involving parents' and teachers' ratings.

DEPENDENT VARIABLES

Some General Issues of Measurement

One of the most complex aspects of drug studies with children is the measurement of the changes induced by the drug (including other independent variables explicitly or inadvertently manipulated). To a large extent the major issues of measurement represent differences in philosophy and manner of approach by clinicians and scientists. Scientific observers tend to be dismayed by the failure of clinicians to appreciate the problems of reliable, valid measurement, while clinicians frequently view more "objective" studies with distrust, especially where there appears to be a lack of appreciation of the full complexities of the clinical situation. A number of such issues repeatedly appear in reviews of drug studies with children.

Molar versus molecular measurement. Clinicians generally prefer to assess the impact of drugs on the total organism, noting reorganizations of personality, mood, and symptom patterns. Most of the earlier uncontrolled drug studies are of this type and have frequently been criticized for attempting complex judgments of unknown reliability. An example of this approach is the early study by Bender and Cottington (1942) who reported the effects of Benzedrine on 40 psychoneurotic, psychopathic, and "organic" children. They reported significant improvement in such factors as feelings of well-being; stimulation of drive for learning; relief of fear, depression, and sexual tension; integration of activity; and ability to relate in therapy. Individual children were analyzed in terms of their unique personality organizations. Thus the worsened behavior of the "psychopathic" children was interpreted in terms of the drug's effect in breaking down a superficial degree of control which hid basically disorganized personalities. Such psychodynamic inferences may make interesting speculation but cannot be easily substantiated.

A scientific observer attempting to replicate such findings is faced with the dilemma of objectively operationalizing* these complex effects, while recognizing that a more piecemeal approach may lose the essence of the original observations. However, it should be noted that complex assessments can be made with excellent reliability by trained observers, and global judgments may often be more reliable than is usually assumed. This does not, of course, relieve an investigator from *demonstrating* that his judgments are in fact replicable and reliable. Psychiatrists interested in operationalizing their judgments of child mental and emotional status would do well to follow the carefully standardized procedure devised by Rutter and Graham (1968).

Molar judgments of behavior are best made with carefully standardized rating scales, while the more molecular behaviors may be assessed by objective performance tests or time-sampling observational methods. In the latter method, carefully specified individual behaviors are counted during fixed periods of observation, as in the careful study of an autistic child described by Hutt et al. (1961), or the study of classroom behaviors by Werry (1969).

* The notion of "operationalism" in science is that "terms, propositions, concepts, constructs, and theories are given all their meaning—in the last analysis—by the methods of observation or investigation used to arrive at them, that they have no other meaning than is yielded by the procedures or operations by which the things or processes to which they refer are known" (English and English 1958).

Relevant versus irrelevant behavior. A major problem in drug studies is that certain behaviors may be quite objectively measured, but the question may be raised as to whether a particular behavior has "clinical relevance." Thus in a study by Schickedanze (1967), he found that retarded boys performed longer on a repetitive task, involving dropping marbles into a box, when treated with methylphenidate than when treated with thioridazine. One might reasonably ask whether such a task measures persistence, attention, motivation to do well, or some other factor. Does the behavior in fact relate to "real-life" behavior? The validity of such measures is often left unexplored. Such tasks may be useful as objective indices of change when combined with more molar observations. The implication is that *both levels of observation need to be employed as dependent variables, since either by itself is likely to be unsatisfactory.* As in the study of thioridazine and amphetamine mentioned earlier (Alexandris and Lundell 1968), the failure of objective test measures to change significantly can cast doubt on the meaning of rating changes observed at a molar level.

*Reliability and validity.** As mentioned above, many studies employ unstandardized ratings by teachers, parents, or physicians, and one is often unsure whether the failure to find drug effects may be due to the inherent lack of control in the methods of observation. The same problem may also apply to objective tests, since the reliability of *change* scores tends to be lower than that of the original scores. However, the real problem is that most measures in the published drug literature are from ad hoc instruments which have not been standardized.

Among rating devices for children's drug studies, a brief, reliable scale for use by parents in rating activity level is available

---

* In brief, *reliability* in psychological measurement generally refers to the stability or replicability of a measurement procedure, while *validity* refers to the ability of a test to measure, in fact, what it purports to measure. However, there are a number of additional meanings attached to these terms, and the reader is referred to the definitions in English and English (1958). A measure is *standardized* when empirical investigation dictates the exact procedures to be used in testing, the permitted variations in environmental conditions, the methods of scoring, and the methods of drawing inferences regarding populations of subjects.

(Werry and Sprague 1970). A symptom checklist for teachers has shown good reliability and sensitivity to drug effects (Conners 1969), and the Devereux Teacher Rating Scale (Spivack and Swift 1967) is a well-designed instrument that should prove useful. These two instruments have been factor analyzed, making it possible to employ separate factors as measures of change or predictors of drug response. Behavior checklists appropriate for parents or clinicians are available from a number of sources (Conners 1970, Peterson 1961, Burks 1964).

Dependent Variables Related to Learning

Attention—vigilance. Various studies have shown that drugs may alter the capacity of children to attend. At a direct level of observation, Sprague, Barnes, and Werry (1970) found that methylphenidate significantly enhanced attending behaviors in 12 underachieving boys, while thioridazine did not differ from placebo. When children with learning disorders were required to monitor a constantly changing display and respond to an infrequently occurring target (continuous performance test), their performance was significantly enhanced over placebo by dextroamphetamine or methylphenidate (Conners 1970, Conners and Rothschild 1968).

Inhibitory control. Impulsive behavior is a characteristic of many poor learners. There is considerable evidence to suggest that drugs may enhance the ability to delay, plan, and respond in a more controlled, integrated manner. This general "inhibitory" quality of drugs is perhaps the single most important effect on behavior in children. In several studies it was found that performance on the Porteus Mazes was significantly enhanced by stimulant drugs in children with learning disorders, behavior problems, or both (Conners, Eisenberg, and Barcai 1967; Conners, Eisenberg, and Sharpe 1965; Conners, Eisenberg, and Sharpe 1964; Conners and Eisenberg 1963; Conners et al. 1969; Conners and Rothschild 1968). This task requires the child to plan his way through a maze on paper, using a pencil, and penalizes impulsive performance. It is generally believed that the test taps the functions of the frontal lobes in decision-making activity (Riklan and Levita 1969, Porteus 1968). In general, *stimulants enhance performance, tranquilizers impair performance* (Helper, Wilcott, and Garfield 1963).

A number of studies of children with learning or behavior disorders have shown that stimulants also enhance skilled motor performance, such as holding a stylus in a small aperture, and finger tapping (Knights and Hinton 1968; Conners and Rothschild 1968; Kleemeier and Kleemeier 1947; Epstein et al. 1968). Such effects may be due to greater capacity to exert control over motor response or to increased motivation to perform well. In one study of reaction times in a continuous performance test, it was found that the stimulant-treated children had longer latencies of response on trials in which signals to respond occurred, compared with the placebo-treated subjects who responded more quickly, thus making more errors. This type of "reflective" (as opposed to impulsive) approach has been demonstrated to be a characteristic of better readers (Kagan 1965).

Several studies have shown that stimulants can also improve performance IQ's. Molitch and Eccles (1937) carried out a double-blind, placebo study of Benzedrine with adolescent juvenile offenders and found that performance IQ's showed about an 18 percent increment over placebo. Bradley and Green (1940), however, stated that "In general, there was no striking change in intelligence quotient when amphetamine sulfate was used" in a study of disturbed, residentially treated children. Zimmerman and Burgemeister (1958) found significant improvement on WISC performance IQ's as a result of methylphenidate treatment, as did Knights and Hinton (1968). The same effect with dextroamphetamine was reported by Epstein et al. (1968), and is reported by Conners (see Fig. 7-2).

Whether these changes in performance abilities are a function of attention to the task, increased motivation, or greater selectivity in response is not clear from the above studies and needs to be clarified.

Mood and personality. Parents frequently describe elevated mood and interest in the environment in children who receive stimulant drugs. Conners, Eisenberg, and Sharpe (1964) used parents' Clyde Mood Scale descriptions of their children

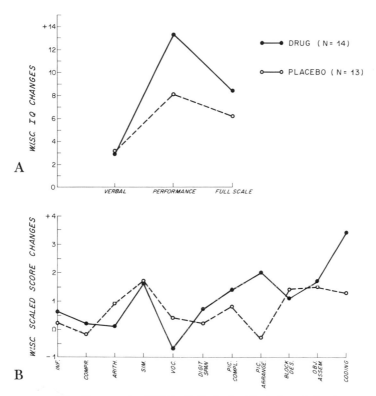

FIGURE 7-2. (A) *Changes in WISC Full Scale, Verbal and Performance IQ with dextroamphetamine and placebo.* (B) *Effect of dextroamphetamine and placebo on WICS subtest scores.*

and found that factors of "friendliness" and "concentration" showed improvements following treatment with dextroamphetamine as compared with placebo controls. This is consistent with the earlier reports of improved attitude in Benzedrine-treated disturbed children (Bradley 1941) and more positive social perceptions in amphetamine-treated delinquents, using a sociometric device (Eisenberg et al. 1963). Occasionally certain children respond with a depressive mood to stimulants (Ounstead 1955). This is a phenomenon whose cause is not understood, but it occurs both in epileptic children with hyperkinesis and in children with behavior problems and hyperkinesis. Some parents become quite concerned with the saddened faces and weepiness, and if these are persistent a change of medication is indicated, or a lower dose of the analeptic may be required.

Language functioning. Considering the important role of subcortical arousal structures in language functions (Riklan and Levita 1969), it is not surprising that language ability should be affected by certain drugs. Creager and Van-Riper (1967) studied 30 children with cerebral dysfunction after the administration of methylphenidate or placebo and found that the total number of words spoken, the number of responses, and the number of incomplete utterances showed significant increases under the active medication. Conners et al. (1969) found that measures of both reading and arithmetic showed small but significant improvement following dextro-amphetamine treatment in a group of children with learning disorders (see Fig. 7-3). Bradley and Bowen (1940) found that the largest gains from Benzedrine treatment occurred in their subjects in arithmetic, while reading performance was somewhat more variable. Language function as a dependent variable requires further research in selected populations, since the evi-

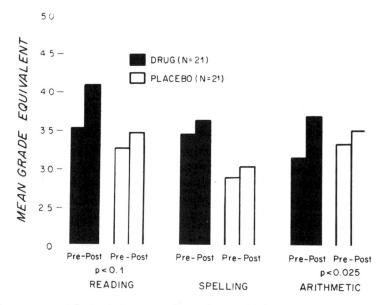

FIGURE 7-3. *Effect of dextroamphetamine and placebo on Wide Range Achievement Tests (Conners et al., Archives of General Psychiatry 21:184, 1969).*

dence seems to indicate that effects of drugs may be significant, but dependent on the initial state of the child.

Auditory perception. Numerous authors have documented the deficiencies in auditory information processing in children with learning disabilities and minimal brain dysfunction (e.g., Sabatino 1969). Relatively little use of auditory tests as dependent variables has been made in drug studies with children. In one recent study (Conners) it was found that the ability to blend sounds into a meaningful pattern (speech synthesis) was improved, while auditory discrimination and auditory memory were not significantly affected, by dextroamphetamine (see Fig. 7-4). It may be important to test auditory figure-ground since children with minimal brain dysfunction appear to be much more impaired in auditory processing in the presence of background noise than without (Sabatino 1969).

Visual perception. Millichap et al. (1968) found that methylphenidate improved scores on the Draw-A-Man Test and the figure-ground subtest of the Frostig Test of Visual Per-

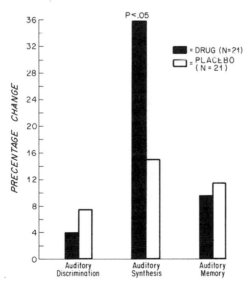

FIGURE 7-4. *Effect of dextroamphetamine on auditory functions.*

ception in a study of 30 children with learning disorders. Conners et al. (1969) found similar effects on some Frostig subtests, though changes in the Draw-A-Man and Bender Gestalt test fell short of significance (see Fig. 7-5).

An important point to be considered when using such measures is that *drug effects may be obscured if some subjects are not impaired on a particular test.* Millichap et al. (1968) found that only when the most impaired patients were separated from those with high scores did the drug effect become apparent. This may be due to either the problem of ceiling effects for a test or the fact that many drugs may be expected to exert positive or "normalizing" effects only when a function is aberrant. Given the rather unique individual patterns of deficit found in most children with learning disorders, *one may expect change in certain functions for certain children, but not in all functions for every child in a drug study.*

Motility.   There are various methods available for reliably measuring the impact of drugs on motility. Millichap and Boldrey (1967) used the actometer, which is a watch con-

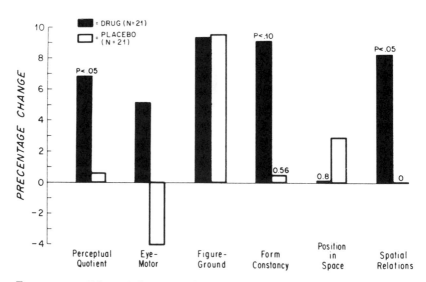

FIGURE 7-5.   *Effect of dextroamphetamine and placebo on Frostig Test of Developmental Perception (Conners et al.,* Archives of General Psychiatry *21:184, 1969).*

structed to count as the child moves about. They found an increase in activity following drug treatment of children with minimal brain dysfunction, though the activity appeared to be more integrated, as judged by parent observations. On the other hand, in a later study (Millichap et al. 1968) it was found that actometer recordings showed a decrease in activity. A stabilometric cushion has been used to measure changes in seat activity during a learning task (Sprague, Barnes, and Werry 1970) following treatment with methylphenidate, thioridazine, or placebo (see Fig. 7-6). The stimulant lowered seat activity while the tranquilizer was no different from placebo. At the same time the stimulant-treated children had faster reaction times, improved accuracy on a discrimination learning task, and improved classroom behavior. In another study Werry (1969) used a time-sampling observational method and found that noisy behavior and non-task-related activity were reduced by methylphenidate in a classroom setting.

There is considerable evidence in animal work to indicate that the initial level of activity determines the response of the animal to stimulant drugs (Irwin 1969, Davis 1957), with highly active animals showing decrease in activity following stimulant medication. This fact may account for some of the discrepancy in the literature regarding effects of drugs on activity level in children and, as mentioned earlier, the crucial variable is probably level of central arousal rather than activity level per se.

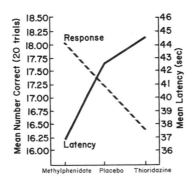

FIGURE 7-6. *Contrasting effects of a stimulant and tranquilizer on discrimination learning performance (Sprague, Barnes, and Werry 1970).*

Learning. Learning is a complex process, so it is not meaningful to consider this as a dependent variable until more specific processes are measured. As yet there are no published studies to indicate that either short- or long-term memory can be enhanced in children, though much recent work from animals suggests that such effects from drugs may be possible (McGaugh and Petrinovich 1965). However, tests of rote learning have shown improvement in stimulant-treated children with learning disorders (Conners, Eisenberg, and Sharpe 1964; Conners et al. 1969). The effect of dextroamphetamine on errors in learning a list of symbols and pictures is shown in Figure 7-7. The children were presented with a symbol followed by the symbol paired with a common object and had to learn to anticipate the object when they saw the symbol again. There were ten such pairs in a list, with a matched list used before and after dextroamphetamine. There was about a 35 percent reduction in errors in the drug-treated group, which is highly significant. Since this task is a lengthy one and requires careful attention, other processes than learning are undoubtedly involved, but the results illustrate how a learning task may be improved through the action of the drug on other factors.

Similar improvement has been found for discrimination learning (Sprague, Barnes, and Werry 1970). Incidentally, these studies and others (Helper, Wilcott, and Garfield 1963)

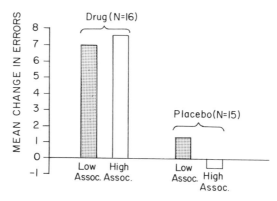

FIGURE 7-7. *Effect of dextroamphetamine and placebo on errors in learning. High and low verbal associations are not differentially affected by the drug (Conners and Rothschild 1968).*

indicate that *tranquilizing drugs tend to impair learning performance in disturbed children,* though one might expect that improvements would occur in those children whose learning is impaired because of abnormally high levels of activation.

SOME CLINICAL CONSIDERATIONS OF DRUG USAGE WITH CHILDREN

In many cases, particularly milder behavior disorders, mood disturbances, personality problems, and learning disorders, it is advisable to consider an initial use of placebos. Many children presenting to outpatient clinics have transient disturbances which respond quite well to minimal therapeutic intervention, brief consultation, and directive advice. Neurotic, anxious children are more likely than those with behavior disorders of the hyperactive type to respond to a placebo. Their response is about as good as that from a brief consultation. However, it is well to remember that the placebo is not simply a phony pill; it is an embodiment of all the physician's magic and symbol and can sometimes provide a channel of communication to both parent and child in cases where either has some investment in somatic therapies or has strong defensive reactions to other treatments which can be lessened by a more directive kind of therapy. The response to a placebo is often helpful in evaluating the reliability of the mother's or teacher's reports of the child's behavior. It is likely that children are somewhat less prone than neurotic adult outpatients to have strong placebo responses per se, but an occasional child and his family appear to need the assurance that a concrete form of treatment, given with the doctor's reassurance that the child will improve, is available. This is in effect the mobilization of hope which Jerome Frank has stressed as such a powerful ingredient in psychotherapy.

It is wise to select a small number of the available agents, get to know their characteristics thoroughly, and use them long enough to ensure that one is completely aware of their value and limitations. *One may easily be misled, both by the literature and one's own partial success rate, into adherence to agents that have no firm basis for their use, and which may in fact be nothing more than expensive placebos.* If anything, response to drugs by children is even more idiosyncratic than in adults, and with even a small number of drugs being combined with wide variations of diagnosis, intelligence, age, family setting, environmental stress, and so on, it is hard indeed to develop rational control over the use of these agents.

One should make systematic efforts to evaluate the drug's benefit in children by the use of multiple points of reference, including the child's subjective response, the parents' report, one's own observations, and—often neglected—the reports of teachers, when not dealing with hospitalized children. The child will frequently be a poor source of information about the effects and will frequently report no effect, or an effect contrary to that noted by other observers. He may fail to verbalize certain aspects of the significance of the drug treatment, such as his resistance to the pills because he thinks they are "crazy pills" or "stupid pills" or because other children say that this proves he is an oddball.

The clinical appearance in the office may be radically different from the appearance in stress situations such as school, home, or playground. A phone call to the teacher, or better a standardized rating form, will often provide the best information about the usefulness of the medication. In general, the parents' reports about how the child is progressing in school are not to be trusted by themselves for a number of obvious reasons, though a careful report of home behavior is necessary.

The parents' observations must be judged carefully in terms of the parents' own needs and expectations, and in terms of the reliability of reporting and the relevance of the home behavior to the symptoms being treated. Parents frequently say, "He is no different," even when the school reports marked improvement, or vice versa. It is wise to evaluate concrete routine such as behavior at the dinner table, television, homework, and play with siblings, since some but not all of these areas may show differential drug effects. Energy level, sleep, appetite, and eliminative functions are foci for detecting unwanted side effects as well as the symptoms in these areas.

Objective measures are important for detecting changes in cognition, impulsiveness, and motor control. Standard brief clinical tests such as the Porteus Mazes, Draw-A-Man, copying of designs, and intelligence subtests (block designs, digit-symbol coding) are very useful monitors of both the intellectual functions involved and manner of approach, impulsiveness, and ability to cooperate. Such standardized observations collected over a number of treated cases help the clinician to evaluate his success in objective terms and give some basis for persuading teachers or parents to continue medication when immediate effects may not be obvious to them. We have constantly been surprised, for example, at the striking gains in test performance in treated patients, despite a general belief by others that the child had shown little change. Such improvements in ability to manage the tests, above and beyond practice and placebo effects, may have long-term benefits on cognitive function not readily apparent. Similarly, one might decide that a lowering of cognitive function with a tranquilizer is too heavy a price to pay for control of psychomotor excitement in some children.

Both objective performance tests and global methods of evaluation are essential in making a decision about the usefulness of a drug. There are many sources of error in clinical observations, parents', teachers', and patients' reports; yet they are indispensable as a measure of relevant clinical behavior change. There are virtues in the quantifiable, objective test measures for determining real changes in psychological states, but used by themselves without careful observation they provide only scores which might be trivial without knowledge of the total behavioral picture. "Drug holidays" are also useful ways of evaluating true effects of the treatment.

Perhaps the most important consideration in the use of psychoactive agents is careful attention to the psychodynamics of the treatment situation. This means knowing the impact of the doctor's attitude on the outcome; understanding the symbolic and perceived significance of pill-taking to the child and his family; and understanding some of the ramifications of radically altered behavior for the total family system. With regard to the doctor's attitude, it is well known that enthusiastic endorsement of medication increases the likelihood of change, while equivocal, doubting attitudes will be picked up by the patient and his family and translated into reported results. Mothers are especially sensitive to the doctor's hints as to the likely outcome of such treatment. We have found it useful to be frank but optimistic; to stress that the chosen drug has been found useful with such problems as this child presents, but that children are highly individual in their response and other drugs may have to be tried. If the physician's own theoretical biases are strongly against the use of the psychopharmacological intervention with children, it is probably best for him not to use such methods until he can feel comfortable in doing so, because the family in most cases will sense his expectations and respond appropriately. As Schachter has nicely phrased it, drugs potentiate the available salient cognitions.

The impact of medication on the family may be most crucial in disturbances of basic temperament, such as in the so-called hyperkinetic behavior disorders. Many parents during the medical history recall long-standing disturbances in motility, often as early as the first months of life, or beginning at the time the child started to walk; or they reveal disturbances in feeding or social responsiveness or in aggression control that have been present from the earliest years. In a well-adjusted family such a child may gradually produce considerable family disruption which comes to be seen by the parents as the cause, rather than the effect, of the disorder of temperament in the child. Many mothers become extremely guilty about their "poor handling" of these children, aided more often than not by rather one-sided psychogenic hypotheses from doctors or teachers or the lay child-rearing literature. Over and over again, we have seen that such children respond well to drug treatment and thus help improve the mother's tolerance for the child. This often permits her to alter her own reactive behavior with her child. She may also discuss her feelings of guilt in the maintenance or aggravation of symptoms. Thus the drug may become a symbolic way of siding with the parent, who usually comes with the expectation of being found guilty for crimes of poor parenthood. There is often tremendous relief in the discovery that much of the child's abnormal behavior is not directly due to parental mismanagement. Secretly most mothers know this and can keep it hidden through long psychotherapy sessions in which the subtle philosophy that they are poor parents may be unwittingly instilled. In short the medication can be seen as a sign that the doctor believes her side of the problem. If there are notable improvements in the child the mother is often able to deal realistically with her own sometimes neurotic involvements with and reactions to the child.

Children form a number of hypotheses about the pills, such as that they are "stupid pills" (or "smart pills" or "crazy pills"). As far as possible, given the limitations of a child's intelligence and age, the child needs a clear rationale to enlist his cooperation in an active way.

Clinical Recommendations for Drugs

The following observations on drug usage in children with learning and behavior disorders are based on the author's experience with stimulant drugs and review of the literature. An experienced physician should always administer and supervise the use of medication with children. All children should have a thorough physical examination before even the safest drugs are employed and should be followed up regularly with periodic examinations by the supervising physician. The latter, unfortunately, are not always done by busy practitioners, and such lack of follow-up is potentially dangerous both physically and psychologically. Drugs are *always only a part* of a total treatment program, and while sometimes crucial to the total progress, they may be useless without educational and psychological management, coordination of school and parent efforts, and long-term planning.

Stimulant drugs. Benzedrine sulfate, dextroamphetamine sulfate, and methylphenidate have the longest histories and are among the safest drugs for children. While there is no specific symptom pattern that invariably responds to these agents, there is general agreement that the hyperkinetic child and the child with fluctuating attention profits most frequently from these drugs. Clinical experience indicates that one stimulant may sometimes be more effective than the others with certain children (Bradley 1950). Side effects of anorexia and insomnia can be troublesome but should not discourage stimulant usage unless persistent. Increased irritability with these medications is probably a sign of an already high arousal state and generally contraindicates further treatment with these agents. Methylphenidate appears to have the best "batting average" of the minor stimulants (Millichap and Fowler 1967). Dosages vary from 5 to 50 mg per day in divided doses for the amphetamines, and approximately twice that amount for methylphenidate, though careful titration for age and body size is important.

Tranquilizers. Of the phenothiazine derivatives, thioridazine and chlorpromazine appear to be most frequently used with children, and although controlled studies are relatively few, experienced clinicians frequently find uses for these more powerful (and potentially toxic) agents with severely excited, psychotic, or uncontrollable children. The reader is referred to the recommendations of Fish (1968) and Eveloff (1966) for clinical views on these agents. It should be borne in mind that most evidence indicates some impairment of learning (for both animals and humans) with these agents, though this undoubtedly needs qualification for the specific symptom complex involved. The use of the more powerful stimulating phenothiazines, such as trifluoperazine, in more severely disturbed children appears warranted from clinical studies, but well-controlled studies are lacking with one or two exceptions (Fish, Shapiro, and Campbell 1966). Minor tranquilizers such as diphenhydramine, meprobamate, and chlordiazepoxide, though frequently used for stimulating speech and euphoria and calming anxiety states in children, have no satisfactory controlled documentation of their effectiveness.

Anticonvulsants. Further work needs to be done to clarify which children profit from anticonvulsants. Though clinical experience indicates that some children who respond unfavorably to the stimulants, and who are characterized by explosive outbursts and hyperactivity, may respond remarkably to diphenylhydantoin, most controlled studies do not support the general usefulness of this agent with children, except those with convulsive or subclinical epileptic disorders. This may be largely due to the subtlety of action of the drug and the fact that careful patient selection is required. Two examples follow of the kind of effect possible with this agent:

CASE ILLUSTRATIONS

Case of D. C.

D. C. is a petite 7-year-old white female who was referred because of her inattentive, overactive, and disruptive behavior at school. At home she had frequent and severe temper outbursts. Her academic achievement was poor, especially in the area of reading. This girl was the oldest of 4 children and none of her 3 brothers was having any difficulty. The birth and developmental history were normal. The past medical history included many febrile illnesses during the first 2 years of life, none requiring hospitalization. There were no convulsions and no delirium. The family history revealed that the mother had a half-sister who was mentally retarded and the father had a sister with epilepsy. The neurological examination of this girl was normal.

This girl's IQ as measured by the WISC was 93 with a Verbal IQ of 85 and a Performance IQ of 103. Her Wide Range Achievement Test scores were at the 2-year grade level in reading, 1 year, 7 month grade level in spelling, and 1 year, 9 month grade level in arithmetic. Throughout the testing her actions were quick and her span of attention was short.

This girl was tried on dextroamphetamine sulfate over a period of four weeks. It was quickly apparent that on any dose greater than 5 mg per day her behavior deteriorated, resulting in more frequent temper outbursts which were harder to control. At school where hyperactivity and distractibility had been the main complaints, she now began to fight other children. While taking only 5 mg per day her behavior was unchanged.

Dextroamphetamine was discontinued and she was placed on diphenylhydantoin, 10 mg daily. An EEG was not done. Within three days the parents reported a marked change in her behavior. Temper outbursts were much less frequent and more easily controlled. By the end of two weeks the parents described the home situation as vastly improved. The school also noted that she now responded to reprimand and was much easier to control. The diphenylhydantoin was begun, however, during the last weeks of school, so a meaningful follow-up could not be obtained. When the family was contacted six months later the improvement was even more dramatic. School performance had improved so that she had advanced a full grade. At home the mother described her as a "changed child." This mother also noted on two occasions when she forgot the medicine during a weekend trip that between twenty-four and forty-eight hours after the last dose a noticeable deterioration in behavior was seen.

Case of C. B.

C. B. is a 12-year-old, obese, Negro male living in a poor area of the city and attending an inner city slum school. His academic progress was excellent, but his teacher reported that he had almost no control of his temper. When things were going smoothly he behaved well, but when he was teased, reprimanded, or told to do something against his will he would have a temper outburst of almost dangerous proportions. In the midst of such rages he had beaten a smaller child and hit a teacher. At home his mood changes could be quite rapid and when he was angry he would break things or threaten to hurt someone. At other times he was described as "sweet and cooperative."

There was no medical history of birth injury or serious illness or injury. The difficulty with his temper began at the time he started school. His school history was one of repeated suspensions. There is one younger brother who has no temper problems. There is no family history of similar disorders or serious psychiatric problems.

Testing of this boy showed Verbal IQ's, as measured by the Peabody Picture Vocabulary Test, of 134 and 123. On the Wide Range Achievement Test his reading grade was 11 years, 7 months, his spelling grade was 5 years, 7 months, and his arithmetic grade was 3 years, 6 months. He was in the sixth grade at the time of testing.

No medications had previously been given for his behavior problem. However, he was taking a dextroamphetamine spansule once a day for weight reduction. The mother stated that there had been no change in behavior with the use of this drug. An EEG had not been done.

The patient was placed on diphenylhydantoin, 100 mg daily. After just four or five days of medication the mother reported a very noticeable change in his behavior. The same precipitating events now seemed to cause much less reaction in the patient. Temper outbursts were both less frequent and much less severe. Because this definite change seemed a little less marked after about one week, the dose was increased to 150 mg daily and remained at that level. The school reinstated this boy (he had been permanently suspended for beating a smaller child), and after four weeks there had been no temper outbursts. Follow-up six months later showed a continuance of this favorable change. The mother noticed on a few occasions when she forgot to give the medicine that there was a deterioration in his behavior between twenty-four and forty-eight hours after the last dose.

Antidepressants. No controlled studies that meet acceptable scientific criteria are available for antidepressants, though studies of imipramine, nortriptyline, and amitriptyline in adolescents with depressive features, and in younger children with learning and behavior disorders, indicate that further research is needed with these agents (Krakowski 1965; Rapoport 1965; Splitter and Kaufman 1966). One relatively well-controlled study suggests that depressive illness in children, associated with poor school progress, may be effectively treated with antidepressants, provided proper patient selection is made (Frommer 1967).

SUMMARY AND CONCLUSIONS

The use of psychotropic drugs in children with learning and behavior disorders is a well-established empirical tradition. Various factors which affect the assessment and outcome of drug treatment in children have been described. While one may conclude on the basis of empirical studies that drug management is an invaluable adjunct for many children, attention has been drawn to the importance of stimulus, organismic, and reaction variables which influence the child's response to medication. Relatively little systematic knowledge is available relating these variables to drug response, though promising beginnings have been made in several areas.

In the absence of definitive rational guidelines for patient selection, drug selection, and indications for drug use, a conservative therapeutic strategy indicates that one should use psychotropic drugs only under careful medical management, with appropriate follow-up of treatment which should involve both the family and the school, and only after clear evidence that placebo response, environmental manipulation, and educational remediation have been investigated.

In general, older drugs with known absence of toxicity, such as the stimulants, are drugs of first choice. Routine prescription of medication without careful physical examination and laboratory studies in children is never justifiable. Multiple points of observation, such as from a clinician, parent, teacher, and the child himself, are recommended for proper evaluation of therapeutic effect; the use of standardized objective measures of cognitive function is also recommended.

REFERENCES

Alexander, D., Walker, H. T., and Money, J.   Studies in direction sense. I. Turner's syndrome. *Archives of General Psychiatry* (Chicago) 10:337, 1964.

Alexandris, A., and Lundell, F. W.   Effect of thioridazine, amphetamine and placebo on the hyperkinetic syndrome and cognitive area in mentally deficient children. *Canadian Medical Association Journal* 98:92, 1968.

Baker, R. R.   The effects of psychotropic drugs on psychological testing. *Psychological Bulletin* 69:377, 1968.

Bender, L., and Cottington, F.   The use of amphetamine sulfate (Benzedrine) in child psychiatry. *American Journal of Psychiatry* 99:116, 1942.

Berlyne, D. E.   *Conflict, Arousal and Curiosity.* New York: McGraw-Hill, 1960.

Bradley, C.   Benzedrine and Dexedrine in the treatment of children's behavior disorders. *Pediatrics* 5:24, 1950.

Bradley, C., and Bowen, M.   School performance of children receiving amphetamine (Benzedrine) sulfate. *American Journal of Orthopsychiatry* 10:782, 1940.

Bradley, C., and Bowen, M.   Amphetamine (Benzedrine) therapy of children's behavior disorders. *American Journal of Orthopsychiatry* 11:92, 1941.

Bradley, C., and Green, E.   Psychometric performance of children receiving amphetamine (Benzedrine) sulfate. *American Journal of Orthopsychiatry* 97:338, 1940.

Burks, H. F.   Effects of amphetamine therapy on hyperkinetic children. *Archives of General Psychiatry* 11:604, 1964.

Conners, C. K. The syndrome of minimal brain dysfunction: Psychological aspects. *Pediatric Clinics of North America* 14:749, 1967.

Conners, C. K. Unpublished data.

Conners, C. K. A teacher rating scale for use in drug studies with children. *American Journal of Psychiatry* 126:152, 1969.

Conners, C. K. Symptom patterns in hyperkinetic, neurotic and normal children. *Child Development* 41:667, 1970.

Conners, C. K., and Eisenberg, L. The effects of methylphenidate on symptomatology and learning in disturbed children. *American Journal of Psychiatry* 120:458, 1963.

Conners, C. K., Eisenberg, L., and Barcai, A. Effect of dextroamphetamine on children. *Archives of General Psychiatry* (Chicago) 17:478, 1967.

Conners, C. K., Eisenberg, L., and Sharpe, L. Effect of methylphenidate (Ritalin) on paired-associate learning and Porteus Maze performance in emotionally disturbed children. *Journal of Consulting Psychology* 28:14, 1964.

Conners, C. K., and Rothschild, G. Drugs and Learning in Children. In *Learning Disorders* Vol. 3. Seattle: Special Child Publications, 1968.

Conners, C. K., Rothschild, G. H., Eisenberg, L., Schwartz, L., and Robinson, E. Dextroamphetamine sulfate in children with learning disorders: Effects on perception, learning and achievement. *Archives of General Psychiatry* (Chicago) 21:182, 1969.

Conrad, W. G. Anticipating the response to amphetamine therapy in the treatment of hyperkinetic children. *Pediatrics* 40:96, 1967.

Creager, R. O., and VanRiper, C. The effect of methylphenidate on the verbal productivity of children with cerebral dysfunction. *Journal of Speech and Hearing Research* 10:623, 1967.

Davis, G. D. Effects of central excitant and depressant drugs on local motor activity in the monkey. *American Journal of Physiology* 188:619, 1957.

DiMascio, A., Brown, J., and Kline, J. Psychological Testing in Psychopharmacology: A Review. In A. DiMascio and R. I. Shader (Eds.), *Clinical Handbook of Psychopharmacology*. New York: Science House, 1970.

Dureman, I., and Palshammar, S. Psychophysiological Reactions in a Serial Approach-Avoidance Conflict Situation: Its Relation to Test Anxiety and School Motivation in Children. Department of Psychology, University of Uppsala, Sweden, 1968.

Dureman, I., and Palshammar, S. The Dynamics of Psychophysiological Activation in Children Performing Under Reward Conditions Involving an Approach-Avoidance Conflict. Department of Psychology, University of Uppsala, Sweden, 1968.

Eisenberg, L., Conners, C. K., and Sharpe, L. A controlled study of the differential application of outpatient psychiatric treatment for children. *Japanese Journal of Child Psychiatry* 6:125, 1965.

Eisenberg, L., Lachman, R., Molling, P., Lockner, A., Mizelle, J., and Conners, C. K. A psychopharmacologic experiment in a training school for delinquent boys. *American Journal of Orthopsychiatry* 33:431, 1963.

English, H. B., and English, A. C. *A Comprehensive Dictionary of Psychological and Psychoanalytical Terms.* New York: Longmans, Green, 1958.

Epstein, L., et al. Correlation of dextroamphetamine excretion and drug response in hyperkinetic children. *Journal of Nervous and Mental Disease* 146:136, 1968.

Eveloff, H. H. Psychopharmacologic agents in child psychiatry. *Archives of General Psychiatry* (Chicago) 14:472, 1966.

Fish, B. Drug therapy in child psychiatry: Pharmacological aspects. *Comprehensive Psychiatry* 1:212, 1960.

Fish, B. Drug therapy in child psychiatry: Psychological aspects. *Comprehensive Psychiatry* 1:55, 1960(a).

Fish, B. Evaluation of Psychiatric Therapies in Children. In P. Hoch and J. Zubin (Eds.), *The Evaluation of Psychiatric Treatment.* New York: Grune & Stratton, 1964.

Fish, B. Drug use in psychiatric disorders of children. *American Journal of Psychiatry* [Feb. Suppl.] 124:31, 1968.

Fish, B. Methodology in Child Psychopharmacology. In D. H. Efron (Ed.), *Psychopharmacology: A Review of Progress 1957–1967.* (Proceedings of the Sixth Annual Meeting of The American College of Neuropsychopharmacology, San Juan, Dec. 1967.) Public Health Service Publication No. 1836, 1968(a).

Fish, B., Shapiro, T., and Campbell, M. Long-term prognosis and the response of schizophrenic children to drug therapy: A controlled study of trifluoperazine. *American Journal of Psychiatry* 1:32, 1966.

Freeman, R. D. Drug effects on learning in children: A selective review of the past thirty years. *Journal of Special Education* 1:17, 1966.

Freeman, R. D. Review of Drug Effects. In *Selected Papers on Learning Disabilities.* (Fifth Annual International Conference of the Association for Children with Learning Disabilities, Boston, Feb. 1968.) San Rafael, Cal.: Academic Therapy Publications, 1969.

Frommer, E. A. Treatment of childhood depression with antidepressant drugs. *British Medical Journal* 1:729, 1967.

Grant, Q. Psychopharmacology in childhood emotional and mental disorders. *Journal of Pediatrics* 61:626, 1962.

Helper, M., Wilcott, R. C., and Garfield, S. L. Effects of chlorpromazine on learning and related processes in emotionally disturbed children. *Journal of Consulting Psychology* 27:1, 1963.

Hutt, C., Jackson, P. M., and Level, M. Behavioral parameters and drug effects: A study of a hyperkinetic epileptic child. *Epilepsia* (Amsterdam) 7:250, 1961.

Irwin, S. The actions of drugs on psychomotor activity. *Revue Canadienne de Biologie* 20:239, 1961.

Irwin, S. A rational framework for the development, evaluation, and use of psychoactive drugs. *American Journal of Psychiatry* 124:1, 1968.

Jones, H. E. The Study of Patterns of Emotional Expression. In M. L. Reymert (Ed.), *Feelings and Emotions*. New York: McGraw-Hill, 1950.

Kagan, J. Reflection-impulsivity and reading ability in primary grade children. *Child Development* 36:609, 1965.

Killam, K. F., and Killam, E. K. Drug Action on Pathways Involving the Reticular Formation. In L. D. Proctor et al. (Eds.), *Reticular Formation of the Brain*. Boston: Little, Brown, 1958.

Kleemeier, L. B., and Kleemeier, R. W. Effects of Benzedrine on psychomotor performance. *American Journal of Psychology* 60:89, 1947.

Knights, R. M., and Hinton, G. The Effects of Methylphenidate (Ritalin) on the Motor Skills and Behavior of Children with Learning Problems. Research Bulletin No. 102, University of Western Ontario, 1968.

Knobel, M. Psychopharmacology for the hyperkinetic child: Dynamic considerations. *Archives of General Psychiatry* (Chicago) 6:198, 1962.

Kraft, I. A. The use of psychoactive drugs in the outpatient treatment of psychiatric disorders of children. *American Journal of Psychiatry* 124:1401, 1968.

Krakowski, A. J. Amitriptyline in treatment of hyperkinetic children: A double-blind study. *Psychosomatics* 6:355, 1965.

Laufer, M. W. Brain Disorders. In A. M. Freedman and H. I. Kaplan (Eds.), *Comprehensive Textbook of Psychiatry*. Baltimore: Williams & Wilkins, 1967.

McGaugh, J. L., and Petrinovich, L. F. Effects of drugs on memory and learning. *International Review of Neurobiology* 8:139, 1965.

Millichap, J. G., Aymak, F., Sturgis, L., Larsen, K., and Egan, R. Hyperkinetic behavior and learning disorders: III. Battery of neuropsychological tests in controlled trial of methylphenidate. *American Journal of Diseases of Children* 116:235, 1968.

Millichap, J. G., and Boldrey, E. E. Studies in hyperkinetic behavior. *Neurology* (Minneapolis) 17:467, 1967.

Millichap, J. G., and Fowler, G. Treatment of "minimal brain dysfunction" syndromes. *Pediatric Clinics of North America* 14:769, 1967.

Molitch, M., and Eccles, A. K.   The effect of Benzedrine Sulfate on the intelligence scores of children. *American Journal of Psychiatry* 94:587, 1937.

Money, J., and Lewis, V.   Longitudinal Study of Intelligence Quotient in Treated Congenital Hypothyroidism. In M. P. Cameron and M. O'Connor (Eds.), *Brain-Thyroid Relationships*. Boston: Little, Brown, 1964.

Ounstead, C.   The hyperkinetic syndrome in epileptic children. *Lancet* 2:303, 1955.

Peterson, D. L.   Behavior problems of middle childhood. *Journal of Consulting Psychology* 25:205, 1961.

Porteus, S. D.   New applications of the Porteus Maze Test. *Perceptual and Motor Skills* 26:787, 1968.

Powell, G. F., Brasel, J. A., and Blizzard, R. M.   Emotional deprivation and growth retardation simulating idiopathic hypopituitarism. I. Clinical evaluation. *New England Journal of Medicine* 276:1271, 1967.

Powell, G. F., Brasel, J. A., Raiti, S., and Blizzard, R. M.   Emotional deprivation and growth retardation simulating idiopathic hypopituitarism. II. Endocrinologic evaluation. *New England Journal of Medicine* 276:1279, 1967.

Rapoport, J.   Childhood behavior and learning problems treated with imipramine. *International Journal of Neuropsychiatry* 1:635, 1965.

Riklan, M., and Levita, E.   *Subcortical Correlates of Human Behavior*. Baltimore: Williams & Wilkins, 1969.

Roberts, L.   Central Brain Mechanisms in Speech. In E. C. Carterette (Ed.), *Brain Function. III. Speech, Language, and Communication*. Berkeley: University of California Press, 1966.

Rutter, M., and Graham, P.   The reliability and validity of the psychiatric assessment of the child. I. Interview with the child. *British Journal of Psychiatry* 114:563, 1968.

Sabatino, D. A.   Identifying neurologically impaired children through a test of auditory perception. *Journal of Consulting and Clinical Psychology* 33:184, 1969.

Satterfield, J.   Personal communication, 1969.

Schachter, S., and Singer, J. E.   Cognitive, social and physiological determinants of emotional state. *Psychological Review* 69:379, 1962.

Schickedanze, D.   Effects of Thioridazine and Methylphenidate on Performance of a Motor Task and Concurrent Motor Activity in Retarded Boys. M. A. Thesis, University of Illinois, 1967.

Silverman, A. J., Cohen, S. I., and Shmavonian, B. M.   Investigation of psychophysiologic relationships with skin resistance measures. *Journal of Psychosomatic Research* 4:65, 1959.

Spivack, G., and Swift, M. *Devereux Elementary School Behavior Rating Scale Manual.* Devon, Pa.: Devereux Foundation, 1967.

Splitter, S., and Kaufman, M. A new treatment for underachieving adolescents: Psychotherapy combined with nortriptyline medication. *Psychosomatics* 1:171, 1966.

Sprague, R. L., Barnes, K. R., and Werry, J. S. Methylphenidate and thioridazine: Learning, reaction time, activity, and classroom behavior in disturbed children. *American Journal of Orthopsychiatry* 40:615, 1970.

Sprague, R. L., Werry, J. S., and Davis, K. Psychotropic Drug Effects on Learning and Activity Level of Children. Paper presented at Gatlinburg (Tenn.) Conference on Research and Theory in Mental Retardation, Mar. 1969.

Werry, J. S. The effects of methylphenidate and phenobarbital on the behavior of hyperactive and aggressive children. Unpublished data, 1969.

Werry, J. S., and Sprague, R. L. Hyperactivity. In C. G. Costello (Ed.), *Symptoms of Psychopathology.* New York: Wiley, 1970.

Wilcott, R. C., Helper, M. M., and Garfield, S. L. Some psychophysiological effects of chlorpromazine on emotionally disturbed children. *Journal of Nervous and Mental Disease* 135:233, 1962.

Zimmerman, F. T., and Burgemeister, B. B. Action of methylphenidylacetate (Ritalin) and reserpine in behavior disorders in children and adults. *American Journal of Psychiatry* 115:323, 1958.

8 Brain Damage and Learning Disabilities

Psychological Diagnosis and Remediation*

JAMES C. REED

THIS CHAPTER is concerned with three problems: (1) the use of psychological tests in the evaluation of patients with brain damage, (2) the relation of brain damage to learning ability, and (3) training and educational procedures for brain-damaged children. In generalizing from the material presented, certain limitations must be observed.

First, there is the problem of accurately defining the term *learning disability* and there is the parallel problem of identifying the brain-damaged patient. A child is seldom said to have a learning disability on the basis of achievement level alone. Rather a disability is usually inferred when there is a discrepancy between the child's achievement level and some measure of potential ability. In terms of reading achievement, Simmons and Shapiro (1968) have shown that in estimating the amount of retardation, there is considerable variation among reading expectancy formulas. They show that an eighth-grade student who has an IQ of 120 and reads at a seventh-grade level would be judged 2 years, 3 years, or 4½ years retarded in reading, depend-

* This paper is supported in part by Grant RT7, Tufts University School of Medicine, Social and Rehabilitation Service, Department of Health, Education, and Welfare.

ing upon the reading expectancy formula employed. Obviously the amount of retardation is not an absolute but depends upon the procedure used to measure it. Reed (1970) has likewise shown that the pattern of deficits found among children with learning disabilities depends upon the index used to estimate the learning potential.

Similar difficulties exist with respect to the use of the terms *brain damage* or *cerebral dysfunction.* Within the neurological sciences, brain damage generally implies actual tissue destruction. The diagnosis may be based upon anamnestic information describing a probable insult to the brain, reflex asymmetry, or divergent or abnormal findings on such specialized diagnostic procedures as electroencephalography, pneumoencephalography, or angiography, neurosurgical and neuropathological information based either on surgical specimens or on autopsy findings. For many educators and for many psychologists, however, the diagnosis of brain damage is based upon behavioral characteristics which may or may not be related to any pathological condition of the brain. Thus there are the perceptually disturbed children, the hyperactive or hyperkinetic pupils, and any number of educational misfits, all of whom have been tagged with the label *brain damaged.* In view of the diverse implications of the terms *learning disability* and *brain damaged,* it is not at all surprising that systematic information concerning the relationship between the two is lacking.

The solution to the foregoing problems depends upon a rigorous operational definition of terms and clear specification of the criterion information used in making the diagnosis of brain damage. However, serious obstacles still stand in the way of understanding the relation between cerebral dysfunction and learning disability. These obstacles stem from the kind of experiments which can be performed when using human beings as subjects. When the experimental design would require strict randomization it is difficult if not impossible to investigate the causes of long-standing chronic disease (or disabilities) in human beings. Where randomization cannot be imposed, the experimenter rarely knows whether group comparability has been achieved. The possibility always exists that whatever associations may be observed are the consequence of factors other than those under study (Yerushalmy and Palmer 1959). If one considers the difficulty in interpreting the statistical associations between lung cancer and smoking, one can begin to appreciate the complexities in deriving meaning from the association between learning disabilities and brain dysfunction.

PSYCHOLOGICAL EVALUATION

The foregoing methodological problems restrict the interpretations made from observational data, but they have not prevented psychologists from developing rather sophisticated procedures and test batteries for evaluating patients with cerebral dysfunction and even inferring the location, lateralization, and type of lesion on the basis of psychological tests alone. Through the use of such tests, a clearer understanding of the relation between brain dysfunction and learning disabilities may eventually be had (Reitan and Heineman 1968). In order to provide a background for understanding the neuropsychological evaluation, it is first necessary to review some of the methods which psychologists have used in the past in evaluating patients with brain dysfunction. Reitan (1967a) gives a more complete discussion of the points that follow.

Methods of Inference

Level of performance. Brain damage (documented by neurological criteria) may result in a lowered level of intellectual functioning. Research has shown that brain-damaged children score lower on a wide range of intellectual, psychomotor, perceptual, and motor tasks than do children of similar age without brain damage (Reed and Fitzhugh 1966). In evaluating patients suspected of having sustained brain damage, psychologists have typically included tests which measure level of functioning. There is a serious danger, however, in inferring cerebral damage or dysfunction on the basis of level of performance alone. Achievement on a given task may be lowered by temporary anxiety, lack of motivation, cultural impoverishment, generally low intelligence, and a host of other variables too numerous to mention here. Tests which measure level of performance should be supplemented by other diagnostic procedures when inferences are made about the integrity of the brain.

Pathognomonic signs of brain damage.   Clinical observation suggests that on selected types of tasks, brain-damaged patients will make certain errors that are rarely found in other patient groups. Illustrative examples are rotations on the Kohs Block Design Test, Piotrowski's ten signs of brain damage on the Rorschach Test (1937), or certain deviations on the Bender Gestalt Test (Bender 1938). Aphasic symptoms constitute a pathological sign. Among adults, the use of a *plus-minus* or *present-absent* approach may have a certain degree of validity. However, the inevitable problem of false negatives arises. Furthermore, in identifying a disease of rare occurrence, the use of pathognomonic signs may result in an overall greater percentage of error than in diagnosing every patient as normal (Meehl and Rosen 1955). The usefulness of the sign approach is even more limited among children. For example, the amount of left-right disorientation, the number of errors on a finger agnosia test, and quality of graphic reproductions are age-related. A factor that is a "sign" of brain damage at one age level may well be a normal performance at a younger age level (Diller and Birch 1964).

Differential score approach.   The differential score approach, which may have originated with Babcock (1930), assumes that one effect of brain damage is selective impairment of cognitive functions. A patient's score on a vocabulary test (a skill of long duration and one where overlearning has occurred) may not be as depressed as his score on a test of immediate problem-solving ability. In other words, the difference between scores on tests relatively resistant to impairment, and scores on measures presumably adversely affected by cerebral damage, has been used to indicate the presence of brain damage. The chief limitation of the differential score approach is that it assumes that brain lesions will have a similar effect regardless of the location of the lesion and regardless of the type of the lesion. Among children with chronic cerebral dysfunction of long duration, it is questionable whether selective impairment of intellectual functions does occur (Reed and Reed 1967). An advantage of the differential score approach is its potential for understanding the effects of type and site of lesion on behavior.

Measurements of the two sides of the body. A fourth method of inferring cerebral damage is derived from the physical-neurological evaluation and depends upon comparing differences in adequacy of performance between the two sides of the body. Clear and consistent lateralized deficiencies probably would rarely if ever result from factors such as anxiety, lack of motivation, or generalized retardation. Indeed it would be unusual for a person to be anxious on a motor or sensory task involving the use of the right upper extremity and then to be non-anxious in using the left upper extremity on the same task.

The Neuropsychological Test Battery

There are several procedures, approaches, and tests recommended for evaluating children with brain damage (Bender 1956, Benton 1955, L'Abate 1968). No single test will suffice because of the diverse and subtle effects of brain lesions. However, Halstead (1947) developed a battery of tests which combines the advantage of each of the inferential approaches described in the foregoing paragraphs and is by far the most comprehensive battery available for the assessment of brain-damaged patients. The tests were validated by Reitan (1955) who also extended them downward for use with adolescents and younger children; validating studies of these tests with children have been done by Reed and Reed (1967), Reed and Fitzhugh (1966), Reed, Reitan, and Kløve (1965). The battery described here is Reitan's adaptation for older children. It includes the Wechsler Intelligence Scale for Children, the Category Test, a modified Trail-making Test, an aphasia screening test which is a modification of the Halstead-Wepman Aphasia Screening Test (Halstead and Wepman 1949), and various tests of sensory perceptual functions.

Category Test. The Category Test is a measure of abstract concept formation. It requires the subject to abstract and apply principles from serially presented visual stimuli. The test at the intermediate level includes 168 presentations divided into six subtests. Each subtest is organized around a single principle, and the task of the subject is to discover this organizing principle.

Slides are individually presented on a screen and at the base of the screen is an answer panel which contains four levers numbered one through four. For each picture that appears on the screen, the subject presses one of the four levers. If his answer is correct, a bell rings; if it is wrong, a buzzer sounds. Only one response is allowed for each item. On the first item in any group, the subject can only guess with regard to the right answer, but as he progresses through the items in the group the sounding of the bell or buzzer with each response indicates whether the guesses are correct or incorrect. The test procedure permits the subject to discover the principle underlying the set of items.

Tactual Performance Test (time, memory, and localization components). The Tactual Performance Test utilizes a modification of the Seguin Goddard Form Board. The subject is required, while blindfolded, to place six blocks of different sizes and shapes into corresponding holes on the form board. The subject performs the task first with his preferred hand, then with his nonpreferred hand, and finally with both hands. The time recorded for each trial provides the comparison. The adequacy of performance of the two hands and the time score for all three trials is an indication of the adequacy of performance from the standpoint of level. After the third trial has been completed, the board and blocks are put away and the blindfold removed. The subject is then asked to draw a diagram of the board, the shape of the blocks, and as well as he can, locate them in their correct positions. The test yields three scores—a score for total time, a score corresponding to the number of blocks correctly drawn from memory, and a third score for the number of blocks correctly localized in the subject's drawing.

This test measures the patient's problem-solving ability in a novel situation and requires him to adapt kinesthetic and sensory cues in a problem-solving situation which would ordinarily be coordinated by vision.

Rhythm Test. The Rhythm Test is a modification of the Seashore Test of Musical Talent. The subject is required to differentiate between thirty pairs of rhythmic beats which are sometimes the same and sometimes different. The test appears to require alertness, sustained attention to the task, and the ability to distinguish between rhythmic sequences.

Speech Sound Perception Test. The Speech Sound Perception Test consists of sixty spoken nonsense words which are variants of the *ee* sound presented in multiple choice form. The test is played from a tape recorder with the intensity of sound adjusted to meet the subject's preference. For younger adolescents the answer form has three alternatives. The subject's task is to underline the letter combination which corresponds to the spoken syllable. The test requires the patient to maintain attention for sixty items, to distinguish between similar auditory stimuli, and to recognize the relation between the visual letter combination and its auditory counterpart.

Finger Oscillation Test. The Finger Oscillation Test is a measure of finger-tapping speed. Measurements are obtained from a Veeder Root Counter. The subject is given five consecutive ten-second trials and is told for each trial to tap as fast as he can. Measurements are obtained for the preferred hand and then the nonpreferred hand. A score is recorded for each hand and the score is the average of the five ten-second trials. Performance on this test is probably dependent upon motor speed.

Time Sense Test (visual and memory components). The Time Sense Test requires the patient to press a key which permits a sweep hand to rotate on the face of the clock. After the hand rotates ten times, he then stops it as close to the starting position as possible. After twenty trials, during which the subject watches the rotation of the sweep hand on the face of the clock, the face of the clock is turned away and the subject is asked to stop the clock after ten trials from memory. A series of ten visual and ten memory trials are interspersed to represent a total of forty visual trials and twenty memory trials in the entire test. A score is obtained for each procedure and represents the amount of error made. The visual aspect of this test requires the patient to maintain attention, and a rather discrete visual motor coordination is required to stop the hand's rotation in the correct position. The memory component requires estimation of the duration of the time necessary for the hand to make ten revolutions.

Aphasia Screening Test. Reitan modified the Halstead-Wepman Aphasia Screening Test so that it would be suitable for younger adolescents and children. The test is designed to sample a large number of language and related behaviors in order to provide a survey of possible aphasia and related deficits. The test requires the subject to name common objects, spell, identify individual numbers and letters, read, write, calculate, enunciate, understand spoken language, identify body parts, and differentiate between right and left. Measures are also obtained of the patient's ability to reproduce simple geometrical forms.

Trail-making Test. The Trail-making Test consists of parts A and B. Part A is a series of twenty-five circles randomly distributed over a white sheet of paper and numbered from 1 to 25. The subject is required to connect the circles with a pencil as quickly as possible beginning with number 1 and proceeding in sequence to the end. Part B consists of twenty-five circles, each of which is identified by either a number or a letter of the alphabet. The patient is required to connect the circles in sequence alternating between numbers and letters. Thus he goes from 1 to A, 2 to B, 3 to C, and so on until he gets to the end. Timed scores are obtained separately for part A and part B. The test appears to require visual scanning as well as the ability to shift set in integrating numerical and alphabetical sequences.

Sensory-perceptual disturbances. Measures of sensory-perceptual intactness for tactile, visual, and auditory stimuli are obtained under conditions of double simultaneous stimulation. For tactile stimuli, for example, each hand is first touched separately in order to determine that the subject is able to respond accurately to the hand touched. Following unilateral stimulation, bilateral simultaneous stimulation is interspersed. The normal response is for the subject to respond with the following alternatives: right hand, left hand, or both hands. A patient with a lateralized cerebral lesion will sometimes fail to perceive the stimulus applied to the hand contralateral to the lesion under conditions of simultaneous stimulation even though he was able to perceive the stimulus under conditions of unilateral stimulation. Corresponding procedures are followed for visual and auditory stimuli.

Tactile finger recognition. Inability to identify the fingers on the basis of tactile stimulation alone is one manifestation of finger agnosia. The patient's hand is shielded from his view and the fingers are touched in a random order. There are four trials for each finger on each hand, yielding a total of twenty trials per hand. The score is recorded as the number of errors for each hand.

Fingertip Number Writing Perception Test. Numbers are written on the tips of the fingers and the patient is required to identify solely on the basis of tactile information which number is being written. Again there is a total of four trials for each finger on each hand. The score is the number of errors for each hand.

Tactile Form Recognition Test. In the Tactile Form Recognition Test the subject must identify through touch alone common geometrical shapes (cross, square, triangle, and circle). The subject's hand is shielded from his view, and one of the objects is placed in the hand. With the other hand, the subject points to a standard set of stimulus figures that are visually exposed and identifies the given object. Measures are obtained for both the right and left hand. An additional procedure requires that the patient identify by touch pennies, nickels, and dimes. Each hand is tested separately and the test also requires recognition of coins placed in each hand simultaneously.

Test Objectives

An analysis of the requirements for each of the foregoing tests indicates the diversity of the procedures through which it is possible to infer cerebral damage. The tests permit scores for level of performance on tasks covering a wide range of psychological functions, from higher-level cognitive skills—such as concept formation—to very basic, simple tactile-perceptual skills. Methods are given for eliciting pathognomonic signs, for deriving differential scores, and for comparing the two sides of the body. The cross-body comparisons include measurements of motor function as well as sensory integrity. Each method of inference used to supplement and complement the others constitutes not only a powerful diagnostic tool, but also a research procedure for increasing understanding of brain–behavior relations.

Let us examine two case studies to illustrate how these tests can be used (1) in the evaluation of an individual patient and (2) to increase our understanding of the relation of brain damage to learning disability. The two cases presented here have been discussed by Reitan (1967b) in another context.

Case of K. D. The first patient, K. D., was a white female, 9 years and 1 month old at the time she was admitted to the hospital. For the previous six months she had experienced episodes of headache, vomiting, and a tendency to stagger. At the time of admission the neurological examination showed a slightly broad-based gait and pronounced bilateral papilledema. She was reported to be usually quite well but to have occasional headaches, irritability, and nausea and vomiting. Electroencephalographic tracings were interpreted as being abnormal and compatible with increased intracranial pressure. Skull x-rays showed poor definition of the dorsum sellae and suggested a possible brainstem enlargement. A ventriculogram showed evidence of some upward displacement of the fourth ventricle and was consistent with the presence of a mass lesion in the midline of the posterior fossa. Surgery followed immediately and revealed a large tumor extending from the superior portion of the cerebellum, all the way through the vermis, filling the fourth ventricle, and emerging from the left cerebellar tonsil as a mass of pure tumor tissue. The pathological diagnosis of the tumor tissue was medulloblastoma. Neuropsychological testing was done three days before surgery and the results are shown in Table 8-1.

At the time of the neuropsychological examination, the patient was just more than halfway through the third grade of school. The Wide Range Achievement Test yielded the following grade equivalents: Reading 3 years, 3 months; Spelling

TABLE 8-1. *A Patient with a Medulloblastoma*

Patient: K. D.		Age: 9 years, 1 month		Education: Grade 3	
Wechsler Intelligence Scale for Children		**Halstead's Neuropsychological Battery for Children**			
VIQ	99	Category Test			42
PIQ	118				
F-S IQ	109	Tactual Performance Test			
VWS	49	Right hand	3.2	Time	6.3
PWS	63	Left hand	1.4	Memory	5
Total WS	112	Both hands	1.6	Location	3
Information	9				
Comprehension	7	Seashore Rhythm Test			8
Arithmetic	13	Raw Score	24		
Similarities	9				
Vocabulary	9	Speech Sound Perception Test			15
Digit span	12				
Picture completion	13	Finger Oscillation Test			34
Picture arrangement	9	Right hand	34		
Block design	15	Left hand	32		
Object assembly	14				
Coding	13	Time Sense Test			
Mazes	11	Visual	87.1	Memory	555.0
Trail-making Test for Children			**Sensory-Perceptual Examinations**		
Trails A	13 sec, (0) errors	Tactile	RH 0 LH 0	Both: RH 0	LH 0
Trails B	23 sec, (1) error		RH 0 LF 0	Both: RH 0	LF 0
Jastak Wide Range Achievement Test			LH 0 RF 0	Both: LH 0	RF 0
		Auditory	RE 0 LE 0	Both: RE 0	LE 0
Reading	3.3	Visual	RV 0 LV 0	Both: RV 0	LV 0
Spelling	3.2	Finger Recognition		RH 0	LH 3
Arithmetic	4.1	Fingertip Number Writing		RH 2	LH 2
Dominance Tests		Coin Recognition		RH 2	LH 1
Hand Dominance	R 6 L 1	Tactile Form Recognition		RH 0	LH 0
Foot Dominance	R 2 L 0	**Strength of Grip**			
Visual Dominance	R 2 L 8	R 7.5 kg L 7.5 kg			

SOURCE: Reitan (1967b).

3 years, 2 months, and Arithmetic 4 years, 1 month. These results were well within the range of normal variability considering the age of the child, the years of formal education, and the level of intellectual functioning.

On the Wechsler Intelligence Scale for Children the child earned a Verbal IQ of 99, which is almost exactly average; but her Performance IQ was 118 and in the upper end of the High Average Range. While some overlap occurred between the scores on the verbal subtests and the scores on the performance subtests, the pattern of performance revealed that the patient had a definite tendency to do better on performance or manipulative tasks than she did on verbal tasks. Certainly there was no evidence in the subtest scores or in the relation of Verbal IQ to Performance IQ to suggest disrupted intellectual function stemming from a brain lesion.

On the neuropsychological tests, the level of performance was well within the range of normal variability. For example, on the Category Test, the child made 42 errors; this would place her in about the sixtieth percentile rank for her chronological age group. The total time on the Tactual Performance Test was 6.3 minutes, and there was no significant deviation between her time scores with the right hand and with the left hand. The child required slightly longer to complete the task when using both hands than when using only the left hand. This discrepancy could easily be due to a momentary delay in locating one block. In other words, the performance with the left hand was so good that it would be difficult to improve on it. Motor speed, as measured by the Finger Oscillation Test, was adequate and her time scores on parts A and B of the Trail-making Test were somewhat above average for her age. The only possible evidence of impairment was provided by the Finger Recognition Test where the patient made 3 errors on the left hand but none on the right. However, in the context of otherwise good performance, there would be no justification for using the discrepancy between the two hands on the Finger Agnosia Test to infer the presence of a brain lesion.

In summary, the patient had a highly destructive brain lesion, documented by surgical and neuropathological criterion procedures, which would result in a foreshortened life span; however, on a comprehensive battery of neuropsychological tests, the results were well within the range of normal variability and there was no evidence whatsoever of a learning disability.

Case of R. L. The next patient, R. L., illustrates the cognitive deficits that can occur when damage is sustained at the level of the cerebral hemispheres. This patient was in good health until 8 years, 9 months of age, when he was hit on the head by a steel pole and suffered a left temporo-parietal depressed skull fracture. The wound was repaired surgically, but a report was made that there was very definite laceration of the brain and it was necessary to remove bone fragments from the brain tissue. The patient was unconscious for a week following this injury and was confined to a wheelchair for three months. Three years after the injury was sustained, the patient began to experience generalized convulsive seizures. For a month prior to his second admission he had as many as two seizures a day. Physical examination at the time of the second admission indicated the presence of a left temporo-parietal surgical scar, a spastic gait, a mild spastic paraparesis, right astereognosis, moderate weakness of the right hand, mild weakness of the left hand, generally hyperactive reflexes, and evidence of dysphasia. Skull films indicated the presence of a large metallic plate on the left side of the skull, and the electroencephalogram was interpreted as being abnormal with evidence of slow waves over the left cerebral hemisphere.

Neuropsychological examination was done at the time of the second admission when the patient was 11 years and 10 months of age, and approximately three years after the injury had been sustained. The results are presented in Table 8-2.

On the Wechsler Intelligence Scale for Children, the patient earned Verbal and Performance IQ values in the lower part of the Dull Normal Range. Even though his best scores were on the Block Design and Object Assembly tests, it did not appear that there were significant differences between his verbal and performance abilities. The child was in grade five and on the Wide Range Achievement Test he earned a reading grade score of 3 years, 5 months, a spelling grade score of 2 years, 2 months and an arithmetic grade score of 3 years, 1 month. Thus in terms of chronological age and years of formal education, there was a definite retardation in academic subject matters. In consideration of the lowered IQ values, the retardation is not as great as implied, but nevertheless the patient was achieving at the time of the examination below an arbitrary level of potential performance as estimated by the WISC Scale IQ value.

The neuropsychological examination provided quite definite information for implicating the cerebral hemispheres. The level of performance as measured by the Category Test was within the average range of variability, but the overall time required to complete the Tactual Performance Test was definitely too slow and the child was unable to score on either the memory or location component of the test. In addition the patient could not complete the task with his right upper extremity. He inserted only three blocks in a ten-minute time period. However, with the left (nonpreferred) hand he successfully com-

TABLE 8-2. *A Patient with Depressed Skull Fracture*

Patient: R. L.	Age: 11 years, 10 months	Education: Grade 5

Wechsler Intelligence Scale for Children		Halstead's Neuropsychological Battery for Children		
VIQ	80	Category Test		43
PIQ	83			
F-S IQ	80	Tactual Performance Test		
VWS	34	Right hand 10.0 (3 in*)	Time	19.8
PWS	38	Left hand 7.9	Memory	0
Total WS	72	Both hands 1.8	Location	0
Information	5			
Comprehension	8	Seashore Rhythm Test		9
Arithmetic	7	Raw score 23		
Similarities	9			
Vocabulary	7	Speech Sound Perception Test		19
Digit span	5			
Picture completion	6	Finger Oscillation Test		31
Picture arrangement	5	Right hand 31		
Block design	11	Left hand 35		
Object assembly	11			
Coding	5	Time Sense Test		
Mazes	—	Visual —	Memory —	

Trail-making Test for Children		Sensory-Perceptual Examinations		
Trails A	37 sec, (1) error	Tactile	RH 0 LH 0	Both: RH 0 LH 0
Trails B	61 sec, (1) error		RH 0 LF 0	Both: RH 0 LF 0
Jastak Wide Range			LH 0 RF 0	Both: LH 0 RF 0
Achievement Test		Auditory	RE 0 LE 0	Both: RE 0 LE 0
Reading	3.5	Visual	RV 0 LV 0	Both: RV 0 LV 0
Spelling	2.2	Finger Recognition		RH 4 LH 0
Arithmetic	3.1	Fingertip Number Writing		RH 9 LH 3
Dominance Tests		Coin Recognition		RH 3 LH 2
Hand Dominance	R 7 L 0	Tactile Form Recognition		RH 6 LH 0
Foot Dominance	R 1 L 1	Strength of Grip		
Visual Dominance	R 9 L 1	R 13.5 kg L 19 kg		

* Three blocks inserted.
SOURCE: Reitan (1967b).

pleted the task. The deficiency of the right upper extremity was also revealed by the Finger Tapping Test. With the right hand the patient averaged 31 taps in a ten-second time period. With his left he was able to tap 35 taps in the same time period. (A normal patient usually taps faster with the preferred hand.)

The deficiency of the right upper extremity was not restricted to tasks limited by motor function. Right-sided impairment was also present on sensory and perceptual measures. On the Finger Recognition Task, the Fingertip Number Writing Perception Test, the Coin Recognition Test, and the Tactile Form Recognition Test, the patient consistently made more errors on the right hand than on the left. The combination of deficiencies of both motor and sensory tasks is of value in drawing inferences that the responsible lesion may be referred to the level of the cerebral hemispheres.

Case discussion. There are obvious limitations in making broad generalizations from a sample of two cases. Nevertheless the first documents quite clearly that even highly destructive lesions of the brain need not affect the learning process nor disrupt higher intellectual functions. The second patient also had a serious injury to the brain, but one from which recovery is possible. However, the head injury may have quite disruptive consequences on the patient's adjustment to the problem-solving demands of his environment. For case R. L. it would be difficult to infer from the tests that the head injury resulted in intellectual loss, although the finding would be quite consistent with clinical reports. Nevertheless there were definite signs of lowered performance for a wide range of tasks. There were definite indications of lateralized cerebral dysfunction, and there was evidence of retardation in reading, spelling, and arithmetic. In consideration of the overall findings indicating left cerebral damage, it is not at all surprising that the patient manifests difficulty in language-related areas.

RELATION OF BRAIN DAMAGE TO LEARNING DISABILITIES

The previous section described certain psychological tests and gave examples of how they could be used in patient evaluation.

Thoughtful consideration of the two cases which were presented reveals the complexity of the relation between brain damage and learning disability. These two cases illustrate that it is necessary to know not only whether damage is present, but where on the neural axis the damage has occurred. Damage below the level of the cerebral hemispheres may have no relation to learning, whereas damage at the level of the cerebral hemispheres may have very pronounced consequences for learning.

The problem is even more complicated. In order to understand the relation between the effects of brain pathology and learning disability, or more broadly speaking, the relation between brain lesions and behavior, it is necessary to distinguish among (1) the effects of a lesion after a skill has been acquired, (2) the effects of a lesion before a skill has been acquired (Reed and Reitan 1969), and (3) whether the lesion represents a recent neurological complaint or a chronic condition which is either slowly progressive or static in course (Fitzhugh, Fitzhugh, and Reitan 1962; Matthews and Reitan 1964). Benton (1962), for example, cites differences between acquired dyslexia which results from a recent lesion in the left cerebral hemisphere of the adult and developmental dyslexia which may be associated with adverse perinatal factors. Similar distinctions can be made between acquired and developmental finger agnosia (Kinsbourne and Warrington 1963; Reed 1967; cf. Semmes, Weinstein, Ghent, and Teuber 1960). Dunn (1968) further elucidates the problem of the relation between brain damage and learning disabilities.

The previous paragraphs provide cautions and qualifications which must be observed in interpreting statements on how the condition of the brain might affect learning. A number of investigators, however, have attempted to determine the incidence of neurological disturbances among children with learning disabilities. A general conclusion from these studies is that when children are selected on the basis of a learning disability and then compared with a comparable age group with respect to the incidence of positive neurological signs, the group with a learning disability consistently shows a higher frequency of neurological disturbances. This conclusion must be viewed with the reservation that in most of the studies sampling procedures were not described, hence it is difficult to know what other biases might affect the sample; there was little or no evidence that the learning disability subjects and their normal controls were selected from the same environment. There are many practical difficulties, but a more precise understanding of the relation between neurological disturbances and learning disabilities might result if a normal sibling were used as the control subject.

Cohn (1961) studied 46 children from a county school system who were selected for detailed study because of failure to acquire reading and writing abilities. All were in the chronological age range of 7 to 10. The neurological study included several tests potentially correlated with structural lesions of the brain. Cohn used measures of language, somatic receiving and expressive systems, personal spatial organization, social adaptation, and electroencephalographic tracings. A number of elements were included under each measure, and each element was graded on a maximum basis of 4. The elements were totaled to arrive at an index of neurological deficit. Two control groups were used. In the first, 130 children who showed no apparent learning disabilities were randomly selected from the regular classrooms. The second consisted of 24 subjects who were tutored for reading problems but were retained in a regular classroom because their disabilities were not as severe as those of the experimental group. The results showed that for the learning disability group, the modal neurological impairment index was in the 25 to 50 range. Of the 46 subjects, 44 had neurological impairment indices above 10. For Control Group I, 54 subjects were in the chronological age range of 7 to 10 and the modal neurological impairment index was in the 0 to 10 range. Only 6 of the 54 subjects had indices in the 10 to 25 range. Control Group II showed a distribution similar to Group I on the neurological impairment index. In the learning disability group, over 50 percent of the subjects showed electroencephalographic abnormalities, whereas in Control Group I only 10 percent of the subjects showed electroencephalographic disturbances. Furthermore, "soft" neurological signs were the primary reason for the normal controls' having impairment indices above 5. Cohn concluded that delayed development in the use of graphic symbols was primarily an expression of a general disturbance in neurological function.

Hertzig, Bortner, and Birch (1969) also studied the incidence of neurological findings in children educationally designated as brain-damaged. Their subjects were 105 children, 90 of whom attended a special educational facility for the brain-injured, and 15 who were in normal school placement and served as controls. The subjects were in the chronological age range of 10 to 12 years. A clinical neurological examination was done on each subject by an examiner who did not know which were the control subjects. Of the group designated as brain-damaged, 85 (or 94%) showed signs of primary neurological dysfunction. Of the 90 brain-damaged subjects, 26 showed at least one hard sign. A "hard" sign was defined as the presence of a pathological reflex or lack of cranial nerve intactness. Of the control group, 5 (or ⅓) showed evidence of neurological dysfunction but no hard signs were found for any control subject. The authors imply that children who are educationally designated as brain-damaged and have learning disorders do in fact show neurological disturbances.

The findings of the foregoing investigation are typical of others that have been reported revealing an association between neurological disturbances and learning disabilities (Kawi and Pasamanick 1959). However, this association may stem from common sampling biases rather than representing a biological–behavioral relationship. Furthermore, the demonstration of an association between neurological disturbances and learning disabilities does not provide any illumination concerning appropriate pedagogical procedures which may be used to ameliorate the learning disability. Attention will now be directed toward some of the procedures that have been recommended for children with learning disabilities who also are suspected of having brain damage.

REMEDIAL PROCEDURES

The amount of gain in academic achievement a brain-damaged child with a learning disability can make depends upon the extent of the brain injury, the child's age when the injury was sustained, the level of intellectual functioning, the degree of learning retardation, the age remediation is begun, the materials used in teaching, and probably the quality of the teaching instruction. Systematic evidence is lacking, but the prognosis for older children with severe retardation is probably less favorable than for younger children. Wide variability is present, but on the average brain-damaged children learn at a slower rate and their eventual achievement level is lower than that of their age peers.

Several instructional methods and training procedures have been recommended. The superiority of any one method over another has not been demonstrated. Strauss and Lehtinen (1947) have written a classic text, but the generality of their procedures has not been independently documented. At the end of this chapter is a selected bibliography of instructional procedures widely used with the brain-damaged child.

Earlier, a learning disability was defined as a discrepancy between the child's manifest level of achievement and some measure of expected potential. Recent opinion is divided over the advisability of (1) attempting to give educational instruction in the skill that is deficient or (2) attempting to train abilities propaedeutic (preparatory) to the skill. Thus, for example, the question centers around whether a brain-damaged child who has a severe reading disability should be trained directly in word-recognition skills (phonetic analysis, syllabification, structural analysis) or the use of context clues (oral reading and silent comprehension skills), or whether these deficiencies are merely symptomatic of a disruption in some underlying modality, e.g., visual perception, auditory discrimination, or even a basic neurological disorganization. Those who adopt the latter point of view recommend training in the underlying deficiency.

The Illinois Test of Psycholinguistic Abilities (ITPA) was designed to provide information concerning specific areas of linguistic strengths or weaknesses and to guide the therapist in planning remediation programs in the area where the deficiency occurred. There are nine subtests which tap abilities in three areas: (1) communication channels—auditory and visual, (2) psycholinguistic processes—decoding, association, and encoding, and (3) levels of organization—automatic-sequential and representational. The ITPA has the advantage of providing operational definitions of underlying abilities, but whether training procedures based on this model will prove efficacious will have to be determined by future research. For an example of how the ITPA may be used in the correction of a reading disability, see Della-Piana (1968).

Frostig (1968) believes that deficiencies in visual perception underlie many learning disabilities and that the remedial process should be directed toward ameliorating the visual-perceptive defect. She reports that the methods, materials, and procedures which she employs are highly successful. Independent experimental evidence is lacking.

The Fitzhughs (1966) (The Fitzhugh Perceptual Learning and Understanding Series) have developed two sets of programed instructional materials. One set is for patients who have deficiencies in visuo-spatial skills. The other set is for those deficient in language and conceptual processes. Again the materials are designed for training in a modality or in a process. One advantage of the Fitzhugh materials is that they are self-teaching. Through an ingenious process, when the child marks a correct answer, a colored line appears, so the child can immediately distinguish right answers from wrong answers.

Others believe that failure to develop proficiency in motor skills results in deficiencies in higher-level cognitive and academic skills. Kephart (1960) gives one rationale for the sequential relation of higher-level to lower-level skills and abilities. He also describes treatment procedures based on this rationale. Delacato (1966) describes a training program which supposedly results in a reorganization of neurological processes. For Delacato, the brain-injured child with a severe learning disability has had a breakdown in the neurological development sequence. Through a series of elaborate training procedures, rehabilitation is effected by retraining in the skills which were disrupted in the neuromotor development pattern. As with other procedures, independent evidence of their merit is lacking. Glass and Robbins (1967) critically analyzed fifteen experiments which were evaluations of the approach recommended by Delacato. They concluded that twelve of the studies were invalid in terms of experimental design, statistical analysis, and interpretation of results. These reviews were not concerned with esoteric subtleties of design or picayune flaws in analysis. Rather they directed their attention to major methodological limitations.

Cruickshank, Bentzen, Ratzeburg, and Tannhauser (1961) describe a comprehensive training program for brain-injured children, based on the methods of Strauss and Lehtinen. One aspect of their procedures is the use of cubicles so that distracting stimuli can be kept at a minimum. These authors' own analysis and evaluation failed to reveal the benefits of their methods, and they base their recommendations on logical considerations. Because of the expense of and the necessity for classroom organization, serious thought and analysis should be given before adopting these procedures.

When a severe learning disability is present, many believe that the remedial procedure should be directed toward correcting the manifest deficiency rather than developing proficiency in the underlying modality. Proponents of this point of view stress that the sequential relation of higher-level to lower-level skills is based on armchair theorizing rather than empirical evidence. With justification, many examples can be cited of children with cerebral palsy who show profound disruption of motor skills, but score quite high on intelligence tests and do not show any signs of learning disability. It is questionable whether a child with chronic, static cerebral dysfunction who has a learning disability requires different methods of teaching from a child with a learning disability but without cerebral dysfunction.

Those who recommend attacking the deficiency directly are concerned with an educational diagnosis emphasizing level of achievement, amount of retardation, and specific proficiencies in reading, arithmetic, spelling, and so on. Since difficulty with reading is one of the most common characteristics of a learning disability, this discussion will center on that skill.

For a classic treatment and description of procedures for remedial teaching in reading, see Monroe (1932) and Fernald (1943). Common to many procedures recommended for the brain-injured child with a learning disability is the use of a multisensory approach. Fernald discusses the use of kinesthetic procedures and Johnson (1966) gives some variants. Briefly, the child is presented with a handwritten stimulus of a word which he has expressed an interest in learning. He traces the word with his finger, looking carefully at it, and pronounces the word slowly as he traces. Thus tactile, visual, and auditory channels are used in learning the word. Next the stimulus is removed from sight and the child writes the word. This procedure is repeated until the child has mastered the word. Favorable reports for this method of teaching have been given, but experimental evidence is deficient. Because of the length of time involved, the kinesthetic method of teaching is generally used after other attempts, such as phonetic or visual, have been tried without success.

A number of developments in operant conditioning raise the question of the need for extensive educational diagnosis. The operant procedures require identification of specific behaviors which are either absent from the child's repertoire (inability to sound initial consonants) or behaviors which occur to the detriment of further developing a desirable skill (reading in a monotone). Through the use of planned schedules of positive reinforcement or negative reinforcment, or both, tasks are presented in increasing level of difficulty for the subject, with the initial task being of such a nature that the child can successfully perform it. Thereupon he is rewarded on a predetermined schedule, e.g., every correct response, every fifth correct response. Lovaas (1966) has described detailed procedures for developing speech in children deemed extremely difficult to teach. Operant conditioning procedures with humans are frequently referred to as *behavior modification* techniques. These techniques have been effective in changing a broad spectrum of specific behaviors for a wide range of subjects. For an extension of some of these procedures to programed instruction and their relation to reading, see Schramm (1962).

SUMMARY

There are many factors which govern the amount of academic progress that a brain-injured child can make but, in general, progress is slow. There is a division of opinion over whether it is better to attempt to train the child directly in his academic deficiency or whether there is a necessity to develop propaedeutic skills. *With all the foregoing methods, the greatest amount of success has been had by the proponent of the method.* Most educators agree that training should be individualized on the basis of a thorough knowledge of the child's needs, strengths, and weaknesses. It should be geared to the child's rate of learning and level of achievement. Teaching procedures which have proved satisfactory for the normal child should be given first preference in working with the brain-injured child. All agree that there is a need for critical evaluation of teaching and instructional programs.

In recapitulation of the main points of this chapter, there are many methodological problems which must be overcome if there is to be a significant increase in knowledge about brain damage and learning disabilities. *Learning disability* must be rigorously and operationally defined. The criteria for identifying brain damage must be made explicit. For a comprehensive evaluation of patients with brain damage, it is necessary to employ a battery of tests which measures a wide range of behaviors —from higher-level abstract cognitive skills to simple tactile and perceptual skills. The relation of brain damage to a learning disability cannot be understood apart from an understanding of the site of the lesion, the age at which it occurred, the time of the lesion in relation to the acquisition of the behavior or skill, and the nature of the task in which the child with cerebral dysfunction is deficient. When children are identified on the basis of learning disabilities, an association has been found with neurological disturbances. However, such an association does not provide knowledge of the most effective instructional procedures that should be used. No one teaching procedure has been demonstrated to be superior to others. Future research should be directed toward a more systematic evaluation of instructional procedures.

REFERENCES

Babcock, H. An experiment in the measurement of mental deterioration. *Archives of Psychology*, 18:5, 1930.

Bender, L. *A Visual-Motor Gestalt Test and Its Clinical Use.* New York: American Orthopsychiatric Association, 1938.

Bender, L. *Psychopathology of Children with Organic Brain Disorders.* Springfield, Ill.: Thomas, 1956.

Benton, A. L. *The Revised Visual Retention Test: Clinical and Experimental Application.* New York: The Psychological Corporation, 1955.

Benton, A. L. Dyslexia in Relation to Form Perception and Directional Sense. In J. Money (Ed.), *Reading Disability: Progress and Research Needs in Dyslexia.* Baltimore: Johns Hopkins Press, 1962. Pp. 81–102.

Cohn, R. Delayed acquisition of reading and writing abilities in children. *Archives of Neurology* (Chicago) 4:153, 1961.

Delacato, C. *Neurological Organization and Reading.* Springfield, Ill.: Thomas, 1966.

Della-Piana, M. *Reading Diagnosis and Prescription: An Introduction.* New York: Holt, Rinehart and Winston, 1968.

Diller, L. and Birch, H. G. Psychological Evaluation of Children with Cerebral Damage. In H. G. Birch (Ed.), *Brain Damage in Children.* Baltimore: Williams & Wilkins, 1964. Pp. 27–43.

Dunn, L. M. Minimal Brain Dysfunction: A Dilemma for Educators. In H. C. Haywood (Ed.), *Brain Damage in School Age Children.* Washington: Council for Exceptional Children, 1968. Pp. 161–181.

Fitzhugh, K. B., Fitzhugh, L. C., and Reitan, R. M. The relationship of acuteness of organic brain dysfunction to Trail-making Test performances. *Perceptual and Motor Skills* 15:399, 1962.

Glass, V., and Robbins, M. P. A critique of experiments on the role of neurological organization in reading performance. *Reading Research Quarterly* 3:5, 1967.

Halstead, W. C. *Brain and Intelligence: A Quantitative Study of the Frontal Lobes.* Chicago: University of Chicago Press, 1947.

Halstead, W. C., and Wepman, J. M. The Halstead-Wepman Aphasia Screening Test. *Journal of Speech and Hearing Disorders* 14:9, 1949.

Hertzig, M., Bortner, M., and Birch, H. G. Neurologic findings in children educationally designated as "brain-damaged." *American Journal of Orthopsychiatry* 39:437, 1969.

Hunt, H. F. Diagnostic Methods: Psychological Testing. In A. B. Biker (Ed.), *Clinical Neurology* Vol. I. New York: Hoeber-Harper, 1955. Pp. 311–329.

Kawi, A. A., and Pasamanick, B. *Prenatal and Paranatal Factors in the Development of Childhood Reading Disorders.* Monographs of the Society for Research in Child Development. Serial No. 73, Vol. 24, No. 4. Lafayette, Ind.: Child Development Publications, Purdue University, 1959.

Kinsbourne, M., and Warrington, E. K. Developmental factors in reading and writing backwards. *British Journal of Psychology* 54:145, 1963.

L'Abate, L. Screening Children with Cerebral Dysfunctions Through the Laboratory Method. In H. C. Haywood (Ed.), *Brain Damage in School Age Children*. Washington: Council for Exceptional Children, 1968. Pp. 128–160.

Lovaas, O. I. Program for Establishment of Speech in Schizophrenic and Autistic Children. In J. Wing (Ed.), *Childhood Autism*. London: Pergamon, 1966.

Matthews, C. G., and Reitan, R. M. Correlations of Wechsler-Bellevue rank orders of subtest means in lateralized and non-lateralized brain-damaged groups. *Perceptual and Motor Skills* 19:391, 1964.

Meehl, P. E., and Rosen, A. Antecedent probability and the efficiency of psychometric signs, patterns, or cutting scores. *Psychological Bulletin* 52:194, 1955.

Monroe, M. *Children Who Cannot Read*. Chicago: University of Chicago Press, 1932.

Piotrowski, Z. The Rorschach ink-blot method in organic disturbances of the central nervous system. *Journal of Nervous and Mental Disease* 86:525, 1937.

Reed, H. B. C., and Fitzhugh, K. B. Patterns of deficits in relation to severity of cerebral dysfunction in children and adults. *Journal of Consulting Psychology* 30:98, 1966.

Reed, H. B. C., Reitan, R. M., and Kløve, H. The influence of cerebral lesions on psychological test performances of older children. *Journal of Consulting Psychology* 29:247, 1965.

Reed, J. C. Lateralized finger agnosia and reading achievement at ages 6 and 10. *Child Development* 38:213, 1967.

Reed, J. C. The ability deficits of good and poor readers. *Journal of Learning Disabilities* 1:134, 1968.

Reed, J. C. The deficits of retarded readers: fact or artifact. *Reading Teacher* 23:347, 1970.

Reed, J. C., and Reed, H. B. C. Concept formation ability and non-verbal abstract thinking among older children with chronic cerebral dysfunction. *Journal of Special Education* 1:157, 1967.

Reed, J. C., and Reitan, R. M. Verbal and performance differences among brain-injured children with lateralized motor deficits. *Perceptual and Motor Skills* 29:747, 1969.

Reitan, R. M. An investigation of the validity of Halstead's measures of biological intelligence. *American Medical Association Archives of Neurology and Psychiatry* 73:28, 1955.

Reitan, R. M. Psychological Assessment of Deficits Associated with Brain Lesions in Subjects with Normal and Abnormal Intelligence. In J. L. Khanna (Ed.), *Brain Damage and Mental Retardation: A Psychological Evaluation*. Springfield, Ill.: Thomas, 1967(a).

Reitan, R. M.　Psychological Effects of Brain Lesions in Children. Mimeographed report, Indiana University Medical Center, 1967(b).

Reitan, R. M., and Heineman, C.　Interaction of Neurological Deficits and Emotional Disturbances in Children with Learning Disorders: Methods for Their Differential Assessment. In J. Hellmuth (Ed.), *Learning Disorders*. Seattle: Special Child Publications, Vol. III, 1968.

Schramm, W.　*Programmed Instruction—Today and Tomorrow*. New York: Fund for Advancement of Education, 1962.

Semmes, J., Weinstein, S., Ghent, L., and Teuber, H. L.　*Somatosensory Changes After Penetrating Brain Wounds in Man*. Cambridge, Mass.: Harvard University Press, 1960.

Simmons, G. A., and Shapiro, B. J.　Reading expectancy formulas: A warning note. *Journal of Reading* 11:626, 1968.

Yerushalmy, J., and Palmer, C. E.　On the methodology of investigation of etiological factors in chronic diseases. *Journal of Chronic Diseases* 10:27, 1959.

SELECTED BIBLIOGRAPHY ON EDUCATIONAL PROCEDURES

Bortner, M. (Ed.).　*The Evaluation and Education of Children with Brain Damage*. Springfield, Ill.: Thomas, 1968.

Cruickshank, W. M. (Ed.).　*The Teacher of Brain-injured Children*. Syracuse: Syracuse University Press, 1966.

Cruickshank, W. M. (Ed.).　*The Brain-injured Child in Home, School and Community*. Syracuse: Syracuse University Press, 1967.

Cruickshank, W. M., Bentzen, F. A., Ratzeburg, F. H., and Tannhauser, M. T.　*A Teaching Method for Brain-injured and Hyperactive Children*. Syracuse: Syracuse University Press, 1961.

Delacato, C.　*Neurological Organization and Reading*. Springfield, Ill.: Thomas, 1966.

Ebersole, B., Kephart, N. C., and Ebersole, J. B.　*Steps to Achievement for the Slow Learner*. Columbus, O.: Merrill, 1968.

Fernald, G. M.　*Remedial Techniques in Basic School Subjects*. New York: McGraw-Hill, 1943.

Fitzhugh, K., and Fitzhugh, L.　*The Fitzhugh PLUS Program*. Galien, Mich.: Allied Education Council, 1966.

Frostig, M.　Education for Children with Learning Disabilities. In H. R. Myklebust (Ed.), *Progress in Learning Disabilities*. New York: Grune & Stratton, 1968.

Gillingham, A., and Stillman, B. W.　*Remedial Training for Chil-*

dren with Specific Disability in Reading, Spelling, and Penmanship (7th ed.). Cambridge, Mass.: Educators Publishing Service, Inc., 1965.

Johnson, J., and Myklebust, H. R. *Learning Disabilities: Educational Principles and Practices.* New York: Grune & Stratton, 1967.

Johnson, M. S. Tracing and Kinesthetic Techniques. In J. Money (Ed.), *The Disabled Reader.* Baltimore: Johns Hopkins Press, 1966. Pp. 147–160.

Kephart, N. C. *The Slow Learner in the Classroom.* Columbus, O.: Merrill, 1960.

Kirk, S. A. *The Diagnosis and Remediation of Psycholinguistic Disabilities.* Urbana: University of Illinois Institute on Exceptional Children, 1966.

Orton, J. L. The Orton-Gillingham Approach. In J. Money (Ed.), *The Disabled Reader.* Baltimore: Johns Hopkins Press, 1966. Pp. 119–146.

Strauss, A. A., and Lehtinen, L. E. *Psychopathology and Education of the Brain-injured Child.* New York: Grune & Stratton, 1947.

Tarnopol, L. (Ed.). *Learning Disabilities: Introduction to Educational and Medical Management.* Springfield, Ill.: Thomas, 1969.

9 Clinical Pharmacology of Psychotropic Drugs*
With Special Reference to Children

LEON J. WHITSELL

GENERAL PRECAUTIONS

Physicians using any potent psychotropic drug should be familiar with its chemistry, animal and human pharmacology, indications, contraindications, precautions, warnings, adverse reactions, available dosage forms, duration of action, and treatment of adverse reactions.

DOSAGE RANGES

The limits of dosages shown here reflect, in many instances, the wide ranges reported as actually used for children or adults, compiled from a large number of sources. These doses do *not* necessarily correspond to those recommended by the author, or the manufacturer, or the United States Food and Drug Administration.

* Adapted from syllabus prepared for course on Learning Disorders, Department of Continuing Education in Health Sciences, University of California, San Francisco, March 24–27, 1969.

Preparation of this material was supported in part by the U.S. Children's Bureau, Grant No. 144, a personnel training grant for handicapped children, and also by the generous help provided by the Junior League of San Francisco.

In most instances dosage should be individually adjusted according to the diagnosis and severity of the condition. In general, small doses should be used initially and increased to the optimal effective level as rapidly as possible, based on the therapeutic response of the patient.

USE IN CHILDREN

The possibilities of still-unreported specific hazards of the long-term use of psychotropic drugs in any child (particularly in view of the immaturity of neural structures) must be considered. One may contrast the experience with long-term use of phenobarbital (1912), amphetamine (1937), diphenylhydantoin sodium (1938), and haloperidol (1966).

In using any of these drugs for children, parents must be properly warned not to exceed prescribed dosage. Arrangements must be made for appropriate observation and medical supervision during the period of administration of any drug.

Special Note

Some of the drugs included in this syllabus have not been approved for use in children or may be restricted or contraindicated at present in certain age groups. For current information, consult manufacturer's package insert.

ASSESSMENT PROBLEMS

Following are some problems in the assessment of drugs used for the management of hyperkinetic and other behavior syndromes affecting learning in children:

1. Heterogeneity of the usual "matched groups" of children
2. Special difficulties in double-blind studies, as fixed dosage problems
3. Complex nature of syndromes:
    a. Lack of standard criteria for diagnosis

    b. Lack of uniformity of symptoms

    c. Variability of symptoms in different settings

    d. Problem of subclinical symptoms (e.g., inner distract-
ibility not overtly discernible)

4. Complexities of measurement of activity level, degree of
distractibility, attention span, impulsivity, and related
symptoms

5. Other, often hidden, factors: e.g., family attitudes toward
drugs, unrecognized psychogenic factors, and early trends
toward psychotic reaction or delinquency

TRANQUILIZERS

Definition

"Tranquilizer is a somewhat idealized term, but carries the
implication of mental calm without proportionate depression
of mental activity or alertness" (Cutting 1969). Synonyms:
ataractic (Greek *ataraxia:* peace of mind), psycholeptic, neuro-
leptic, neurolytic, tensitropic.

General Features

Tranquilizers differ from sedatives in showing less dulling of
sensorium, easier arousal, less ataxia, less anesthesia, more muscle tone, no excited stage, and less addiction. Tranquilizers may
lower convulsive threshold despite potentiation of sedative action of barbiturates. The major tranquilizers are also known as
"antipsychotic" agents, but many have a wide variety of other
uses.

MAJOR TRANQUILIZERS:
PHENOTHIAZINE DERIVATIVES

Phenothiazines

    Phenothiazines were introduced (ca. 1950) as antihistamines
and antiparkinsonism agents. They overshadow other tranquilizers, especially as "antipsychotic" agents. Their site of action

Phenothiazine nucleus

is presumed to be largely subcortical, chiefly on structures that involve emotion.

TOXICITY

Milder effects include:

1. constipation (adynamic ileus)
2. orthostatic hypotension
3. dermatitis (photosensitivity)
4. galactorrhea, amenorrhea
5. impotence or inhibition of orgasm
6. urinary retention
7. fluid retention
8. EKG changes
9. weight gain

Rare severe effects include:

1. jaundice
2. aplastic anemia, agranulocytosis
3. asthma
4. hyperpyrexia, circulatory collapse, cerebral edema
5. sudden death (asphyxia, failure of cough reflex, cardiac arrhythmia, cardiac arrest)

Central nervous system effects include:

1. weakness, akinesia, apathy, chilliness
2. extrapyramidal syndromes (motor restlessness, muscle spasms, tremors, torsion spasms, opisthotonus, jaw-tongue and face-neck syndromes, catatonic-like states, oculogyric crises, parkinsonism)
3. activation of psychotic reactions (especially depressions)
4. convulsions

Rare long-term effects include:

1. pigmentary retinopathy; narrowed visual fields; lenticular, corneal, or conjunctival changes (melanosis)

2. skin pigmentation (melanosis)
3. melanosis of internal organs, apparently related to prolonged high dosage
4. persistent extrapyramidal (dyskinetic) syndromes

Promethazine (Phenergan, Wyeth, 1951)

a. Potent antihistamine; weaker tranquilizer, but used as sedative and antiemetic
b. Chemistry: separation of nitrogen atoms by 2 carbon atoms
characteristic of antihistamines
c. Dose: 25–200 mg daily

Aliphatic Type of Side Chain (Open Chain)

Aliphatic open chain is an original type of derivative, characterized by both extrapyramidal effects and danger of agranulocytosis and hepatitis.

Chlorpromazine (Thorazine, Smith Kline and French, 1954)

a. Chemistry: separation of nitrogen atoms by 3 carbon atoms
characteristic of tranquilizers
b. The model for comparison of action of other phenothiazines and other major tranquilizers

All dosages include adult range.

  c. Mechanism:
  1. depresses reticular system, brainstem, and so on; EEG resembles sleep
  2. adrenolytic: blocks epinephrine receptor sites peripherally
  3. inhibits deamination of serotonin
  4. interferes with action of brain's norepinephrine; decreased sympathetic discharge from CNS
  d. Actions: reduction in motor activity, quietness, drowsiness (but not strongly hypnotic), apathy; antiemetic
  e. Uses: tranquilizer, especially in excited psychoses and hyperkinetic behavior in children; antiemetic. Used intravenously only for hiccups and preparation for surgery
  f. Dose: 30–1,000 mg daily

Promazine (Sparine, Wyeth, 1955)

$CH_2CH_2CH_2-N$ $\big\langle{}^{CH_3}_{CH_3}$

  a. Weaker and less toxic than chlorpromazine
  b. Dose: 30–1,000 mg daily

Triflupromazine (Vesprin, Squibb, 1957)

CF_3 $CH_2CH_2CH_2-N$ $\big\langle{}^{CH_3}_{CH_3}$

  a. Potent and more toxic
  b. Some use in neuroses and hyperkinetic behavior in children

All dosages include adult range.

c. Antiemetic
d. Dose: 20–200 mg daily

> Piperazine Type of Side Chain (two nitrogen atoms in ring)

Piperazine ring inside chain tends to increase extrapyramidal effects and antiemetic effects but reduces adrenolytic and anticholinergic activity, e.g., less effect on blood pressure.

Prochlorperazine (Compazine, Smith Kline and French, 1956)

a. More potent than chlorpromazine, also more toxic, especially in children
b. Toxicity includes bizarre convulsions, especially in children; opisthotonus, eye rolling, tongue protrusion, confusion, catatonia, dystonias, tremors, coma
c. Dose: 5–200 mg daily

Perphenazine (Trilafon, Schering, 1957)

All dosages include adult range.

    a. More potent and more toxic than chlorpromazine; less sedation

    b. Strongly antiemetic

    c. Dose: 6–24 mg daily (pediatric dosage not yet established)

Trifluoperazine (Stelazine, Smith Kline and French, 1959)

    a. Higher potency and toxicity than chlorpromazine

    b. Widely used for anxiety, psychoses, and more severe behavior disorders in children

    c. Dose: 1–80 mg daily

Fluphenazine (Prolixin, Squibb; Permitil, White, 1959)

    a. More potent (25 times) than chlorpromazine

    b. Parkinsonism in 30 percent; controlled by antiparkinsonism agents

    c. Leukopenia in 4 percent of cases in one series

    d. Dose: 0.5–10 mg daily

        Piperidine Type of Side Chain (one nitrogen atom in ring)

All dosages include adult range.

Thioridazine (Mellaril, Sandoz, 1959)

a. Minimal extrapyramidal effects; reduced cataleptic effect in animals
b. Equally potent but less toxic than chlorpromazine
c. Reported useful in hyperkinetic, anxious, emotionally labile, aggressive, and disturbed children; also some apparent value in enuresis
d. Special side effects:
    1. pigmentary retinopathy in adults following doses of 3,000–4,000 mg daily for forty days (different from chronic retinopathy reported from long-term use of phenothiazines)
    2. frequent impotence and inhibition of orgasm (more common than with other phenothiazines)
e. Dose: 10–1,000 mg daily

TABLE 9-1. *Dosage Conversion for Phenothiazine Tranquilizers*

Approximate Therapeutic Equivalents (mg)		
promazine	200	Sparine
chlorpromazine	100	Thorazine
thioridazine	100	Mellaril
triflupromazine	50	Vesprin
prochlorperazine	25	Compazine
perphenazine	10–12	Trilafon
trifluoperazine	5	Stelazine
fluphenazine	2	Prolixin, Permitil

All dosages include adult range.

Emergency Treatment of Drug-Induced Extrapyramidal Reactions

Extrapyramidal reactions include face-neck syndrome, opisthotonus, torsion spasms, dystonia, hemiballismus, severe akathisia, and oculogyric crises.

1. Early gastric lavage, intestinal purge; maintain open airway; oxygen; maintain adequate hydration
2. *Meperidine* (Demerol) 25–100 mg by intramuscular injection
3. *Benztropine* (Cogentin) 2 mg per 2 cc by intramuscular injection or intravenously
4. *Biperiden* (Akineton) 1–2 mg intramuscular injection or 5 mg per 1 cc intravenously (watch for possible postural hypotension)
5. *Diphenhydramine* (Benadryl) 50–100 mg intramuscular injection or intravenously
6. *Sodium phenobarbital* (Luminal Sodium) 130 mg intramuscular injection
7. *Caffeine sodium benzoate* 500 mg may be used by injection as stimulant; avoid picrotoxin or pentylenetetrazol (Metrazol) because of danger of convulsions
8. *Methocarbamol* (Robaxin) 1 gm per 10 cc by intramuscular or intravenous injection *slowly* as muscular relaxant
9. Dialysis *apparently not helpful*

Emergency Treatment of Hypotensive Neurocirculatory Collapse

1. Shock position; pressure bandages to lower limbs
2. *Methylphenidate* (Ritalin) 30–50 mg by injection every 30 minutes
3. *Levarterenol bitartrate* (Levophed) 2–4 μg per minute in 5 percent dextrose in water or saline as intravenous drip (4 cc of 0.2 percent solution in 1,000 cc of fluid). Phenylephrine (Neo-Synephrine) solution may also be used intravenously
4. Intravenous fluids, plasma
5. *Contraindicated:* epinephrine, mephentermine (Wyamine), and so on, may lower blood pressure further

All dosages include adult range.

MAJOR TRANQUILIZERS: THIOXANTHENE DERIVATIVES

Thioxanthene derivatives are structurally related to a class of drugs under study for treatment of schistosomiasis, e.g., lucanthone (Miracil D., Nilodin) in present use.

Chlorprothixene (Taractan, Roche)

a. Differs structurally from chlorpromazine only in replacement of nitrogen atom in central ring of phenothiazine nucleus by carbon atom
b. Similar to chlorpromazine in actions, potency, and side effects; effective in children
c. Dose: 20–600 mg daily

Thiothixene (Navane, Roerig)

a. High potency and toxicity
b. Chiefly used for chronic, withdrawn, refractory schizophrenics
c. Dose: 6–60 mg daily

All dosages include adult range.

MAJOR TRANQUILIZERS: BUTYROPHEN-ONE DERIVATIVES

Haloperidol (Haldol, McNeil 1966)

a. Highly potent (and toxic) antipsychotic agent
b. Actions resemble phenothiazines; less tendency to produce hypothermia or hypotensive-sympatholytic effects
c. Reported useful in management of acute mania
d. Markedly effective in Gilles de la Tourette's disease (vocal barking, tics, and coprolalia in children)
e. Not yet approved for use under 12 years of age
f. Dose: 0.5–15 mg daily

MAJOR TRANQUILIZERS: RAUWOLFIA DERIVATIVES

Rauwolfia serpentina (Raudixin, Squibb, and others, 1953)

a. Long used in India as depressant; recent (1953) application to hypertension and mental disorders
b. Contains reserpine and other alkaloids
c. Dose: Raudixin 200–300 mg equivalent to reserpine 0.5 mg

All dosages include adult range.

Reserpine (Serpasil, CIBA, 1953 and others)
  a. Alkaloid from *Rauwolfia serpentina;* synthesized (1956)
  b. Indole derivative
  c. Mechanism: stimulates activity of parasympathetic division of subcortical integrating structures by:
    1. inhibiting normal binding and inactive storing of serotonin in brain cells, especially in hypothalamus and reticular formation
    2. interference with stored supply of norepinephrine at peripheral nerve endings
  d. Actions:
    1. induces calm sleep with easy arousal, decreased aggressiveness
    2. sympatholytic (blocks or exhausts catecholamines), lowers blood pressure
    3. hyperglycemic
    4. slow onset of action and slow recovery from effects after discontinuation
  e. Toxicity:
    1. lethargy, agitation, insomnia, confusion, nightmares, parkinsonism, convulsions, *depression* (CNS effects)
    2. nasal congestion, diarrhea, hypertension, circulatory collapse (sympatholytic)
    3. amenorrhea, gastric ulceration and bleeding, edema
    4. similarity to malignant carcinoid
  f. Uses:
    1. phenothiazine-resistant excited psychoses, hypertension, chorea
    2. hyperkinetic behavior disorders of children
  g. Doses: 0.1–10 mg daily

MINOR TRANQUILIZERS: GLYCEROL DERIVATIVES

General
  a. Include propanediols and related open chain (aliphatic) alcohols, some with carbamate or amide groups
  b. Main use in milder (psychoneurotic) anxiety reactions and tension states; limited usefulness in major psychoses

All dosages include adult range.

c. Some are also mild muscle relaxants (internuncial neurone blockers), may contribute to tranquilizing action
d. Some have limited anticonvulsant activity
e. Little or no direct effect on autonomic nervous system
f. May aggravate hyperkinetic behavior disorders of children because of sedative effect

$$H_2C-OH$$
$$H\text{-}C\text{-}OH$$
$$H_2C-OH$$

Meprobamate (Miltown, Wallace; Equanil, Wyeth, 1955)

$$H_2C-O-CONH_2$$
$$C_3H_7-C-CH_3$$
$$H_2C-O-CONH_2$$

a. Derived from mephenesin
b. Mild tranquilizer and muscle relaxant: question whether more effective than phenobarbital
c. Mild anticonvulsant action
d. Toxicity:
   1. fever, rash, hypotensive crisis, angioneurotic edema, gastrointestinal symptoms
   2. leukopenia, purpura, aplastic anemia
   3. habituation
   4. ataxia with large doses
   5. convulsive seizures on abrupt withdrawal from high doses
e. Uses:
   1. anxiety states, tension
   2. occasionally used as adjunct anticonvulsant, especially in petit mal
   3. cerebral palsy, as muscle relaxant
f. Dose: 200–2,400 mg daily

All dosages include adult range.

Tybamate (Solacen, Wallace)

$$\underset{\underset{\displaystyle CH_2CH_2CH_3}{|}}{\overset{\displaystyle O \quad CH_3 \quad O}{H_2NCOCH_2CCH_2OCNHCH_2CH_2CH_2CH_3}}$$

a. Tranquilizer, primarily for anxiety and tension states
b. Reported to act subcortically with selective effects on thalamus
c. Suppresses EEG effects of LSD-25 in rabbits
d. Dose: 250–3,000 mg daily

Methocarbamol (Robaxin, Robins, 1957)

$$\begin{array}{l} H_2C-O-CONH_2 \\ HC-OH \\ H_2C-O -\!\!\!\!\bigcirc \\ \qquad\quad OCH_3 \end{array}$$

a. Primarily a muscle relaxant
b. Occasional drowsiness, nausea
c. Used in muscle spasm, tetanus, cerebral palsy, extrapyramidal syndromes
d. Dose: 1.5–9 gm daily

Carisoprodol (Soma, Wallace; Rela, Schering, 1959)

$$\begin{array}{l} H_2C-O-CONH_3 \\ C_3H_7C-CH_3 \qquad\qquad CH_3 \\ H_2C-O-CONH-CH \\ \qquad\qquad\qquad\qquad CH_3 \end{array}$$

a. Isopropyl derivative of meprobamate

All dosages include adult range.

b. Used primarily as muscle relaxant to relieve pain and stiff-
ness in muscles and joints

c. Occasional use in spastic cerebral palsy and dyskinesia

d. Claimed to have analgesic, antipyretic, and atropine-like
action in addition to relaxing power

e. Dose: 350–2,800 mg daily

MINOR TRANQUILIZERS: DIPHENYL-METHANE DERIVATIVES

Chemistry

a. Relationship to atropine

b. Relatives: spasmolytics, antiparkinsonism agents, antihistamines, analgesics (methadone), local anesthetics, choline
esters, stimulants (pipradol)

Trihexyphenidyl (Artane, Lederle, 1949)

HC-COH-CH$_2$CH$_2$-N

a. Antiparkinsonism agent

b. No sedative action

c. Dose: 4–20 mg daily

Diphenhydramine (Benadryl, Parke Davis, 1946)

HC-O-CH$_2$CH$_2$-N(CH$_3$)(CH$_3$)

a. Antihistamine

b. Mild action in parkinsonism

All dosages include adult range.

c. Mild sedative
d. Large doses may precipitate convulsive seizures
e. Effective in quieting emotionally disturbed children, especially under age 10 to 12 years
f. Dose: 25–400 mg daily; caution if seizure-prone

Hydroxyzine (Atarax, Roerig; Vistaril, Pfizer, 1956)

$$\text{HC-N} \underbrace{}_{} \text{N-CH}_2\text{CH}_2\text{-O-CH}_2\text{CH}_2\text{OH}$$

a. Antihistamine with mild sedative, antiemetic, and antianxiety actions
b. May potentiate barbiturates, narcotics, alcohol, and anticoagulants
c. Dose: 20–1,000 mg daily

MINOR TRANQUILIZERS: BENZODIAZEPINES

Benzodiazepines have more potent tranquilizer activity than glycerol and diphenylmethane derivatives. They are reported to produce marked tranquilization and taming of hostile monkeys and vicious rats without sedation or lessening of motor activity. They act chiefly on limbic system, thalamus, and hypothalamus and produce anticonvulsant and muscle relaxant activity with limited peripheral autonomic action and extrapyramidal side effects.

Toxicity: drowsiness, fatigue, muscular weakness, ataxia, dizziness, hypotension, vertigo, syncope, constipation, incontinence, menorrhagia, changes in libido, rash, edema, blood dyscrasias, jaundice, and so on. Less commonly, hyperactivity, excitement, confusion, depersonalization, and paradoxical rage reactions.

All dosages include adult range.

Chlordiazepoxide (Librium, Roche, 1960)

a. Rapidly absorbed; peak in eight hours
b. Excreted partly in urine; continues several days after last dose
c. Used chiefly for tension and anxiety in adults
d. Used by injection for acute agitation and delirium tremens
e. Used in hyperactive aggressive children. *Caution:* May have paradoxical stimulating action!
f. Dose: 10–300 mg daily

Diazepam (Valium, Roche)

a. More potent tranquilizer than chlordiazepoxide
b. Muscle relaxant, reported effective in spasticity and athetoid cerebral palsy
c. Valuable adjunct, by injection, in status epilepticus and severe recurrent convulsive seizures
d. May be effective in control of acute agitation

All dosages include adult range.

e. Dependence and habituation may follow extended use of larger doses
f. May be contraindicated for use in children under 6 months of age
g. Dose: 2–40 mg daily

Oxazepam (Serax, Wyeth)

a. Used mainly in anxiety, agitation, and irritability
b. Not indicated for children under 6 years of age
c. Use with caution in older patients (orthostatic hypotension)
d. Dose: 20–120 mg daily

ANTIDEPRESSANT DRUGS

Definitions

Antidepressant drugs include minor psychomotor stimulants and major psychic energizers. The term *psychic energizer* emphasizes ability to alleviate psychotic depression and implies a true antidepressant effect beyond mere stimulation and euphorization. *Analeptic* is an old term for a "restorative" medicine, especially a cordial; it is now limited to drugs that antagonize the action of CNS depressants.

All dosages include adult range.

MILD ANTIDEPRESSANTS (PSYCHOMOTOR STIMULANTS)

Amphetamines

Amphetamine (Benzedrine, Smith Kline and French, and others)

Dextroamphetamine (Dexedrine, Smith Kline and French, and others)

$$\text{C}_6\text{H}_5\text{—CH}_2\overset{\overset{\displaystyle CH_3}{|}}{\underset{\underset{\displaystyle NH_2}{|}}{CH}} \cdot \tfrac{1}{2}\, H_2SO_4$$

a. Used as analeptic; also used in treatment of narcolepsy, oculogyric crises, mild depression with organic illness, and enuresis
b. Mild antidepressant; depresses appetite
c. Excitatory action on reticular activating system
d. Widely used for hyperkinetic behavior disorders since 1937
e. Toxicity: insomnia, palpitation, gastrointestinal disturbances, collapse (sympathetic action)
f. Habituation a problem in adults
g. Dose: 2.5–60 mg daily

Methamphetamine (Methedrine, Burroughs Wellcome; Desoxyn, Abbott, and others)

$$\text{C}_6\text{H}_5\text{—CH}_2\overset{\overset{\displaystyle }{|}}{\underset{\underset{\displaystyle HN}{|}}{CH}}\text{-CH}_3 \quad \overset{CH_3}{} \cdot HCl$$

a. Less circulatory action than amphetamine
b. Dose: 2.5–30 mg daily

All dosages include adult range.

Piperidine Derivatives

Pipradol (Meratran, Merrell, 1955)

a. Mild stimulant and antidepressant
b. Main use in mild neurotic (reactive) depressions; no longer widely used
c. Reported to relieve torticollis but contraindicated in chorea and obsessive-compulsive states
d. Toxicity: agitation, insomnia, gastrointestinal disturbances, rash, dizziness, chest pains
e. Dose: 1–7.5 mg daily

Methylphenidate (Ritalin, CIBA, 1956)

a. Psychic stimulant and analeptic; acts on reticular activating system; may stimulate sympathetic output of hypothalamus
b. Widely used for hyperkinetic behavior disorders in children
c. Improves muscular coordination
d. Less habituating than amphetamines
e. Most effective available drug for narcolepsy; also used for torticollis and tics

All dosages include adult range.

  f. Useful as mild cerebral stimulant in some adults with mild apathy and depression complicating organic illness; also used to relieve drowsiness with anticonvulsants and sedative phenothiazines

  g. May increase activity of anticonvulsants, tricyclic antidepressants, and anticoagulants

  h. Toxicity: similar to pipradol; rare cardiac arrhythmia

  i. Dose: 10–80 mg daily

Tertiary Amines

Deanol (Deaner, Riker, 1958)

$$HOCH_2CH_2N \overset{CH_3}{\underset{CH_3}{\diagdown}} \cdot HOOC-\langle \rangle-NH\overset{O}{\overset{\|}{C}}CH_3$$

  a. Apparently acts as acetylcholine precursor

  b. Stimulant action: originally used in mild depressions and organic fatigue, slow onset of action

  c. Controversial reports of efficacy in hyperkinetic behavior disorders of children

  d. Side effects (dose-related): muscular tension, twitching, insomnia, occipital headaches, pruritis, rash, constipation, postural hypotension (rare)

  e. Toxicity: no serious long-term toxic effects reported within range of tolerated doses

  f. *Contraindicated* (relatively) in epilepsy; large doses may precipitate seizures in predisposed children

  g. Dose: 25–300 mg daily

MAJOR ANTIDEPRESSANTS:
IMINODIBENZYL DERIVATIVES
(TRICYCLIC ANTIDEPRESSANTS)

General

Iminodibenzyl derivatives are analogues of phenothiazine compounds. Their antidepressant action apparently depends on in-

All dosages include adult range.

hibition of storage of norepinephrine and serotonin in deeply bound inactive form, allowing greater concentration and more prolonged action of amines at the receptor site with slow onset of action. The action on enuresis probably depends on an altered sleep state, allowing more response to the stimulus of a full bladder; anticholinergic activity may also contribute. These drugs have been reported useful for relief of cataplectic attacks, sleep paralysis, and hypnagogic hallucinations (apparently by effect on pontine reticular formation). The dibenzazepines differ structurally from phenothiazines only by substitution of an ethyl bridge for a sulfur atom in the central ring.

Imipramine (Tofrānil, Geigy, 1959)

a. Dibenzazepine analogue of promazine (Sparine)
b. Not a monoamine oxidase inhibitor
c. Toxic effects similar to phenothiazines (e.g., tremor, hypotension)
d. Highly effective and widely used antidepressant, especially in neurotic and milder psychotic depressive reactions
e. Widely used for childhood enuresis but "not recommended for use at the present time in patients under 12 years of age" (Huff 1969)
f. Dose: 10–200 mg daily

Desipramine (Pertofrane, Geigy; Norpramin, Lakeside)

All dosages include adult range.

a. Monomethyl derivative of imipramine
b. Reported to have more rapid onset of action and fewer side effects than parent drug
c. Dose: 25–200 mg daily

Omipramol (Ensidon, Geigy)

$$\text{CH}_2\text{CH}_2\text{CH}_2-\text{N}\overline{}\text{N}-\text{CH}_2\text{CH}_2\text{OH}$$

a. Dibenzazepine analogue of perphenazine
b. Reported effective in severe emotional disturbances of children
c. Not yet available for general use
d. Dose: 25–200 mg daily

Dibenzcarbepines

Carbon atom substituted for nitrogen atom in central ring of dibenzazepine ring

Amitriptyline (Elavil, Merck Sharp and Dohme, 1961)

$$\text{CHCH}_2\text{CH}_2-\text{N}\overset{\text{CH}_3}{\underset{\text{CH}_3}{\diagdown}}$$

a. Antidepressant action very similar to imipramine
b. Dose: 10–200 mg daily

All dosages include adult range.

Nortriptyline (Aventyl, Lilly)

$$\text{(dibenzocycloheptene ring system)}$$
$$\overset{\shortparallel}{C}HCH_2CH_2-NHCH_3$$

a. Potent antidepressant
b. Monomethyl form of amitriptyline
c. Widely used for children with enuresis
d. Dose: 10–200 mg daily

PRINCIPLES OF DRUG TREATMENT

The following is reprinted with permission from L. Eisenberg, Psychopharmacology in Childhood: A Critique, in E. Miller (Ed.), *Foundations of Child Psychiatry* (Oxford, Pergamon Press Ltd., 1968), pp. 639–640:

No drug should be employed without firm indication for its use, without careful control of the patient to be treated, and without due precautions for toxicity. With any potent drug, toxicity is inevitable; to justify its use, the severity of the presenting condition and the likelihood of benefit must outweigh the risk of toxicity. Toxicity studies on adults cannot be safely extrapolated to children because of differences in the immature organism. Clinical decisions must be based upon data from pediatric studies.

An old and familiar drug is to be preferred to a new drug unless evidence for superiority for the latter is preponderant. This principle of pharmacologic conservatism is based upon the fact that unexpected toxicity from a new agent may be apparent only after prolonged experience with its use. . . . This is not a statement of pharmacologic nihilism. Drugs can make a decisive difference in treatment but their very potency commends us not to use them lightly.

Despite these cautions, drugs can be useful agents in the management of pediatric psychiatric disorders when chosen appro-

All dosages include adult range.

priately and applied with discrimination. . . . They can be effective in controlling symptoms not readily managed by other means and can facilitate other methods of psychiatric treatment by allaying symptoms that disrupt learning. If they are not the panaceas portrayed in advertisements, neither are they the poisons claimed by those wedded to exclusively psychological methods of treatment.

Every drug study reveals the potency of placebo effects; that is, benefits occurring from the relationship between physician and patient and from positive expectations in the patient. . . . Skill in the use of drugs requires, in addition to knowledge of their pharmacologic properties, sensitivity to their psychologic implications.

Drugs should be used no longer than necessary. Dosage should be reduced periodically with the goal of cessation of treatment if symptoms do not return on lower dosage. Dosage must be individualized. Undertreatment, as well as overtreatment, can result in incorrect judgments about the appropriateness of particular drugs for the patient.

The use of drugs does not relieve the physician of the responsibility for seeking to identify and eliminate the factors causing or aggravating the psychiatric disorder. All of the currently available psychopharmacologic agents treat symptoms, not diseases. Clearly symptomatic relief is not to be disparaged; indeed it will remain a major part of medicine so long as causes are unknown and cures unattainable in many diseases. However, symptom suppression may also delay diagnosis and hence effective treatment. To prescribe drugs for a child whose symptoms stem from correctable social, familial, biological or intrapersonal disturbances without attempting to alter the factors causing the symptoms is poor medicine.

ACKNOWLEDGMENT

Indebtedness is gratefully acknowledged to my former teacher, Dr. Windsor S. Cutting, whose superb outline style served as model for this syllabus.

ANNOTATED REFERENCES

Caffey, E. M., Hollister, L. E., Kairn, S. C., and Pokorny, A. D. *Antipsychotic, Antianxiety, and Antidepressant Drugs,* Medical Bulletin # 11, Veterans Administration, Washington, D.C., Sept. 15, 1966.

Council on Drugs, American Medical Association. Notes on the Package Insert, *Journal of the American Medical Association* 207:1335 (Feb. 17) 1969. Discusses physician's responsibilities and potential liabilities in use of drugs beyond the range of the manufacturer's recommendations. Also considers value and shortcomings of package inserts. (See editorial in same issue, p. 1342.)

Cutting, W. C. *Handbook of Pharmacology: The Actions and Uses of Drugs.* New York: Appleton-Century-Crofts, 1969. Authoritative, highly useful compendium of modern knowledge of the action and uses of drugs, in outline form. Copiously illustrated with structural formulas.

DiMascio, A., and Shader, R. I. *Clinical Handbook of Psychopharmacology.* New York: Science House, 1970. Special sections on neuro-electrophysiologic and biochemical studies of drugs, psychodynamics of psychotropic medications, and interaction of pharmacotherapy with total treatment. Also brief discussion of guidelines for drug treatment of children.

Eisenberg, L. Basic Issues in Drug Research with Children: Opportunities and limitations of a pediatric age group. In S. Fisher (Ed.), *Child Research in Psychopharmacology.* Springfield, Ill.: Charles C Thomas, 1959.

Eisenberg, L. Psychopharmacology in Childhood: A critique. In E. Miller (Ed.), *Foundations of Child Psychiatry.* Oxford: Pergamon Press, 1968. Concise discussion of uses of drugs in child psychiatry, scope of physician's responsibilities, principles of management.

Eveloff, H. H. Psychopharmacologic agents in child psychiatry: A survey of the literature since 1960. *Archives of General Psychiatry* 14:472, 1966. Discusses neuroanatomy and neurophysiology to be considered in drug therapy; drug groups in terms of clinical usage. Gives recommendations for drug treatment in order of preference for various syndromes in children: (minimal to moderate) (a) *Hyperactive:* 1) dextroamphetamine, 2) methylphenidate, 3) chlorpromazine, and 4) diphenhydramine (patients under 10 years of age); and (b) *Withdrawn:* trifluoperazine.

Fish, B. Psychiatric Treatment of Children: Organic therapies. In A.M. Freedman and H. I. Kaplan (Eds.), *Comprehensive Textbook of Psychiatry.* Baltimore: Williams & Wilkins, 1967. Concise review, including personal views and recommendations of a child psychiatrist having special and wide experience in this field.

Haas, H., Fink, H., and Härtfelder, G. Das Placeboproblem (The Placebo Problem). *Fortschritte der Arzneimittelforschung* 1:279 1959. Translation published in *Psychopharmacology Service Center Bulletin.* 2:1 (July) 1963. Comprehensive review of placebo studies.

Hishikawa, Y., Ida, H., Nakai, K., and Kaneko, Z. Treatment of narcolepsy with imipramine (Tofrānil) and desmethylimipramine (Pertofrane). *Journal of the Neurological Sciences* 3:453, 1966. Discusses probable sites of chief activity of tricyclic antidepressants discovered from work relating to effects of these agents on subcortical and brain stem structures with special reference to clinical effects in treatment of narcolepsy syndrome.

Honigfeld, G. Non-specific factors in treatment: I. Review of placebo reactions and placebo reactors. *Diseases of the Nervous System* 25:145, 1964. II. Review of Social-Psychological Factors. *Diseases of the Nervous System* 25:225, 1964. Well-written, provocative discussion of the clinical evaluation of drug effects.

Huff, B. B. (Ed.). *Physicians' Desk Reference to Pharmaceutical Specialties and Biologicals* (24th ed.). Oradell, N.J.: Medical Economics, 1970. Revised annually; frequent supplements. Most valuable single reference on drugs currently available to American physicians; listings include reprints of manufacturers' package inserts, product identification, and therapeutic index.

Killam, E. K. Drug action on the brain-stem reticular formation. *Pharmacological Reviews* 14:175, 1962. Careful review of research studies on actions of drugs on reticular activating system.

Klein, D. F., and Davis, J. M. *Diagnosis and Drug Treatment of Psychiatric Disorders.* Baltimore: Williams & Wilkins, 1969. Outlines the diagnostic process and principles of psychotropic drug management. Presents authoritative reviews of the world's literature on antipsychotic drugs, mood-stabilizing drugs, and minor tranquilizers; critique of treatment studies. Valuable, well-organized, integrated text.

Lucas, A. R. Psychopharmacologic Treatment. In C. R. Shaw (Ed.), *The Psychiatric Disorders of Childhood.* New York: Appleton-Century-Crofts, 1966. "Psychotropic drugs have now achieved status as important tools in the treatment of the psychiatric disorders of childhood, but the day when they can replace psychotherapy has not arrived, nor is it in the foreseeable future."

Meissner, W. W. Hippocampus and learning. *International Journal of Neuropsychiatry* 3:298 (July–Aug.) 1967. Reviews recent research findings to develop thesis that hippocampus has complex integrating function touching multiple levels of cognitive experience.

Morelli, H. F., and Melmon, K. L.   The clinician's approach to drug interactions. *California Medicine* 109:380 (Nov.) 1968. Stresses the hazards of drug interactions and importance of avoiding multiple drug therapy. When such multiple treatment is unavoidable, patients must be carefully observed.

Schildkraut, J. J., Schanberg, S. M., Breese, G. R., and Kopin, I. J. Norepinephrine metabolism and drugs used in affective disorders. *American Journal of Psychiatry* 124:600 (Nov.) 1967. Reviews evidence for hypothesis that antidepressant drugs exert their clinical effects by increasing levels of norepinephrine and other monoamines at neuronal receptors; includes a tentative summary of drug actions.

Simpson, G. M., and Angus, J. W. S.   Drug induced extrapyramidal disorders. *Acta Psychiatrica Scandinavica,* Supplement 212, 1970. Extensive review of literature, discussion of mechanisms, and report of original studies.

Smythies, J. R.   *The Neurological Foundations of Neuropsychiatry: An Outline of the Mechanisms of Emotion, Memory and the Organization of Behavior, with Particular Regard to the Limbic System.* New York: Academic Press, 1966. Reviews recent research relating higher cerebral functions involved in learning and behavior to limbic and brain stem structures.

Today's Drugs: Monoamineoxidase inhibitors. *British Medical Journal* 2:35, 1968.

Today's Drugs: Tricyclic antidepressants. *British Medical Journal* 2:102, 1968.

Werry, J. S.   The use of psycho-active drugs in children. *Illinois Medical Journal* 131:785, 827 (June) 1967. Formulates general rules regarding use of psychoactive drugs; reviews problems of pediatric psychopharmacology; discusses drugs most likely to be useful in hyperactivity; less predictive but probably useful in anxiety-produced symptoms, enuresis, tics, phobias, sleep disturbances.

Wurtman, R. J.   *Catecholamines* (New England Journal of Medicine Medical Progress Series). Boston: Little Brown, 1966. Comprehensive review, clinically oriented, of recent studies relevant to modes of action of MAOI and tricyclic antidepressants and their uses. Brief review of clinical uses of these agents and experimental evidence of their probable modes of action.

Wyke, B.   *Principles of General Neurology: An Introduction to the Basic Principles of Medical and Surgical Neurology.* New York: Elsevier, 1969. Extensive review and discussion in depth of basic aspects of neurophysiology and neuropharmacology, with special attention to recent advances in knowledge of sites and modes of action. Lengthy sections on pharmacodynamics of central, visceral neuronal, and neuromuscular communication processes.

Index